The Art of Wandering

The Writer as Walker

MERLIN COVERLEY

OLDCASTLE BOOKS

First published in 2012 by
Oldcastle Books Ltd,
PO Box 394, Harpenden,
Herts, AL5 1XJ
www.oldcastlebooks.com

A CIP catalogue record for this book is available from the British Library

ISBNs
978-1-84243-370-6 (print)
978-1-84243-640-0 (epub)
978-1-84243-639-4 (kindle)
978-1-84243-641-7 (pdf)

6 8 10 9 7

Typeset by Avocet Typeset, Chilton, Aylesbury, Bucks
in 12.75pt Bembo
Printed and bound in the UK by 4edge Limited

To my parents

Contents

Tullio had resumed talking about his illness, which was also his chief hobby. He had studied the anatomy of the leg and the foot. Laughing, he told me that when one walks at a rapid pace, the time in which a step is taken does not exceed a half-second, and that in that half-second no fewer than fifty-four muscles are engaged. I reacted with a start, and my thoughts immediately rushed to my legs, to seek this monstrous machinery. I believe I found it. Naturally I didn't identify the fifty-four moving parts, but rather an enormous complication went to pieces the moment I intruded my attention upon it.

I limped, leaving that café, and I went on limping for several days. For me, walking had become hard labour, also slightly painful. That jungle of cogs now seemed to lack oil, and in moving, they damaged one another reciprocally. A few days afterwards, I was assailed by a more serious illness, of which I will speak, that diminished the first. But even today, as I write about it, if someone watches me when I move, the fifty-four muscles become self-conscious and I risk falling.
Italo Svevo, *Zeno's Conscience*[1]

Is it not truly extraordinary to realise that ever since men have walked, no-one has ever asked why they walk, how they walk, whether they walk, whether they might walk better, what they achieve by walking, whether they might not have the means to regulate, change, or analyse their walk: questions that bear on all the systems of philosophy, psychology and politics with which the world is preoccupied?
Honoré de Balzac, *Théorie de la Démarche*[2]

Introduction: The Writer as Walker

Walking has been so natural and so ordinary that few thought of writing about it [...] it is only in this age, as a protest against the wheel, walking as a literary cult has come into being. Stephen Graham[3]

Both walking and writing are simple, common activities. You put one foot in front of the other; you put one word in front of another. What could be more basic than a single step, more basic than a single word? Yet if you connect enough of these basic building blocks, connect enough steps, enough words, you may find that you've done something quite special. The thousand-mile journey starts with the single step; the million-word manuscript starts with a single syllable. Geoff Nicholson[4]

For such a seemingly innocuous activity, and one which is commonly conducted with the participant largely oblivious to its operation, the act of walking has acquired a surprising degree of cultural significance. How can it be that something so straightforward, so instinctive, should have attained such a role? The answer, of course, lies not so much in the movement of one's legs but in what such movement symbolises and where such movement may lead. For, as ever, walking is a means to an end, rarely an end in itself. For much of human history and in most parts of the world today, this end is, as it always has been, simply locomotion, a way of passing from A to B; and yet the history of walking is one which has seen this end gradually evolve. For as walking has been superseded by other forms of transportation, so has it taken on or been attributed with other less obvious designations.

11

As a means of cutting across established routes and challenging the enclosure of public space, walking has long since held a well-established political function which has animated walkers and radicals from John Clare to Guy Debord; as an aesthetic act walking has played a crucial role in many of the twentieth century's most notable avant-garde movements, from Dada and Surrealism to Situationism and beyond; more recently it has become associated with the Land Art movement and the practices of performance art. In all these cases, however, walking is valued less for what it is or does, than for what it resembles, replicates or facilitates. For millennia the act of walking and the bodily rhythms it incorporates have been felt to somehow reflect or engender the mental processes of abstract thought, as if the metronomic beat of the walker's step could mark time, shaping the thoughts it provokes into a coherent narrative. Here, then, we can locate the source of the astonishing cultural legacy which walking has accrued, a legacy embodied in the figure of the writer as walker.

Many writers and commentators have remarked upon the apparent reciprocity between walking and writing, but none perhaps with the acuity of the anthropologist, Tim Ingold, who has outlined in some detail his belief that such fundamental activities as walking, writing, reading and drawing all display characteristics or gestures common to each of them. What unites these activities, argues Ingold, is the way in which they reflect a particular form of movement, 'breaking a path through a terrain and leaving a trace, at once in the imagination and on the ground.'[5] This movement Ingold calls 'wayfaring', a practice which he claims is 'the fundamental mode by which living beings inhabit the earth.'[6] As a consequence, Ingold sees human life as defined by 'the line of its own movement', a process which inscribes a trace across the landscape which can be 'read' by subsequent generations. Of course, in such a schema the act of walking takes on a highly significant, indeed pivotal role, becoming the means through which human beings learn to understand the world about them as they pass through it; and the trace they leave behind them is not merely recorded in the paths that are left in their wake but also in the oral histories and texts through which such actions are recorded. Using such diverse examples as the 'perambulatory meditations' of medieval monasticism, the Dreamtime of the Australian Aborigines, and the abstract art of Wassily Kandinsky, Ingold demonstrates the ways in which the act of walking imposes a trace that can be mapped across both time and space, revealing a common heritage. 'How, then,' asks Ingold, 'does reading differ from walking in the landscape?' The answer: 'Not at all. To walk is to journey in the mind as much as on the land: it is a deeply meditative practice. And to read is to journey on the page as much as in the mind. Far from being rigidly partitioned, there is constant traffic between these terrains, respectively mental and material, through the gateway of the senses.'[7] Elsewhere, Ingold emphasises the clear parallels between the flow of the narrative in the act of storytelling and the steady pace of the walker or wayfarer as he moves from place to place:

> To tell a story, then, is to *relate*, in narrative, the occurrences of the past, retracing a path through a world that others, recursively picking up the threads of past lives, can follow in the process of spinning out their own [...] in the story as in life there is always somewhere further one can go. And in storytelling as in wayfaring, it is in the movement from place to place – or from topic to topic – that knowledge is integrated.[8]

As will soon become evident as this book progresses, Ingold is by no means alone in observing the fact that walking and writing are so clearly complementary activities. Indeed, not only have many of the writers whom I will be discussing here come to the same conclusion, but they have also demonstrated in their own works the ways in which the act of walking provokes and engenders the act of writing. Furthermore, in many instances the results of this union of mind and foot, the texts which collectively form the pedestrian canon, themselves reflect the walks which inspired them, often presenting exactly that metronomic rhythm and digressive form which are themselves the hallmarks of the idle stroll.[9]

Of course, walking is such a commonplace activity that its literary history could be extended almost indefinitely to encompass the entire literary canon within its pages. But a history in which walking is regarded as a conscious activity and in which it is ascribed a significance in itself is much less extensive, and it is such a history that I will be surveying in the following account. Yet at what point does the walker move to the foreground and become a subject worthy of discussion in his (he remains, despite notable exceptions, predominantly male) own right? In the introduction to his book, *Walkers* (1986), Miles Jebb writes: 'As I see it, the main criterion of the true walker is that he makes something of it and does not consider it merely as drudgery.'[10] Identifying exactly what this 'something' is which distinguishes the true walker from his counterfeit companions is, of course, difficult; what seems more obvious, however, is that this elusive attribute, which elevates a seemingly straightforward activity to something rather more than simple locomotion, is one which has preoccupied an astonishing array of philosophers, poets, writers and artists for more than two thousand years. Throughout this period, as intellectual and cultural fashions have changed, so has the act of walking been subject to widely fluctuating literary representations, as too have the criteria for establishing what constitutes a 'true' walker: from the pilgrim to the pedestrian, the flâneur to the stalker. The language may change but the activity remains essentially the same.

In the following pages I have attempted to maintain, wherever possible, a chronological sequence that demonstrates the ways in which walking has evolved over time, from antiquity to the present day; and yet so disparate and so frequently contradictory are the myriad forms that walking has taken that I have chosen also to corral the many figures and works discussed here into thematic categories which illustrate the many guises that the walker has assumed, from philosopher to revolutionary, vagrant to visionary. One consequence of such an approach is that writers who normally inhabit very different parts of the literary spectrum, rarely, if ever, coming into contact, are brought into conjunction here through their common regard for walking: for example, Hilaire Belloc and Werner Herzog, Xavier de Maistre and Albert Speer. Indeed, the strange and unexpected connections generated here are unimaginable in perhaps any other literary sphere.

Such categories can, however, never wholly be maintained, particularly where an activity as prone to drift as walking is concerned, and these divisions are at times resisted by their subjects, whose wanderings allow them to move easily between them. One distinction, however, that has been more rigorously enforced is geographical: the writers discussed here are without exception drawn from the Western literary tradition; and while the walks which they undertake frequently take them beyond the boundaries of Europe and North America, it is to these two continents that I have restricted my account.[11]

Just as the writers and texts discussed here constitute their own distinct pedestrian canon, so too must this book take its own place alongside those earlier accounts which have sought to outline and illustrate the history of the writer as walker. I am very conscious of the works that have preceded my own in this regard, many of which can be found in the bibliography to this book; and just as each of these reflects its own author's personal preferences in the choice of writers it seeks to celebrate or to omit, so too have I been faced with similar decisions. Of course, a number of writers demand inclusion here simply because it would be perverse to exclude them: Rousseau, De Quincey, Wordsworth and Dickens, for example. Other names, however, are routinely absent from such surveys, and it is these, amongst them Arthur Machen and Robert Walser, whom I have paid particular attention to in my account. Of course, each new book updates its predecessors, and just as new accounts acquire new writers and their works, so too are others shed along the way: the names of Iain Sinclair and Will Self, for example, seem indispensable here, at least from a Londoner's perspective; equally indispensable, however, to writers and walkers of previous generations, were figures such as Leslie Stephen and Christopher Morley, and yet their names are not to be found amongst those gathered here.

'Mankind in general has seldom regarded walking as a pleasure', writes Morris Marples in his history of walking, *Shanks's Pony* (1959).[12] Yet throughout the following pages the sentiment expressed by writers as diverse as Wordsworth and Whitman, Woolf and O'Hara, is predominantly one of joy; a joy that is to be found in the freedom of the open road; in the wonder of the natural world; in the solitude of the crowded street; and in the unlikeliest corners of the suburban city. Of course, such pleasure is often eroded by fatigue and may even be a prelude to the darker emotions of melancholy and despair, but in every instance such walks reveal new aspects of the landscape they pass through, both urban and rural, which had hitherto been ignored or overlooked. Every walk can be expressed as a story narrated by the walker; it is these stories and the lives of those who walked them which are examined here.

Notes

[1] Italo Svevo, *Zeno's Conscience* (1923), ed. and trans. by William Weaver, London: Penguin, 2002, p. 105

[2] Honoré de Balzac, *Théorie de la Démarche* ('Theory of Walking'; 1833), trans. by Tim Ingold in *Being Alive: Essays on Movement, Knowledge and Description*, London: Routledge, 2011, p. 33

[3] Stephen Graham, 'The Literature of Walking', in *The Tramp's Anthology*, ed. by Stephen Graham, London: Peter Davies, 1928, vii–xi, p. viii

[4] Geoff Nicholson, *The Lost Art of Walking: The History, Science,*

Philosophy, Literature, Theory and Practice of Pedestrianism, Chelmsford: Harbour Books, 2010, p. 262

[5] Tim Ingold, *Being Alive: Essays on Movement, Knowledge and Description,* London: Routledge, 2011, p. 178

[6] Ingold, *Being Alive,* p. 12

[7] Ingold, *Being Alive,* p. 202

[8] Tim Ingold, *Lines: A Brief History,* London: Routledge, 2007, pp. 90–91

[9] Ingold extends his analogy between storytelling and walking to include both the story that is voiced or sung, as well as the handwritten text. Yet he also recognises that such a comparison, based as it is upon the uninterrupted flow of the hand across the page and that of the foot across the earth, is not applicable to the text which has been typed or printed. Indeed, the transition from the written to the printed word presents, for Ingold at least, a fundamental disruption of the relationship between writing and walking, as the unbroken line which is symbolic of both is fractured: 'It was when writers *ceased* to perform the equivalent of a walk', concludes Ingold, 'that their words were reduced to fragments and in turn fragmented.' Ingold, *Lines,* pp. 91–93

[10] Miles Jebb, *Walkers,* London: Constable, 1986, Introduction, p. ix

[11] This is a distinction which remains broadly true of all the major walking histories I have encountered. One exception to this rule is *Journeys: An Anthology,* edited by Robyn Davidson (London: Picador, 2001) in which walking plays only a part, but which is categorised by region and is truly global in scope.

[12] Morris Marples, *Shanks's Pony: A Study of Walking,* London: Dent, 1959, p. xiii

The Walker as Philosopher

To travel on foot, is to travel like Thales, Plato, and Pythagoras. Jean–Jacques Rousseau.[1]

Philosophers walked. But philosophers who thought about walking are rarer. Rebecca Solnit.[2]

In one of the less celebrated accounts of literary walking, *Of Walks and Walking Tours: An Attempt to find a Philosophy and a Creed* (1914), the author, Arnold Haultain, draws up a shortlist of 'notable walkers' in which the usual suspects, De Quincey and Stevenson, are joined by their classical forebears, Plato, Virgil and Horace. At the top of the list are Jesus and Mohammed.[3] This attempt to trace the genesis of the literary walk to its biblical roots is by no means uncommon, often taking as its starting point the expulsion of Adam and Eve from Eden, a symbolic moment memorialised in the closing lines of Milton's *Paradise Lost* (1667): 'The world was all before them, where to choose/ Their place of rest, and Providence their guide: / They hand in hand with wand'ring steps and slow, / Through Eden took their solitary way.'[4] It is not Adam and Eve, however, but their offspring, Cain and Abel, who have been identified as establishing the primordial division between the walker or nomad and his more sedentary cousin, the settler. In his book, *Walkscapes: Walking as an Aesthetic Practice* (2002), Francesco Careri describes a division between what he calls 'nomadic' and 'erratic' space, the consequence of two different ways of living and working in the world, to which he ascribes a biblical source:

The sons of Adam and Eve embody the two souls in which the human race is divided from the outset: Cain is the sedentary soul, Abel the nomadic one [...] Cain can be identified with *Homo Faber*, the man who works and tames nature to materially construct a new universe, while Abel, whose job was, all told, less tiring and more amusing, can be seen as *Homo Ludens* [...] the man who plays and constructs an ephemeral system of relations between nature and life.[5]

'So from the very beginning,' concludes Careri, 'artistic creation, as well as that rejection of work [...] was associated with walking.'[6] While Abel, the prototype nomad, wanders in the hills, free to play while his sheep graze, Cain stays and tills the land, no doubt feeling increasingly embittered. It is clear how this story is going to end. And yet, in the aftermath of Abel's murder at the hands of his brother, divine punishment lends this tale an ironic twist:

It is interesting to note that after the murder Cain is punished by God by being condemned to roam the face of the earth: Abel's nomadism is transformed from a condition of privilege to one of divine punishment. The *error* of fratricide is punished with a sentence to *err* without a home, eternally lost in the land of Nod, the infinite desert where Abel had previously roamed. And it should be emphasized that after the death of Abel the first cities are constructed by the descendents of Cain: Cain, the farmer condemned to wander, gives rise to the sedentary life and therefore to another sin, he carries with him the origins of the stationary life of the farmer and those of the nomadic life of Abel, both experienced as a punishment and an error [...] The nomads came from the lineage of Cain, who was a settler forced to become a nomad, and they carry the wanderings of Abel in their roots.[7]

For those seeking the historical antecedents with which to establish a philosophy of walking, however, and in particular for those Enlightenment thinkers who were to regard the philosopher-walker as emblematic of their newfound intellectual freedom, such biblical foundations were insufficient or irrelevant. What was really required was the support of the classical tradition.

As Rousseau's remark above indicates, to travel on foot is, indeed, to travel in the manner of Thales, Plato and Pythagoras. Yet for those searching for evidence of walking as an intentional act, rather than simply as a means of locomotion, the classical age appears to have very little to offer. Plato's *Phaedrus*, for example, has been repeatedly identified as the text in which Socrates emerges as an early, if not the earliest, philosopher-walker. On closer inspection, however, this becomes a highly questionable assertion, for the *Phaedrus* remains the only one of Plato's dialogues in which we see Socrates depart from his familiar urban haunts, and rather belying his status as the archetypal walker, he is admonished for his reluctance to stray beyond Athens' city walls:

> *Phaedrus*: […] it's proof of how you never leave town either to travel abroad, or even, I think, to step outside the city walls at all.

> *Socrates*: You'll have to forgive me, my friend. I'm an intellectual, you see, and country places with their trees tend to have nothing to teach me, whereas people in town do. But I think you've found a way to charm me outside […][8]

Socrates, the city-dwelling intellectual, is only lured out of the city by the prospect of reading a speech which Phaedrus has prepared, and this walk is by no means an epic, as Socrates wastes no time in finding the nearest tree under which he can consult Phaedrus' work. Walking here provides a background to the ideas discussed and is never more than ancillary to them.

In fact, the stroll was a well-established classical device for providing the setting for philosophising, if not itself regarded as a subject fit for philosophical discussion. Hence, Virgil's *Georgics*, the pastoral idylls of Theocritus and Horace, and even Homer's *Odyssey*, have all been identified as further examples of the integral role the act of walking plays in the classical canon. But in all these cases, if the walk is to have a role, it is not a philosophical but a literary one, providing a handy structural device in which the physical rhythm of the walk lends a degree of dynamism to the text. Walking and talking regularly coincide here, but the conjunction of these two everyday activities is never formalised in any way, let alone as the basis to any philosophical position. In short, as Morris Marples has reminded us, 'we find the Greeks taking pleasure in the combined operation of walking and talking [...] But no Greek or Roman ever went for a walking-tour.'[9]

Amidst the scant evidence that the classical world elevated the act of walking to anything more than a means to an end, there remains one Greek school of thought which, although contested by modern scholars, is consistently identified as the point at which Western philosophy and walking first intersect. 'Western philosophy finds its beginnings in walking, with the Peripatetic philosophers' writes David Macauley, 'who walked boldly out of the dark and deep realm of myth and into the lighted house of logos.'[10] The persistent claim that the bodily rhythms of walking somehow correspond to mental processes appears to originate here, in the Athenian school of philosophy founded by Aristotle. While emphasising the link between walking and thinking, however, the belief that the Peripatetic school provides a philosophical grounding for this position, a belief which later writers have been so keen to promote, itself appears to be little more than a myth arising from a linguistic misunderstanding.

The term Peripatetic is used to describe the followers of Aristotle's school of philosophy, founded in Athens in around 335 BC, and continued by his successors, amongst them Theophrastus and Strato. A transliteration of the ancient Greek word περιπατητικός, meaning 'of walking' or 'given to walking about', the term has evolved to apply to any act of itinerant wandering or meandering. The school itself, however, or peripatos, the Lyceum gymnasium in which the members met, derives its name from the peripatoi (περίπατοι), the colonnades or covered walkways through which Aristotle is alleged to have walked while lecturing. It is out of this confusion that the belief arose that walking was somehow an intrinsic part of the philosophical method employed by Aristotle and his followers. In reality, however, and rather more prosaically, it appears that the Peripatetics owe their name not to their philosophy, but to the setting in which it was conducted; and not only has this myth arisen from linguistic confusion, but the Peripatetics have since been subjected to further misrepresentation, as later writers wilfully overlooked reality in favour of the more romantic image of the strolling philosopher. According to Rebecca Solnit, the chief culprit here was John Thelwall, whose work, *The Peripatetic*, was first published in 1793. Thelwall's peculiar but highly influential blend of biography and philosophical treatise is almost completely neglected today but his misguided attempt to 'consecrate the act of walking' has survived him, and the spurious classical tradition he endorsed lives on.[11]

Beyond the fact that, architecturally at least, walking was accommodated within the Lyceum as the basis for conversational, if not philosophical, activity, it is by now impossible to determine with any certainty what role, if any, the act of walking held in classical philosophy. If, at the very least, the Peripatetics can be said to exemplify a tradition of meditative walking, in which philosophical thought is in some way harnessed to the physical movements of the walker, then this activity, as Socrates indicates in the *Phaedrus*, is one more usually reserved for the enclosed spaces of the *peripatos*. Such a tradition, in which walking comes to be seen as primarily a contemplative, even educative, act, is one which was continued, albeit in a more spiritual fashion, within the monastic confines of the Middle Ages. In this respect, it has little in common with the unbounded, and less structured excursions favoured by the Romantics, to whom the walk and the walker were to become symbolic not of systematic thought, but of intellectual freedom and solitary creativity. And, as we shall see in the following chapter, while this former position helps to establish the figure of the walker as pilgrim, a tradition with a significant literary history of its own, it is out of this latter current, that the episodic and often fragmentary history of philosophical walking was to emerge.

In reality, this philosophical tradition can largely be reduced to little more than a walking-themed selection of quotations and biographical sketches: Saint Thomas Aquinas, for example, is reputed to have walked more than 9,000 miles during his excursions across Europe; while Thomas Hobbes did so much of his thinking on foot that he had an ink-horn fitted to his staff, allowing him to record his ideas as they occurred to him. Likewise, Jeremy Bentham maintained a strict regime of 'post-jentacular circumgyrations'[12]; and Immanuel Kant's lunchtime strolls around Königsberg were taken with such metronomic regularity that his neighbours were said to set their watches by him. This may suggest a highly disciplined if not pedantic personality, but can such a fact really shed any light on his *Critique of Pure Reason*? Hegel and John Stuart Mill, and later Heidegger and Husserl, the list of philosopher-walkers seems so comprehensive that it is perhaps only the stationary philosopher who can be said to display true originality.

There is, of course, a single and overriding exception here: the figure that is said to have 'laid the groundwork for the ideological edifice within which walking itself would be enshrined.'[13] Jean-Jacques Rousseau's *Reveries of a Solitary Walker* was his final work, and was not published until 1782, four years after his death. But by then, both in his *Confessions* and elsewhere, Rousseau had consecrated the hallowed role of the philosopher-walker in the iconography of Enlightenment thinking, blazing a trail that the Romantics were soon to follow:

Never did I think so much, exist so vividly, and experience so much, never have I been so much myself – if I may use that expression – as in the journeys I have taken alone and on foot. There is something about walking which stimulates and enlivens my thoughts. When I stay in one place I can hardly think at all; my body has to be on the move to set my mind going. The sight of the countryside, the succession of pleasant views, the open air, a sound appetite, and the good health I gain by walking, the easy atmosphere of an inn, the absence of everything that recalls me to my situation – all these serve to free my spirit, to lend a greater boldness to my thinking, to throw me, so to speak, into the vastness of things, so that I can combine them, select them, and make them mine as I will, without fear or restraint.[14]

Rousseau was born in Geneva in 1712, and the history of Rousseau the walker predates that of Rousseau the philosopher, beginning in 1727 when, aged fifteen, he returned to the city from a country stroll only to find that the city gates had been shut. In an act of extraordinary impulsiveness, he turned his back on his birthplace, and literally walked away from his previous life to begin a long period as an itinerant wanderer. Leaving Switzerland for France and Italy, Rousseau worked and walked his way through the experiences that were to shape both his character and his work.[15] It was a habit that he was never fully able or willing to overcome and it was to shape his life: 'I like to walk at my leisure, and halt when I please. The wandering life is what I like. To journey on foot, unhurried, in fine weather and in fine country, and to have something pleasant to look forward to at my goal, that is of all ways of life the one that suits me best.'[16]

According to his recollections of this period, later recorded in the *Confessions* (1782), his transition from walker to writer was itself prompted by a decision taken while on foot. For it was in 1749, while walking the six miles from Paris to the gaol in which his friend Denis Diderot was incarcerated, that he came across a question posed by the Dijon Academy in the pages of the *Mercure de France*. His response was to launch his writing career and to set himself on a highly controversial course in which he would challenge the established principles of monarchy, religion and the state. For Rousseau's prize-winning essay questioned the moral benefits of the arts and sciences, arguing that their effects were to weaken and corrupt mankind. His conclusion, that man was the victim rather than the beneficiary of so-called progress, was to form the basis of his *Discourse on the Origin and Foundation of Inequality* (1754) in which he outlined his belief that man was only truly free within a state of nature, a condition of pure simplicity and self-reliance beyond the harmful interventions of human society. In such an idealised existence, the act of walking itself takes on an elemental role, as a means of pure mobility, unadorned by any of the unwelcome and unnecessary accoutrements which weigh down the modern traveller.

Having located the ideal walker in a state of nature outside society, Rousseau's own walks can be seen as an attempt to replicate the purity of this experience. But the role that walking was to play in Rousseau's life and philosophy was to evolve over time, and while it symbolised unfettered freedom in his early life, the walking described in the *Confessions* and the *Reveries* reveals a sense of persecutory fear, in which Rousseau is no longer walking towards an unknown future but escaping from an unwelcome past and an intolerable present. For inevitably Rousseau was unable to recapture the intoxicating sense of freedom inspired by his flight from Geneva, nor was he able to access the solitude he sought, free from what he perceived as the betrayals and disappointments of life in society, a position paradoxically heightened by the fame his work had brought him.

The *Reveries of a Solitary Walker* holds an ambiguous position within the literature of walking. For it is less a book about walking than an account of those thoughts that walking has prompted. Strictly speaking neither philosophy nor biography, the series of ten essays that comprise the book (the eighth and ninth in draft, the tenth unfinished at the time of Rousseau's death) form a walker's diary in which reminiscence and reflection intermingle with botanical observation in an unstructured and free-ranging style. 'My whole life has been little else than a long reverie divided into chapters by my daily walks', writes Rousseau, a sentiment perfectly encapsulated in the form of the *Reveries*.[17]

From the outset, Rousseau is keen to establish himself as the true subject of his book, writing in the First Walk: 'These pages will be no more than a formless record of my reveries. I myself will figure largely in them, because a solitary person inevitably thinks a lot about himself.'[18] Indeed, in a similar vein, in the Second Walk Rousseau identifies these hours of solitude as providing the only opportunity for him to be 'completely myself and my own master, with nothing to distract or hinder me, the only ones when I am what nature meant me to be.'[19] The Second Walk holds a noteworthy position within the book in that it is one of the few times at which Rousseau recalls in any detail, an event, rather than an impression, idea or observation; and within the context of the book, it is an event which holds a highly incongruous, if not surreal, position. For walking home one evening, Rousseau sees a Great Dane rushing towards him, and attempts to take evasive action:

> I judged that my only hope of avoiding being knocked down was to leap into the air at precisely the right moment to allow the dog to pass underneath me. This lightning plan of action, which I had no time either to examine or to put into practice, was my last thought before I went down. I felt neither the impact nor my fall, nor indeed anything else until I eventually came to.[20]

Rousseau made his way home, minus several teeth, and slowly convalesced. But soon the story had spread across Paris and sometime later Rousseau was faced with the rumour that he had in fact died from his fall.[21] This whole event shows Rousseau to be a strangely vulnerable figure but it is his response which is most revealing. For unable to recognise the humour that might attach itself to such an absurd event, Rousseau greets the news of his premature departure with morbid suspicion, recognising 'a foretaste of the tribute of insults and indignities which are being prepared to honour my memory by way of funeral oration.'[22] And it is precisely this sense of heightened paranoia which pervades the entire book, transforming the act of walking into an escape mechanism, a means of evading a society which is seen as wholly malevolent. For it is only amidst nature that Rousseau can once again reassert control over his surroundings, his botanical forays providing him with a semblance of the status denied to him, or so he believes, by society.[23]

The unfinished Tenth Walk, along with the Fifth Walk, both recount periods of relative happiness for Rousseau: the former as a teenager at the home of his lover and patroness, Madame de Warens; the latter in solitude on the island of Saint-Pierre on Lake Bienne. The tenor of these two episodes is, however, conspicuously at odds with the prevailing mood of melancholy which informs the *Reveries*, and nowhere is this obsessive sense of victimhood more apparent than in the Ninth Walk, which begins with his observation that 'Happiness is a state which does not seem to be made for man in this world.'[24] For it seems that if we are to recognise Rousseau's position in inaugurating the literature of philosophical walking, then we must also credit him with establishing a parallel tradition of melancholic walking, a tradition which continues to this day.[25]

If Rousseau can be identified as the prototype philosopher-walker, those who have followed in his footsteps have been reluctant to elevate the act of walking to quite the same position within their own work. In fact, the only other figure to share in Rousseau's apotheosis of the pedestrian is one who also reflects his ambiguous position within the Western philosophical canon. For like Rousseau, Søren Kierkegaard is a figure whose evocative, descriptive and highly personal accounts of Copenhagen street life place him at odds with a philosophical tradition dominated by rigorous logical reasoning.

Whilst sharing Rousseau's peripatetic habits, Kierkegaard (1813–1855) was a walker who thrived not in the countryside but amidst the throng of city life. The setting was almost exclusively Copenhagen, the city in which Kierkegaard spent his entire life, and it was here, amidst the crowds, that he was able to detach himself from his surroundings whilst remaining keenly observant of them. As the result of a childhood fall, Kierkegaard suffered from a pronounced curvature of the spine, an anatomical fact which made him lean backwards as he walked, causing his gait to take on a dislocated, mechanical manner and making his movements appear overly deliberate.[26] Such an appearance was, of course, deceptive, for there was little deliberation to be found in Kierkegaard's wandering. His was the aimless drift that was to become that hallmark of the *flâneur* on the streets of Paris a generation later.[27] 'When you go for a walk', he wrote, 'let your thoughts wander aimlessly, snooping about, experimenting with first one thing and then another.'[28] Walking was, however, much more than just an aesthetic practice for Kierkegaard; it was a source of diversion and pleasure; both a source and a cure for solitude, as well as a crucial support to his productivity as a writer. In short, it was a way of life:

Above all, do not lose your desire to walk: every day I walk myself into a state of well-being and walk away from every illness. I have walked myself into my best thoughts, and I know of no thought so burdensome that one cannot walk away from it. Even if one were to walk for one's health and it were constantly one section ahead – *I would still say walk!* Besides, it is also apparent that in walking one constantly gets as close to well-being as possible, even if one does not quite reach it – *but by sitting still, and the more one sits still, the closer one feels to feeling ill.* Health and salvation can only be found in motion. If any denies that motion exists, I do as Diogenes did, I walk. If anyone denies that health resides in motion, then I walk away from all morbid objections. *Thus if one keeps on walking, everything will be all right.*[29]

For Kierkegaard, however, walking was unable to provide him with the panacea for all of life's ills and, despite his best attempts to keep walking, everything did not quite turn out all right in the end. In fact, rather than acquiring the serenity of the idle stroller, his life appears to have been a catalogue of crises and humiliations, in which a childhood dominated by the overpowering influence of his father was soon to be followed by a broken engagement with his fiancée, an event which was to colour the rest of his life. The final blow, however, appears to be the one which denied him his sole pleasure, that of walking the city streets. For following a very public dispute with the satirical magazine, the *Corsair*, he was subjected to a merciless campaign of mockery which made him something of a figure of ridicule on Copenhagen's streets. No longer the watcher, but the watched, Kierkegaard was now unable to find solace in the crowd: 'My atmosphere has been tainted for me. Because of my melancholy and my enormous work I needed a situation of solitude in the crowd in order to rest. So I despair. I can no longer find it. Curiosity surrounds me everywhere.'[30] Unable to break the habit of a lifetime, however, he continued to walk the streets, and it was on one such walk that he collapsed and later died.

'Sitting still is precisely the *sin* against the holy ghost,' writes Nietzsche. 'Only thoughts which come by *walking* have any value.'[31] Like Kierkegaard before him, Nietzsche was to repeatedly affirm the importance of walking (the ideas later expressed in *Thus Spoke Zarathustra* came to him while walking in the hills above Rapallo in Italy), without ever granting the activity an explicit philosophical position within his work. Despite this, however, Nietzsche's walking can be seen clearly to shape the form that his work takes. Hence, his love of the 'müssiggang', or leisurely stroll, is reflected in a literary style that avoids systematic thought in favour of a notoriously digressive and fragmented approach, itself a direct result of his practice of jotting down ideas while on foot.[32] Furthermore, his habit of solitary walking in the open air (like Rousseau and Thoreau he walked to escape the city and the crowd), has been seen to explain the central importance of *place* in his philosophy.[33]

Nietzsche's walking is described in terms of the same expression of solitude and alienation that animated both Rousseau and Kierkegaard before him, and it is a form of expression that anticipates the existential angst associated with modernity rather than recalling the walkers and thinkers of an earlier age. And it is perhaps for this reason that the link between walking and philosophy remains so stubbornly elusive – the solitude which these figures give voice to is inevitably grounded within an intensely personal vision of the world, a vision that places their writing at odds with any form of systematic thought and which renders them resistant to inclusion in any one tradition. The history of the philosopher–walker is, then, one which ultimately questions the very nature of philosophy as a suitable medium for engaging with an action seemingly at odds with it; and the philosopher–walker is shown to stand outside the very philosophical tradition he was thought to represent.

In recent years, however, there has been something of a resurgence in the theorising of walking. Of course, such theories are not in themselves new – there is a well-established tradition of attempts to 'explain' the activity of walking in something approaching a scientific manner, amongst them Honoré De Balzac's 'Théorie de la Démarche' (Theory of Walking, 1833) and Oliver Wendell Holmes' 'The Physiology of Walking' (1878). But what we witness today is not a return of theory, at least not in the sense that these two writers might have understood the term. Instead, we are talking about *theory*, that rather awkward term that promises (and frequently delivers) something rather abstruse, impenetrable, and more often than not, French.[34]

Fulfilling all these criteria, and by far the most influential of such accounts, Michel de Certeau's *The Practice of Everyday Life*

(1984) invokes both Henri Lefebvre's *Critique of Everyday Life* (1947) and Raoul Vaneigem's *Revolution of Everyday Life* (1967) in seeking to understand and theorise the practices of the 'common man' through an analysis of the patterns of his everyday existence. Thus de Certeau provides an epigraph to his work dedicated, 'To the ordinary man. To the common hero, an ubiquitous character, walking in countless thousands on the streets.'[35]

De Certeau's highly abstract take on those everyday practices that characterise modern life, from speaking and reading to walking and cooking, displays a curious logic that reveals, through a semiotic and poetic analysis of these practices, patterns and strategies common to each of them. In this way he attempts to illustrate the hidden structure of modern urban life that governs the relationship between a city and its inhabitants. Under the heading of 'Walking in the City', de Certeau takes New York as his example, distinguishing between two opposing perspectives on the city: that of *voyeur* and *walker*. To de Certeau, New York is the apotheosis of the modern city precisely because it is here that the division between the walker at street level and the voyeur inhabiting the summit of the skyscrapers above is at its most stark: 'The ordinary practitioners of the city live "down below", below the thresholds at which visibility begins. They walk – an elementary form of this experience of the city: they are walkers.'[36] But looking down upon them from up above, with a panoptical god–like view, are the voyeurs who experience the city as a vast totality far removed from any individual perspective: 'To be lifted to the summit of the World Trade Center is to be lifted out of the city's grasp. One's body is no longer clasped by the streets [...] when one goes up there, he leaves behind the mass that carries off and mixes up in itself any identity of authors or spectators [...] His elevation transfigures him into a voyeur. It puts him at a distance.'[37]

This, then, for de Certeau at least, is the distinction governing modern urban life, that between walker and voyeur, and it is one which emphasises the democratic importance of the street–level perspective to be gained from walking the city and reconnecting with individual life. In the light of this distinction it is clear how the simple act of walking can take on a subversive hue, abolishing the distancing and voyeuristic perspective of those who view the city from above. For the totalising gaze of the voyeur, who sees the city as a homogenous whole, encompasses an anonymous urban space that sees no place for individual or separate identities and which erases or suppresses the personal and the local.

'De Certeau's metaphor suggests a frightening possibility', writes Rebecca Solnit, 'that if the city is a language spoken by walkers, then a postpedestrian city not only has fallen silent but risks becoming a dead language, one whose colloquial phrases, jokes, and curses will vanish, even if its formal grammar survives.'[38] It is only by resisting such an outcome that the individual can re-establish an emotional engagement with his surroundings. 'Their story begins on ground level, with footsteps,' concludes de Certeau, and it is here, not up above, that the true history of the city is recorded.[39]

Notes

[1] Jean-Jacques Rousseau, *Émile, or On Education* (1762), trans. by Allen Bloom, New York: Basic Books, 1979, p. 412

[2] Rebecca Solnit, *Wanderlust: A History of Walking*, London: Verso, 2001, p. 16

[3] Arnold Haultain, *Of Walks and Walking Tours: An Attempt to Find a Philosophy and a Creed*, London: T Werner Laurie Ltd, 1914, pp. 9–15

[4] John Milton, *Paradise Lost* (1667), ed. by John Leonard, London: Penguin, 2003, Book XII, Line 646, p. 288. Elsewhere, Roger Gilbert writes: 'The earliest literary walk occurs quite literally in the beginning; that is, in Genesis. I refer, of course, to Yahweh's walk "in the garden at the breezy time of day", during which he discovers Adam and Eve's primal transgression.' Roger Gilbert, *Walks in the World: Representation and Experience in Modern American Poetry*, Princeton, NJ: Princeton University Press, 1991, p. 35

[5] Francesco Careri, *Walkscapes: Walking as an Aesthetic Practice,* Barcelona: Editorial Gustavo Gili, 2002, pp. 29–30. The concept of *Homo Ludens*, or 'playing man' was the brainchild of Dutch historian, Johan Huizinga, who was to stress the importance of the element of play in the development of culture and society. See Johan Huizinga, *Homo Ludens: A Study of the Play Element in Culture* (1938), trans. by RFC Hull, Boston, MA: Beacon Press, 1955

[6] Careri, p. 33

[7] Careri, pp. 33–34. Careri's brilliant analysis of the evolution and significance of walking in pre-history owes (and acknowledges) a great deal to comments on the same theme made by Bruce Chatwin in *The Songlines* (1987), an account of his travels in central Australia. Chatwin devotes much of his book to extracts from his notebooks, an eclectic selection of quotations and observations on the subject of walking and nomadism, amongst which one finds the following remarks: 'The names of the brothers are a matched pair of opposites. Abel comes from the Hebrew '*hebel*' meaning 'breath' or 'vapour': anything that lives and moves and is transient, including his own life. The root of 'Cain' appears to be '*kanah*': to 'acquire', 'get', 'own property', and so 'rule' or 'subjugate'. 'Cain' also means 'metal-smith'. And since in several languages – even Chinese – the words for 'violence' and 'subjugation' are linked to the discovery of metal, it is perhaps the destiny of Cain and his descendants to practice the black arts of technology.' Bruce Chatwin, *The Songlines*, London: Viking, 1987, pp. 192–193

[8] Plato, *Phaedrus*, trans. by Robin Waterfield, Oxford: OUP, 2002, p. 7. According to Thoreau, Plato's reluctance to leave the city was by no means atypical. Athenians of Plato's status would be more inclined to plant groves within which to walk rather than to leave the confines of the city: 'Even some sects of philosophers have felt the necessity of importing the woods to themselves, since they did not go to the woods. "They planted groves and walks of Platanes," where they took *subdiales ambulationes* in

porticos open to the air.' Henry David Thoreau, 'Walking' (1862), in *The Pleasures of Walking*, ed. by Edwin Valentine Mitchell, Bourne End, Bucks: Spurbooks, 1975, 129–172, p. 135

[9] Marples, p. xiii

[10] David Macauley, 'A Few Foot Notes on Walking', *Trumpeter: Journal of Ecosophy*, (Vol. 10: 1, Winter, 1993) at http://trumpeter. athabascau.ca/content/v10.1/Macauley.html. Macauley notes that in the Eastern philosophical tradition 'walking has always been a part of the philosophical way, as in Taoism and Zen Buddhism, where the sages and monks sauntered the countryside in search of enlightenment. Walking is even given a special place as one of the four Chinese 'dignities' (modes of being in the world), along with Standing, Sitting and Lying.' (Note 14, p. 5)

[11] Solnit, p. 14. Although, as appears to be the case, we have not been bequeathed a philosophy of walking from antiquity, we may well have inherited our gait: 'The historian Jan Bremmer has traced the western ideals of upright posture, and a gait with long measured strides and straight legs, to the culture of Ancient Greece, passed on to early modern Europe by way of the works of Cicero, Saint Ambrose and Erasmus. The origin of the Greek gait, Bremmer suggests, lies in an earlier age when every man had to carry arms, and be ready to fight to protect both reputation and possessions.' Ingold, *Being Alive*, p. 40. See also Jan Bremmer, 'Walking, standing and sitting in ancient Greek culture', in *A Cultural History of Gesture*, ed. by J. Bremmer & H. Roodenburg, Oxford: Polity Press, pp. 15–35

[12] Leslie Stephen, 'In Praise of Walking', in *The Pleasures of Walking*, ed. by Edwin Valentine Mitchell, 18–38, p. 24

[13] Solnit, p. 17

[14] Jean-Jacques Rousseau, *Confessions* (1782), trans. by JM Cohen, Harmondsworth: Penguin, 1954, p. 167

[15] The details of Rousseau's peripatetic existence following his flight from Geneva have been summarised as follows: 'He then made his own way as a footman in Turin, a student in a choir school in Annecy, a lover of a baroness in Chambéry, an

interpreter to a Levantine mountebank, an itinerant musician, a private tutor, and then a secretary in Venice. He did all this before establishing himself in Paris when he was still in his early thirties.' Joseph A. Amato, *On Foot: A History of Walking*, New York: New York University Press, 2004, p. 109

[16] Rousseau, *Confessions*, p. 382

[17] Comment jotted down by Rousseau on the back of a playing-card while writing the *Reveries* (1776–78). See Peter France, ed., Jean-Jacques Rousseau, *The Reveries of the Solitary Walker*, London: Penguin, 2004, Introduction, p. 12

[18] Rousseau, *Reveries*, p. 32

[19] Rousseau, *Reveries*, p. 35

[20] Rousseau, *Reveries*, p. 38

[21] The *Courier d'Avignon* of December 20, 1776 was to mistakenly report Rousseau's death.

[22] Rousseau, *Reveries*, p. 43

[23] Jeffrey Robinson writes, 'Rousseau's walks are expressions of power [...] All plants are subject to his or Linnaeus's categories, which he subdues by knowing them. He walks through his kingdom, paying his respects to his subjects.' Jeffrey Robinson, *The Walk: Notes on a Romantic Image*, Norman, OK: University of Oklahoma Press, 1989, p. 73

[24] Rousseau, *Reveries*, p. 137

[25] In this regard, the most obvious contemporary successor to Rousseau has been the writer and walker, WG Sebald, whose account of walks taken along the Suffolk coast in his acclaimed *The Rings of Saturn* (1995) frequently manages to replicate, if not surpass, the melancholy tone to be found in Rousseau's *Reveries*. See WG Sebald, *The Rings of Saturn*, trans. by Michael Hulse, London: Harvill, 1998

[26] *The Journals of Kierkegaard, 1834–1854*, ed. and trans. by Alexander Dru, London: Fontana, 1958, Introduction, p. 8

[27] In fact, were he 'less prolific and less Danish', argues Rebecca Solnit, it might be Kierkegaard and not Benjamin who is today regarded as the first true philosopher of *flânerie*. Solnit, p. 200

28 Søren Kierkegaard, 'Letter to Emil Boesen' in *Written Images: Søren Kierkegaard's Journals, Notebooks, Booklets, Sheets, Scraps, and Slips of Paper*, ed. by Niels Jorgen Cappelhorn, Joakim Garff and Johnny Kondrup, trans. by Bruce H Kirmmse, Princeton, NJ: Princeton University Press, 2003, p. 135

29 Søren Kierkegaard, 'Letter to Henrietta Lund' (1847), trans. by Henrik Rosenmeier and qtd. in *The Vintage Book of Walking*, ed. by Duncan Minshull, London: Vintage, 2000, p. 6

30 Søren Kierkegaard, *Søren Kierkegaard's Journals and Papers*, ed. and trans. by Howard V. Hong & Edna H. Hong, Bloomington, IA: Indiana University Press, 1967–1978, Vol. 5, p. 386

31 Friedrich Nietzsche, *The Twilight of the Idols*, ed. and trans. by Duncan Large, Oxford: Oxford University Press, 2008, p. 9. 'And look what happened to him', notes Iain Sinclair, quoting Nietzsche's remark, 'seething till his eyes popped out, conversations with horses.' Iain Sinclair, *London Orbital*, London: Granta, 2002, p. 31

32 Duncan Large notes that Nietzsche's notebook material was largely recorded on foot, away from his desk and the dangers of 'conceptual cobwebbing.' Nietzsche, *Twilight of the Idols*, Introduction, p. xx

33 Friedrich Nietzsche, *Thus Spoke Zarathustra*, ed. and trans. by Graham Parkes, Oxford: Oxford University Press, 2008, Introduction, p. xiii

34 'One glory remains to Paris', writes Rebecca Solnit, 'that of possessing the chief theorists of walking.' In addition to Debord (1950s) and de Certeau (1980s), Solnit adds the name of Christophe Bailly (1990s). Bailly describes the act of walking as the *'grammaire generative de jambes'* (generative grammar of the legs), speaking of the city as 'a collection of stories, a memory of itself made by the walkers of the streets.' 'Should walking erode,' warns Solnit, 'the collection may become unread or unreadable.' Solnit, pp. 212–213. One further name which one might add to the roster of Parisian pedestrian-theorists is that of Jacques Réda, whose wanderings through the city place him firmly within the

tradition of Baudelaire and Rimbaud. See Jacques Réda, *The Ruins of Paris* (Les Ruines de Paris; 1970), trans. by Mark Treharne, London: Reaktion, 1996

[35] Michel de Certeau, *The Practice of Everyday Life*, trans. by Steven Rendall, Berkeley, CA: University of California Press, 2002, epigraph

[36] de Certeau, p. 93

[37] de Certeau, p. 92

[38] Solnit, p. 213

[39] de Certeau, p. 97

The Walker as Pilgrim

I raised me, as good walkers should, and bore
My body upright, though the thoughts in me
Remained bowed down and shrunken as before. Dante[1]

For we are all pilgrims. William Langland[2]

In contrast to the often awkward relationship between walking and philosophy, in which the aimless and digressive nature of the former may appear at odds with the more systematic objectives of the latter, the pilgrimage dominates the pre-romantic literature of the walk by achieving a harmony of thought and action in which the movement of the narrative is reflected and reinforced by the characters as they move through the landscape towards their sacred goal. This spiritual dimension has its roots in the earliest literary representations of walking, and in the Christian tradition it originates in the expulsion of Adam and Eve from Eden. But it is Christ himself who provided the template for the medieval pilgrim, through his own three-year period of intensive walking and preaching across Judea, an area extending some 130 miles from Sidon and Tyre in the north to Jerusalem in the south.[3]

In early poems of pilgrimage, such as Dante's *Commedia* (1308–21) and William Langland's *Piers Plowman* (c. 1360–87), the essentially plotless character of the walk is contained within a highly structured poetic form, and the activity of walking is itself framed within the allegorical device of the dream. Rather than walking, then, we see dreams of walking, in which the pedestrian is abstracted from his physical surroundings and the hardships of true pilgrimage, to become 'the walker', an Everyman, the universal symbol of the common man. Yet despite this sense of spiritual abstraction, the pilgrim is never wholly divorced from the realm of direct experience and however visionary and unearthly the imaginary landscape becomes, a material geography lies beneath, recognisably the world inhabited by the reader.

From a twenty-first century perspective, however, in which the religious impulse of the pilgrimage has been largely transmuted into a more secular desire for political or cultural change, the literary pilgrimages of Dante, Chaucer and Bunyan are often viewed with a mistaken reverence that overlooks the fact that, by the Middle Ages, the ascetic purity of the pilgrimage had already diminished to the extent that its participants were as likely to ride as walk.[4] Of course, the authors of these poems were well aware of the manner in which many of their contemporaries viewed the spiritual significance of the pilgrimage, and the disdain which they felt for the pilgrim. Indeed, it is in recognition of such an outlook that Thoreau speculates upon the etymology of the word 'sauntering': 'beautifully derived "from idle people who roved about the country, in the Middle Ages, and asked charity, under pretense of going *à la Sainte Terre*," to the Holy Land, till the children exclaimed, "There goes a Sainte-Terrer", a Saunterer, a Holy-Lander.' 'They who never go to the Holy Land in their walks, as they pretend, are indeed mere idlers and vagabonds', writes Thoreau, 'But they who do go there are saunterers in the good sense, such as I mean.'[5]

But despite the ridicule with which the figure of the pilgrim is often portrayed in the work of Chaucer and Langland, in which the act of pilgrimage is already seen as largely divorced from its religious component, one should note also the derivation of another word, 'travel', with its origins in *travail*, meaning not only work, but also suffering and the pangs of childbirth.[6] For the travel undertaken by the pilgrims of the early medieval age had little in common with the bawdy, playful, and often equestrian variety pursued on the road to Canterbury. Indeed, such accounts obscure the very real hardship experienced by those who, from the very beginnings of church history, set out for Rome and Jerusalem. For these pilgrims, the journey was truly an act of penance, an ordeal to be endured in the hope of forgiveness:

> In Galicia there are thick forests and few towns [...] mosquitoes infest the marshy plain of south Bordeaux where the traveller who strays from the road can sink up to his knees in mud. Some of the rivers are impassable. Several pilgrims had been drowned at Sorde, where travellers and their horses were ferried across the river on hollowed-out tree trunks. Other rivers were undrinkable, like the salt stream at Lorca, where the author of the *Guide* found two Basques earning their living by skinning the horses who had died after drinking from it.[7]

This summary is taken from the twelfth-century *Guide for Pilgrims to Santiago* and reveals what was awaiting those medieval pilgrims who set out on the road to Santiago de Compostela, while half of those setting out for Rome in 1350 were believed to have been robbed or killed.[8] Yet despite the hazards and hardships, pilgrims flocked to the holy sites of medieval Europe in huge numbers, encouraged by the Church and helped in particular by the Benedictine Rule which instructed that every guest should be welcomed as if he or she were Christ himself.[9] Of course, neither the Church nor the local shopkeepers were blind to the economic potential presented by this traffic in penitents, and the principal routes of medieval pilgrimage were soon to be characterised both by an array of churches, cathedrals and abbeys as well as the ready availability of icons and relics purportedly from the Holy Land. In this respect, the pilgrim acted as a trailblazer; and armed with his walking staff and dressed in his uniform of large-brimmed hat, long, coarse tunic and scrip, or pouch, for food and money, the pilgrim was to become the emblematic traveller of his day.

It was in the later Middle Ages that the pilgrimage began to lose its reputation for hardship and piety as the pilgrim himself became an untrustworthy figure, a liar whose 'pilgrim's tales' were to be treated with mockery and suspicion.[10] This transition was the result of the Church's policy of permitting the would-be pilgrim to substitute the pilgrimage itself, with all its inherent dangers, for a rather less unpleasant form of penance, perhaps conducted vicariously by others, or even undertaken from home:

> On the eve of the Reformation, a Strasbourg preacher calculated for a prisoner confined to his cell an indoor walking penance equivalent to making a pilgrimage to Rome for the 1500 Jubilee. Offering a kind of spiritual pedometer, he proposed that a prisoner could walk his cell for forty-two days and then devote himself to prayer for seven days to win an indulgence. This equalled the actual time required to get to and from Rome as well as the time spent visiting its holy stations. Erasmus scoffed at this kind of calculation. He suggested that by walking about his house, going to his study, checking on his daughter's chastity, and so forth, he too was doing his Roman stations.[11]

The role of the pilgrimage within literature is similar to that of the quest, for the pilgrimage is one of the fundamental forms the walk can take, the quest in search of something, the journey towards a goal, however intangible, and in this case the search for one's own transformation through God. The pilgrimage only differs from the quest in that its protagonist is essentially passive, 'his primary activity is precisely that of *passing*, rather than confronting'.[12] From Malory to Milton, and Cervantes to Bunyan, the metaphors of walking and travelling are central to the narrative, so central in fact that we hardly notice them. In fact, just as the act of writing expresses a journey through the terrain of the imagination, so too does the act of reading itself mirror this journey, as the reader is conducted on a journey with the author as guide. In this way, the distinction between walking and reading can be seen to dissolve as the act of walking becomes the means of 'reading' a landscape; and nowhere is this elision of reading and walking more apparent than in the archetypal poem of pilgrimage, Dante's *Commedia*.

'The question occurs to me', wrote the walker and writer, Bruce Chatwin, 'and quite seriously – how many shoe soles, how many ox-hide soles, how many sandals Alighieri wore out in the course of his poetic work, wandering about on the goat paths of Italy.'[13] For Dante's journey through the three realms of the soul after death, with Virgil and later Beatrice as Dante's (and the reader's) guide, is also a tour through the imaginative landscape of fourteenth-century Italy, the landscape that Dante himself wandered for more than two decades in exile from his native Florence. Notoriously complex in structure and sophisticated in symbolic meaning, the *Commedia* is at heart a travel story, in which the movement of the narrative is dictated by the movement of the characters as they complete their circular journey through Hell, Purgatory, and Heaven. And, like all good pilgrims, Dante conducts his journey on foot, setting out on the night before Good Friday and arriving a week later on the Wednesday after Easter, 1300. An allegorical epic that seemingly distances itself from the realm of direct experience which the literary walk usually inhabits, Dante's poem is in fact a twofold journey in which the struggle of Everyman to attain knowledge of God is conjoined to Dante's memories of his younger self and his own journey through life. This doubling is also reflected in the twofold division between Dante the pilgrim and Dante the poet, the first appearing as a character within the story recounted by the second. From the outset, then, truth, memory and fiction are intermingled, as Dante finds himself alone in a dark wood:

Half way along the road we have to go,
I found myself obscured in a great forest,
Bewildered, and I knew I had lost the way.[14]

It is beyond the scope of this book to attempt to explore Dante's work in any detail, and his inclusion here is simply as a means of illustrating the way in which the pilgrim comes to symbolise, not only the allegorical journey towards God, but also the journey through life itself, a journey which, in the Middle Ages, was inevitably taken, regardless of one's position in society, largely on foot. So just as the celebrated opening to Dante's poem may well symbolise man's sinful existence as he stumbles along the path to redemption, it may also recall Dante's own description of his early struggles, as an outcast, banished from his homeland in 1302 and forced to lead the life of a wanderer: 'I have wandered through almost every region to which this tongue of ours extends, a stranger, almost a beggar [...] Truly I have been a ship without sail and rudder, wafted to divers havens and inlets and shores, by the parching wind which woeful poverty exhales.'[15]

If Dante's poem emphasises the spiritual dimension of the pilgrimage, using allegory to distance his journey from the realities of everyday life, then Chaucer goes some way to reversing this process in his *Canterbury Tales* (1380–92), in which ('The Parson's Tale' apart) the spiritual is almost wholly overlooked in favour of the more secular and everyday aspects of the pilgrimage. As mentioned above, however, in Chaucer's depiction, the pilgrims who depart from the Tabard Inn tend to do so on horseback, and in doing so they not only invalidate their own attempts at gaining penance, but also prevent *The Canterbury Tales* from taking up a place in this account. A more rigorously pedestrian alternative to Chaucer's work, however, and one which shares his less than idealised vision of the pilgrim, is William Langland's *Piers Plowman* (c. 1360–87).

Little is known about the author of *Piers Plowman* and much of our knowledge is based upon the autobiographical evidence of the poem which, like Dante's *Commedia*, is narrated by the character of the author himself. First printed in the sixteenth century and mistakenly attributed to various authors, Chaucer amongst them, *Piers Plowman* owes less to Chaucer's poem than it does to Dante's; for like the *Commedia*, Langland's poem is also a mixture of allegory and social commentary, and it too outlines a circular pilgrimage, a transformative process which returns the pilgrim to himself through the knowledge of God. Written in unrhymed alliterative verse, and divided into sections which are, in keeping with an account of pilgrimage, called *passus*, the Latin for steps, *Piers Plowman* is structured around three distinct forms of pilgrimage layered upon one another, all three of which implicitly ridicule the institution: the first of these describes the narrator Will and his quest to find St Truth and to gain salvation; the second is the search for the allegorical characters Do-Well, Do-Better and Do-Best; and the third lies in the book's ending in which the search for *Piers Plowman* begins. These three interwoven goals all represent aspects of the individual's own journey through life, combining the physical journey with the inner spiritual journey towards God.[16]

The poem begins in the Malvern Hills in Worcestershire where, once again, the pilgrim begins his journey on foot, a solitary figure, a wanderer who has lost his way:

One summer time, when the sun was mild, I dressed myself in sheepskin clothing, the habit of a hermit of unholy life, and wandered abroad in this world, listening out for its strange and wonderful events. But one May morning, on Malvern Hills, out of the unknown, a marvellous thing happened to me. I was tired after wandering astray, and I turned aside to rest under a spacious bank beside a stream. And as I lay down and leaned back, and looked at the water, I grew drowsy and fell asleep, so sweet was the music that it made.[17]

From the outset, then, the motif of the journey is central, and throughout the poem we are reminded that 'the activity proper to a poet, dreamer and reader is that of journeying.'[18] Once again the narrative is driven by the unceasing movement of the characters, a purposeful movement through life which is encapsulated in the figure of the simple wayfaring man, perhaps the most evocative symbol in all the literature of the Middle Ages. Here the activity of walking is lent a moral significance, as a symbol of both poverty and simplicity; and in making a mere ploughman the hero of his poem, Langland implicitly questions the established social structure of fourteenth-century England, contrasting the everyday life of the commoner with the abuses of the established Church.

Will's dream in the prologue is a prelude to a series of visions, in which the 'Middle Earth' of fourteenth-century England is shown to exist precariously between the extremes of heaven and hell; for the world that *Piers Plowman* explores is both timeless and rooted in the everyday: 'England and nowhere. Never and always.'[19] On his journey through a landscape which is both supernatural and yet recognisably his own, Will meets a series of characters, some of whom are allegorical personifications of ideas, such as Reason and Conscience, while others would be a familiar sight to the traveller in the Middle Ages:

He was holding a staff round which was wrapped a broad strip of cloth, that wound all about it like a woodbine plant. By his side he carried a bowl and a bag; on his hat were perched a hundred tiny phials, as well as tokens of shells from Galicia, cross-ornaments on his cloak, a model of the keys of Rome, and on his breast a vernicle. All these emblems were designed to inform the world at large of all the pilgrim-shrines he had visited. The first thing everyone asked him was, where did he come from?

'From Sinai', he replied, 'and from the tomb of our Lord. I've been in Bethlehem, in Babylon, in Armenia, Alexandria, and various other places. You can tell from the souvenirs sitting on my hat that I've gone walking far and wide in quest of sundry holy saints, for the good of my soul.'[20]

The 'palmer', a pilgrim who has visited the Holy Land, is unable to help Will on his quest to find St Truth. For despite all his pilgrim badges and relics he has moved no further on the true journey towards God, his presence merely symbolic of the hypocrisy of the institution of pilgrimage.

The poem ends as the dreamer wakes, and the final word is given not to Will but to Conscience: 'Dear Christ!' cried Conscience. 'I'll become a pilgrim, then. I shall walk as wide as the distant horizon's bounds, and hunt the whole earth for Piers the Plowman.'[21] There is no epilogue or afterword to the poem, for at this point the voice of Conscience is that of the wakened dreamer, and his promise to keep 'walking the world' can be taken as both the true message of the poem – the call to embark on the inner pilgrimage towards God – as well as an exhortation to the reader to do the same.[22]

Such an exhortation to the would–be pilgrim finds more explicit confirmation in the 'author's apology for his book' with which John Bunyan begins *The Pilgrim's Progress* (1678):

This book will make a traveller of thee,
If by its councel thou wilt ruled be;
It will direct thee to the Holy Land,
If thou wilt its directions understand:
Yea, it will make the slothful active be,
The blind also delightful things to see.[23]

Bunyan's book is truly a walker's call to arms, developing the Christian metaphor of life as pilgrimage to provide concrete support for the reader in his own journey towards God. And once again the symbolic figure of the wayfaring man steadfastly walking through an inhospitable landscape is employed from the outset: 'As I walked through the wilderness of this world, I lighted on a certain place, where was a den; and I laid me down in that place to sleep: and as I slept I dreamed a dream.'[24] The journey revealed in this dream, in which the pilgrim, Christian, travels from his hometown, the City of Destruction, to the Celestial City of the hereafter, is perhaps the most famous allegorical work in the English language, ensuring that such well-known landmarks as Vanity Fair and the Slough of Despond have acquired a literary afterlife beyond the confines of the text.

'Pilgrimage', writes Rebecca Solnit, 'is premised on the idea that the sacred is not entirely immaterial, but that there is a geography of spiritual power'; and within the literature of pilgrimage, Bunyan's topographical landmarks remain the most widely recognisable.[25] Yet despite the familiarity of these surroundings, both to Bunyan and his subsequent readership, the way of the pilgrim remains unimaginably hard, as if Bunyan wished to deliberately emphasise the treachery inherent within the most reassuringly familiar landscapes.[26] For the act of walking is not always as straightforward as it seems, Bunyan reminds us, and may as often take a pilgrim off his true path as advance him along it:

> Now I beheld in my dream that they had not journeyed far but the River and the way for a time parted. At which they were not a little sorry, yet they durst not go out of their way. Now the way from the River was rough, and their feet tender by reason of their travels; so the soul of the pilgrims was much discouraged, because of the way. Wherefore still as they went on they wished for better way. Now a little before them there was on the left hand of the road, a meadow, and a stile to go over into it, and that meadow is called By-Path Meadow. Then said Christian to his fellow, 'If this Meadow lieth along by our wayside, let's go over into it.' Then he went to the stile to see, and behold a path lay along by the way on the other side of the fence. ''Tis according to my wish,' said Christian, 'here is the easiest going; come, good Hopeful, and let us go over.'[27]

In taking the easier path the pilgrims condemn themselves to greater suffering, and of course their attempted short-cut leads not to the Celestial City but to Doubting Castle and the grounds of Giant Despair. For not only must the footsore pilgrim complete his arduous journey, he must complete it in the correct manner, as any deviation from the true path will end not in salvation but in damnation.

Despite Bunyan's unfamiliarity with literary tradition, *The Pilgrim's Progress* presents clear similarities with both Dante's *Commedia* and Langland's *Piers Plowman*.[28] Bunyan's Puritan theology may be at odds with that of his predecessors, yet *The Pilgrim's Progress* shares many of the allegorical devices of these earlier works, such as the dream-vision and the personification of human characteristics. And just as Langland, and to a lesser extent Dante, drew upon the familiar landscapes of their homelands in the depiction of their imaginary journeys, so too does Christian's journey originate in 'a muddy, poorly signposted seventeenth-century road, over hills, through dark valleys and across bleak moors', in which 'the weariness of aching legs, is never far away.'[29] For Bunyan's imaginary landscape is grounded in the harsh physical realities of his own rural Bedfordshire, and the obstacles that Christian must overcome originate in the journeys he himself would have made. It is for this reason that another literary walker, Iain Sinclair, has described Bunyan's work as 'the ultimate English walking book, where the physical journey that he does then becomes fabulated into this Christian mythology, but all the places are actually mappable.'[30] Indeed, there have been numerous scholarly attempts to identify the topographical counterparts to Bunyan's imaginary landmarks: the Delectable Hills are thought to be based upon the Chilterns, and Christian's entire pilgrimage may well find its roots within Bunyan's regular journey from Bedford to St Albans and on to London. Yet the remarkable success of Bunyan's work (it was at one time the most widely read and translated book in the English language apart from the Bible) originates precisely in its ability to transcend the specificities of his own time and place, and it is the imaginative power of *The Pilgrim's Progress* which has ensured its universal appeal.

As the religious impulse for pilgrimage, at least in Western, predominantly Christian societies, has subsided, so too has the literature that it inspired. The act of pilgrimage remains, however, although the spiritual goals that animated its medieval participants have gradually given way to cultural and political alternatives, with the result that such pilgrimages are now often indistinguishable from other forms of travel or wider political protest.[31] Providing an unexpected addendum to the literature of pilgrimage, however, are two figures whose work must have rarely, if ever, appeared on the same page before: Hilaire Belloc and Werner Herzog.

The work of Hilaire Belloc (1870–1953), the Anglo-French Catholic convert who was both a prolific writer and prodigious walker, is nowadays almost entirely neglected, his reputation largely sustained by his book of children's verse, *Cautionary Tales* (1907). At the turn of the last century, however, he was, along with his contemporaries HG Wells and GK Chesterton, one of the most widely read authors of his day. In his essay, 'The Idea of a Pilgrimage' (1904) Belloc acknowledges that the modern–day pilgrim may be motivated by little more than a desire to see the world and to share his experiences with others:

> For a man that goes on a pilgrimage does best of all if he starts out [...] with the heart of a wanderer, eager for the world as it is, forgetful of maps or descriptions, but hungry for real colours and men and the seeming of things [...] pilgrimage ought to be nothing but a nobler kind of travel, in which, according to our age and inclination, we tell our tales, or draw our pictures, or compose our songs.[32]

For Belloc, a committed Catholic, the pilgrimage was both an act of religious devotion and a source of creative stimulus, the act of walking intimately linked to the tales such an activity inevitably generated. For this reason, Belloc is dismissive of other forms of locomotion, describing bicycling as 'flurried', while driving by car is judged to be too luxurious as well as dangerous (although not in the conventional sense, but 'because it brings us constantly against servants and flattery').[33] It is only by walking that one can overcome the divisions of social class and be at one with our surroundings: 'the best way of all is on foot, where one is a man like any other man, with the sky above one, and the road beneath, and the world on every side, and time to see all.'[34]

Belloc certainly practised what he preached, publishing a series of books documenting his walks, amongst them an account of his many visits to the Pyrenees (*The Pyrenees*, 1909), as well as an arduous recreation of the medieval pilgrimage between Winchester and Canterbury (*The Old Road*, 1904). The Pilgrims' Way, as this 120 mile stretch is known, was undertaken by Belloc and his companion in mid-winter, without a pack, and at a rate of eighteen to twenty miles a day, 'so that he might try to feel as they felt, and recapture to some extent the experiences of those who had travelled the Pilgrims' Way six or seven hundred years before.'[35] Preceding these accounts, however, was the book that established Belloc's reputation, selling more than 120,000 copies and almost single-handedly reviving the then dormant market for pilgrimage literature.

The Path to Rome (1902) recalls the journey made by Belloc the previous year, embarking from Toul in France, where he had conducted his military service, and following as direct a route as possible towards Rome where he was to conclude his journey by hearing mass at St Peter's. Before his departure, Belloc, like generations of pilgrims before him, had made a vow: 'I will walk all the way and take advantage of no wheeled thing; I will sleep rough and cover thirty miles a day, and I will hear mass every morning.'[36]

If Belloc had stuck to these resolutions then *The Path to Rome* would have been a quite different book, rather shorter perhaps and certainly less entertaining; but thankfully he soon found himself unable to keep to the harsh regimen he had set himself, and, having spent the first night in the open, most of his subsequent nights were spent in a bed.[37] Walking was also rejected at times in favour of carts and the occasional train. Travelling light, in a linen suit and carrying the obligatory staff, Belloc did, by his own admission 'live very hard', although such hardships were largely due, not to an enforced asceticism, but rather the result of insufficient planning and a lack of funds. In any event, Belloc stuck to his plan by taking the most direct route, often departing from the road if it diverted him too widely from his course. But as Bunyan's pilgrim learned to his cost, such shortcuts could often have dire consequences, in one case leading Belloc on a 'mirific and horripilant adventure' as he attempted to cross from France into Italy through an Alpine pass, narrowly avoiding death in a blizzard.[38] Forced to retrace his footsteps, Belloc completed his journey, but his experiences of Europe's rural landscapes, and in particular those of the mountains, left an indelible mark on his writing, transforming his ardent Catholicism into something approaching nature worship:

> The great clouds stood up in the heaven, separate, like persons; and no wind blew; but everything was full of evening. I worshipped them so far as it is permitted to worship inanimate things. They domed into the pure light of the higher air, inviolable. They seemed halted in the presence of a commanding majesty who ranked them all in order. The vision filled me with a large calm [...] I fell asleep, still thinking of the shapes of clouds and of the power of God.[39]

Belloc's faith survived the lure of the mountains, his journey ultimately reaffirming his spiritual beliefs, but this was not the sole or even the predominant component of his pilgrimage; for he admits to completing his journey with a good story to tell, and it is this, the creative rather than the religious benefit, which he was to acknowledge as the major objective all along.[40]

Some seventy years later and Werner Herzog was to cross Europe on foot, this time in the opposite direction, once again according the act of walking a significance far beyond its everyday usage. Herzog is better known, of course, as a filmmaker, but he is also the author of *Of Walking in Ice* (1978), one of the strangest and most heartfelt accounts of walking ever published. It takes the form of a diary, recording an epic journey made on foot over a period of three weeks in winter 1974 from his home in Munich to the hospital bedside of fellow German filmmaker Lotte Eisner, in Paris:

> At the end of November 1974, a friend called and told me that Lotte Eisner was seriously ill and would probably die. I said that this must not be, not at this time, German cinema could not do without her now, we would not permit her death. I took a jacket, a compass and a duffel bag with the necessities. My boots were so solid and new that I had confidence in them. I set off on the most direct route to Paris, in full faith, believing that she would stay alive if I came on foot.[41]

Perhaps nowhere else in the literature of walking has this activity been endowed with such extraordinary power. For Herzog believed that such a walk would discharge a sacred function, an act of will that would somehow prevent the death of his friend and mentor. Walking through often atrocious conditions and subject to a startling array of maladies, Herzog produced an account which veers wildly, from the euphoric: 'A rainbow before me all at once fills me with the greatest confidence. What a sign it is, over and in front of him who walks. Everyone should Walk'; to the morose: 'While I was taking a shit, a hare came by at arm's length without noticing me. Pale brandy on my left thigh, which hurts from my groin down with every step. Why is walking so full of woe?'[42] These sudden switches in register as Herzog stumbles towards his goal lend the book a feverish, almost delirious tone, in which seemingly mundane observations - 'You pass a lot of discarded rubbish when you walk' - are interspersed with moments of heightened awareness, in which the detritus of the everyday takes on a surreal, if slightly sinister aspect – 'The cigarette packets on the roadside fascinate me greatly, even more when left uncrushed, then blow up slightly to take on a corpse-like quality, the edges no longer sharp and the cellophane dimmed from inside from the dampness, forming water droplets in the cold.'[43] The journey is eventually completed, as a footsore Herzog arrives in Paris to find Eisner alive and recovering from her illness:

As afterthought just this: I went to Madame Eisner, she was still tired and marked by her illness. Someone must have told her on the phone that I had come on foot – I didn't want to mention it. I was embarrassed and placed my smarting legs up on the second armchair, which she pushed over to me. In the embarrassment a thought passed through my head and, since the situation was strange anyway, I told it to her. Together, I said, we shall boil fire and stop fish. Then she looked at me and smiled very delicately, and since she knew that I was someone on foot and therefore unprotected, she understood me. For one splendid, fleeting moment something mellow flowed through my deadly tired body. I said to her, 'Open the window. From these last days onward I can fly.'[44]

The spell cast by Herzog's monumental act of pilgrimage was a highly potent one – Eisner not only survived, but went on to live for another decade. Indeed, it appears that she might have lived on forever if Herzog hadn't interceded on her behalf, releasing her from the charm that he had wrought:

Lotte lived until the age of ninety or thereabouts, and years after the walk, when she was nearly blind, could not walk or read or go out to see films, she said to me, 'Werner, there is still this spell cast over me that I am not allowed to die. I am tired of life. It would be a good time for me now.' Jokingly I said, 'OK, Lotte, I hereby take the spell away.' Three weeks later she died.[45]

Herzog is something of a philosopher when it comes to walking, if we can call it that, for he claims there is no real expression in English, preferring 'travelling on foot.'[46] He has discussed the subject at some length, arguing that the activity has a fundamental quality which is essential to our true nature, a nature increasingly at odds with the sedentary aspect of modern life:

Humans are not made to sit at computer terminals or travel by aeroplane; destiny intended something different for us. For too long now we have been estranged from the essential, which is the nomadic life: travelling on foot. A distinction must be made between hiking and travelling on foot. In today's society – though it would be ridiculous to advocate travelling on foot for everyone to every possible destination – I personally would rather do the existentially essential things in my life on foot. If you live in England and your girlfriend is in Sicily, and it is clear that you want to marry her, then you should walk to Sicily to propose. For these things travel by car or aeroplane is not the right thing. The volume and depth and intensity of the world is something that only those on foot will ever experience.[47]

In 1999 Herzog was to publish a manifesto of sorts, the 'Minnesota Declaration.'[48] Ostensibly a twelve point charter incorporating the fundamentals of documentary cinema, it is in fact a highly eccentric document, incorporating such statements as 'The moon is dull. Mother Nature doesn't call, doesn't speak to you, although a glacier eventually farts. And don't you listen to the Song of Life.' At number seven on the list is a mercifully concise summary of his philosophy of walking: 'Tourism is sin, and travel on foot virtue.' For Herzog, walking is an act of pilgrimage in which, unlike for his medieval forbears, the sacred is embodied in the act of walking itself rather than through the attainment of any spiritual goal. His friend and fellow walker, Bruce Chatwin, shared this philosophy, describing what he called the 'sacramental' aspect of walking and confirming Herzog's belief that walking 'is not simply therapeutic for oneself but is a poetic activity that can cure the world of its ills.'[49] It was as a consequence of this belief that Chatwin was himself to call on his friend for help while stricken by illness, no doubt hoping that Herzog could once again summon up the healing powers that he had employed to such good effect for Lotte Eisner. In the event, Herzog could do little to prevent Chatwin's death, but his account of their final meeting is both a poignant reflection on the central role that walking had played in their relationship, as well as a reminder of the powerful emotional response this activity is still able to evoke:

Bruce had summoned Werner Herzog because he thought the director had healing powers [...] He was a skeleton, there was nothing left of him, and all of a sudden he would shout at me: 'I've got to be on the road again, I've got to be on the road again.' And I said to him, 'Yes, that's where you belong.' And he said: 'Can you come with me?' And I said: 'Yes, sure, we will walk together.' And then he said: 'My rucksack is so heavy.' And I said: 'Bruce, I carry it.' And we spoke about where we were walking and had a walk together and he all of a sudden had a lucid moment when his blanket was off him and every few minutes I turned him around because his bones were aching and he called his legs 'the boys'. He said: 'Can you put the left boy around to this side and the right boy?' And he looked down at himself and he saw the legs were only spindles and he looked at me in this very lucid moment and he said: 'I'm never going to walk again.' He said: 'Werner, I'm dying.' And I said, 'Yes, I am aware of that.' And then he said: 'You must carry my rucksack, you are the one who must carry it.' And I said: 'Yes, I will proudly do that.' And I have his rucksack and it's such a dear thing to me. Let's say if my house was on fire, I would throw my children out of the window, but of all my belongings it would be the rucksack that I would save.[50]

Notes

[1] Dante Alighieri, *The Divine Comedy: Purgatory*, trans. by Dorothy L. Sayers, London: Penguin, 2004, Canto XII, Lines 7–9, p. 158

[2] William Langland, *Piers Plowman*, ed. and trans. by AVC Schmidt, Oxford: Oxford University Press, 1992, p. 119

[3] Amato, *On Foot,* p. 45

[4] Anne D. Wallace notes that in *The Canterbury Tales*, 'horses are as indispensable as cloaks or boots, and the riding styles of their owners serve as natural parts of the pilgrim's portraits.' Anne D. Wallace, *Walking, Literature, and English Culture: The Origins and Uses of the Peripatetic in the Nineteenth Century*, Oxford: Clarendon, 1993, p. 51

[5] Thoreau, 'Walking', in *The Pleasures of Walking*, ed., by Edwin Valentine Mitchell, 129–172, p. 129. 'Despite Thoreau's assertion, a recent attempt to find evidence to support his claim has drawn a blank, as has a similar effort to prove that 'roam' derives from the pilgrimage to Rome. In support of Chaucer's depiction of his pilgrims' reluctance to walk, however, it appears that 'canter' was first used to describe 'the mode of horse-travel to Canterbury and known as the "Canterbury Gallop"[...] Though pilgrims, if they rode, would have to dismount and walk the final part of the journey for it to be efficacious.' See Julia Bolton Holloway, *The Pilgrim and the Book: A Study of Dante, Langland and Chaucer*, New York: Peter Lang, 1992, p. 282

[6] Solnit, p. 46

[7] Jonathan Sumption, *Pilgrimage: An Image of Medieval Religion*, London: Faber, 1975, p. 177

[8] Sumption, p.182

[9] Amato, p. 52

[10] Holloway, p. xiii

[11] Amato, p. 52

[12] Gilbert, p. 36

[13] Chatwin, *The Songlines*, p. 227. Illustrating the degree to which Dante's poetry was bound up with the act of walking, Chatwin quotes from Osip Mandelstam's essay 'Conversation about

Dante': 'The *Inferno* and especially the *Purgatorio* glorify the human gait, the measure and rhythm of walking, the foot and its shape. The step, linked to the breathing and saturated with thought: this Dante understands as the beginning of prosody.' Osip Mandelstam, 'Conversation about Dante', trans. by Clarence Brown (1965) and qtd. in Chatwin, *The Songlines*, p. 228

[14] Dante, *The Divine Comedy*, ed. by David H Higgins and trans. by CH Sisson, Oxford: Oxford World's Classics, 2008, p. 47

[15] Dante, 'Il Convivio' (I, 3) in *The Portable Dante*, ed. by Paolo Milano, Harmondsworth: Penguin, 1977, p. xiv

[16] Barbara A. Johnson, *Reading Piers Plowman and The Pilgrim's Progress: Reception and the Protestant Reader*, Carbondale, IL: Southern Illinois University Press, 1992, p. 115

[17] Langland, p. 1

[18] Elizabeth Salter, *Piers Plowman: An Introduction*, Oxford: Blackwell, 1969, p. 90

[19] AVC Schmidt, ed., Langland, *Piers Plowman*, Introduction, p. xxvii

[20] Langland, pp. 59–60

[21] Langland, p. 254

[22] Langland, p. 351(n. 254)

[23] John Bunyan, *The Pilgrim's Progress*, ed. by Roger Sharrock, London: Penguin, p. 8

[24] Bunyan, p. 11

[25] Solnit, p. 50

[26] Kim Taplin, *The English Path*, Woodbridge, Suffolk: The Boydell Press, 1979, p. 134

[27] Bunyan, pp. 97–98

[28] In fact, so clear are the similarities, particularly between its opening lines and those of the *Commedia*, that Bunyan was forced to defend himself against charges of plagiarism.

[29] N H Keeble, ed., Bunyan, *The Pilgrim's Progress*, Introduction, p. xiv

[30] Nicholson, *The Lost Art of Walking*, p. 52

[31] Rebecca Solnit writes: 'In the last half century or so, a wide

variety of secular and non-traditional pilgrimages have evolved that extend the notion of the pilgrimage into political and economic spheres [...] from appealing for divine intervention or holy miracle to demanding political change, making the audience no longer God or the gods, but the public.' Solnit, pp. 54–57

[32] Hilaire Belloc, 'The Idea of Pilgrimage' in *Hills and the Sea*, London: Methuen, 1906, 229–234, pp. 230–1

[33] Belloc, 'The Idea of Pilgrimage', p. 234

[34] Belloc, 'The Idea of Pilgrimage', p. 234

[35] Marples, p. 160

[36] Hilaire Belloc, *The Path to Rome*, London: George Allen, 1902, p. viii

[37] Belloc quickly rejected his 'bookish plan' of sleeping rough, and out of a total of 26 nights, 17 were spent in hotels or inns. See Marples, p. 157

[38] Marples, p. 156

[39] Belloc, *The Path to Rome*, pp. 328–9

[40] Marples, p. 155

[41] Werner Herzog, *Of Walking in Ice* (1978), trans. by Marje Herzog & Alan Greenberg, New York: Free Association, 2007, Foreword

[42] Herzog, *Of Walking in Ice*, pp. 42 & 17

[43] Herzog, *Of Walking in Ice*, pp. 7 & 14

[44] Herzog, *Of Walking in Ice*, p. 68

[45] Werner Herzog, *Herzog on Herzog*, ed. by Paul Cronin, London: Faber, 2002, p. 281

[46] In conversation with Paul Holdengräber, Herzog comments: 'I would be careful to call it walking. There is no real expression in English. I would call it travelling on foot. And travelling on foot is something that we have lost out of our civilisation. But we are made for travelling on foot – physically we are made for travelling on foot, and in our minds to move at a certain pace, and seeing things with intimacy and seeing the details and having en route, you have only substantial encounters.' See 'Werner Herzog: The Legend Returns', March 23, 2011, at http://www.

intelligencesquared.com/micro-site/herzog

[47] Herzog, *Herzog on Herzog*, p. 280

[48] Werner Herzog, *Minnesota Declaration: Truth and Fact in Documentary Cinema*, Walker Art Center, Minneapolis, April 30, 1999 at http://www.wernerherzog.com/52.html

[49] Bruce Chatwin, 'Werner Herzog in Ghana' in *What Am I Doing Here*, London: Vintage, 2005, 136–149, pp. 138–9

[50] Nicholas Shakespeare, *Bruce Chatwin*, London: Vintage, 2000, pp. 530–1

The Imaginary Walker

One does not need legs to be a nomad. Zygmunt Bauman[1]

September 18, 1956 *Today I ended the second year of my walking tour [...] As long as I continue my tramping, I shall remain on an even keel.* Albert Speer[2]

In his introduction to *The Pleasures of Walking* (1934), Edwin Valentine Mitchell notes: 'One kind of walking which I do not recall seeing mentioned anywhere in the literature of the subject is imaginary walking.'[3] Unknown to Mitchell, however, the act of imaginary walking has in fact a distinguished history, having its roots in the wider practice of armchair travel, through which the imagination of the would-be traveller allows him to transcend the bounds of time and space. Richard Holmes has identified the pre-Romantic poet, William Cowper, as a pioneer of this technique, a process which helped him to overcome his disabling depression, enabling him to escape momentarily from the confines of his home in the Buckinghamshire village of Olney. Transported by Cook's account of his second expedition, *A Voyage Towards the South Pole and Round the World* (1777), Cowper was to write: 'My imagination is so captivated upon these occasions that I seem to partake with the navigators, in all the dangers they encountered. I lose my anchor; my main-sail is rent into shreds; I kill a shark, and by signs converse with a Patagonian, and all this without moving from my fireside.'[4]

Cowper was to put such reveries to good use, accompanying Cook on board an imaginary *Resolution*, in his long, reflective poem, *The Task* (1784):

He travels and I too. I tread his deck,
Ascend his topmast, through his peering eyes
Discover countries, with a kindred heart
Suffer his woes and share in his escapes,
While fancy, like the finger of a clock,
Runs the great Circuit, and is still at home.[5]

If Cowper provides the armchair traveller with a maritime voyage of discovery in 1784, then a more domestic, but equally adventurous, pedestrian equivalent was to arrive shortly afterwards in the form of Xavier de Maistre's *A Journey Around my Room* (1795):

My room is situated on the forty-fifth degree of latitude [...] it stretches from east to west; it forms a long rectangle, thirty-six paces in circumference if you hug the wall. My journey will, however, measure much more than this, as I will be crossing it frequently lengthwise, or else diagonally, without any rule or method. I will even follow a zigzag path, and I will trace out every possible geometrical trajectory if need be.[6]

Born in Chambéry, Savoy in 1763 to French parents, Xavier de Maistre was the younger brother of the philosophical writer and counter-revolutionary Joseph-Marie de Maistre who, having read the manuscript, arranged for the book to be published in 1795. A military man, Xavier de Maistre was also a traveller in the more conventional manner, visiting Italy and the Alps as well as surviving a Russian campaign in the Caucasus. It is as a pioneer of room-travel, however, that he is best remembered; and it was in the spring of 1790, while confined to his Turin apartment for forty-two days under house arrest following a duel, that he embarked upon a voyage around his bedroom; a trip every bit as arduous as that of Magellan and Cook but one that took place almost entirely within the boundaries of his imagination. The result was *A Journey Around My Room* (1795) and it was to be followed by the equally adventurous *A Nocturnal Expedition Around My Room* (1825). These accounts, as de Maistre was to proudly proclaim, would introduce the world to a new form of travel involving little of the risk or expense facing the conventional traveller. "Would even the most indolent of men," he asks, "hesitate to set off with me in search of a pleasure that will cost him neither effort nor money?"[7]

This pioneering mode of travel is a curious hybrid in which pedestrian and armchair traveller meet. For while de Maistre sets out on foot across his room: 'Once you've left my armchair, walking towards the north, you come into view of my bed'; he also encourages the reader 'to send his soul off on its travels all by itself', leaving the legs to reach their destination unaided while the mind is elsewhere.[8] Furthermore, there is an additional form of locomotion, in which armchair travel finds a more literal interpretation: 'I was in my armchair, in which I had leant back so that its two front legs were raised two inches above the ground; and by leaning to the right and the left, and thereby advancing slowly forward, I had imperceptibly come right up to the wall – This is the way I travel when I'm not in a hurry.'[9] Employing all of these techniques, de Maistre follows a haphazard route across his room, his lack of direction reflected in an equally meandering and digressive narrative:

There's no more attractive pleasure than following one's ideas wherever they lead, as the hunter pursues his game, without even trying to keep to any set route. And so, when I travel through my room, I rarely follow a straight line: I go from my table towards a picture hanging in a corner; from there I set out obliquely towards the door; but even though, when I begin, it really is my intention to go there, if I happen to meet an armchair en route, I don't think twice about it, and settle down in it without further ado.[10]

As he nears the final day of his incarceration, de Maistre finally approaches his armchair next to the fire and this epic journey reaches its conclusion. Eager to justify the new form of travel he has inaugurated, de Maistre is at pains to emphasise that his journey has not been one enforced upon him by his limited freedom: 'I wouldn't for anything in the world want to be suspected of having embarked on this journey merely because I couldn't think of anything else to do', he writes; for on the contrary, 'This enforced retreat was merely an opportunity to set out on my journey earlier.'[11] Indeed, the reader would be mistaken in presuming that de Maistre's house-arrest had in any way restricted his freedom or curtailed his movements. For rather than punishing him, the authorities have in fact liberated him, allowing him to explore a world more commonly overlooked:

> As if they had taken freedom from me! [...] They have forbidden me to roam around a city, a mere point in space; but they have left me with the whole universe: immensity and eternity are mine to command [...] Was it to punish me that they locked me up in my room – in that delightful country that holds every good thing, and all the riches of life, within its realm? You may as well exile a mouse in a granary.[12]

Returning to Turin some years later, de Maistre finds that his room has been destroyed, but staying elsewhere for the night, he picks up the thread and continues his journey in *A Nocturnal Expedition around my Room* (1825). On this occasion, however, he employs a slightly different technique for exploring the expanses of his room:

> Four hours gave me ample time to carry out my plan, since on this occasion I merely wanted to perform a simple excursion around my room. If the first journey lasted forty-two days, this was because I had not been in any position to ensure that it took a shorter time. Nor did I wish to be constrained by travelling much in a coach, as before, since I am

convinced that a traveller on foot sees many things that escape a man who travels with the post. So I decided to go on foot and on horseback alternately, depending on the circumstances: a new method which I have not yet revealed, and whose usefulness will soon be apparent.[13]

Travelling to his window, de Maistre's observations of the night sky trigger a reverie in which his imagination transports him through the heavens, effortlessly conveying him 'to a distance which few travellers before me have ever reached.'[14] Tiring from his exertions, however, he continues his journey on horseback, astride his window, 'leaving my legs to dangle to the left and the right'; and it is in this position that he spends the night, until finally, finding his saddle less comfortable than he hoped, 'he is obliged to get off my horse in rather a hurry.'[15] He dismounts and returns to bed.

Alain de Botton has claimed that de Maistre's room–travel was inspired by a single, profound insight: 'That the pleasure we derive from journeys is perhaps dependent more on the mindset with which we travel than on the destination we travel to.'[16] In which case, de Maistre simply follows this observation to its logical, not to say absurd, conclusion, in which our surroundings, however mundane or familiar they may seem, can be transformed through little more than an act of will into something new and unexpected. The chief characteristic of this mindset is a heightened receptivity to our surroundings, in which we treat new (and familiar) places with humility, withholding our habituated responses in favour of a willingness to see things afresh.[17] 'De Maistre tried to shake us from our passivity', writes de Botton, and putting his, or rather de Maistre's, words into practice, he attempts to walk his familiar route to the Underground station in Hammersmith, as if experiencing his surroundings for the first time. The results are mixed.[18]

Elsewhere, de Maistre has been compared to another great walker, John Bunyan. For like de Maistre, Bunyan also experienced imprisonment, albeit in less comfortable surroundings, and both writers were forced to supplement the paucity of their situation by falling back upon memory, imagination, daydream, and storytelling. Indeed, like all prisoners, they were forced to overcome the claustrophobia of their position through an imaginative leap which allowed then to transcend their surroundings and the isolation of their condition.[19]

Amongst his many literary successors, de Maistre's translator, Andrew Brown, has identified the artist, Daniel Spoerri, along with writer Georges Perec, both of whom have studied in detail the minutiae of everyday life. But another, perhaps less obvious, practitioner of de Maistre's house-bound flights of mental travel is Arthur Rimbaud. Rimbaud's many real, as opposed to imaginary, acts of walking have been well documented and he is discussed here in greater length in a later chapter. But his lesser known contribution to the realms of imaginary travel is memorialised in the verb *Robinsonner*, coined by Rimbaud and meaning 'to let the mind wander – or to travel mentally.'[20] In his poem, *Roman* (1870) Rimbaud writes 'Le Coeur fou Robinsonne à travers les romans' or 'The wild heart Crusoes through a thousand novels.'[21]; and Rimbaud's term is, of course, born of Crusoe's imaginary voyage, conveying its essential themes of both isolation and imaginary escape. And Robinson has indeed escaped, as Rimbaud suggests, to become the symbol of the imaginary traveller in, amongst others, the works of Defoe, Céline and Kafka.[22]

The most celebrated literary representation of the armchair traveller, however, is that of Rimbaud's countryman and contemporary, Joris-Karl Huysmans, whose notorious decadent novel *À Rebours* (Against Nature) introduced the world to the arch-dandy and domesticated flâneur, Duc Jean Floressas des Esseintes. First published in 1894, Huysmans's novel was used by Oscar Wilde as the template for his *Dorian Gray*, depicting a sickly and indolent aesthete, surrounded by the trappings of his fantastically appointed home in Paris and increasingly unwilling to venture out. For while de Maistre explores his room whilst confined under house arrest, des Esseintes is a willing captive who has withdrawn voluntarily from the world outside to devote more time to voyages of the mind. That is until, fuelled by the novels of Charles Dickens, des Esseintes formulates an impetuous and energetic plan to visit London for himself. Having ordered a taxi, he sets off, stopping en route for some last minute research at an English tavern:

> Des Esseintes let his mind drift, picturing, under the influence of the crimson tints of the port wine filling the glasses, the Dickensian characters who so enjoyed drinking it, and in his imagination populating the cellar with quite different beings [...] The city of the novels, the well-lit, well-heated, well-cared-for, well-ordered houses of the novels [...] appeared to him in the form of a cosy ark sailing through a flood of mud and soot. He settled down comfortably in this fictional London, happy to be indoors, listening to the sepulchral hooting of the tugs travelling down the Thames, behind the Tuileries, near the bridge.[23]

Gradually, however, as inertia begins to hold sway, des Esseintes becomes unable to distinguish between the London of his mind and that of his supposed destination. For not only is imaginative travel an appealing alternative to the real thing, it is, for des Esseintes at least, far superior:

> Des Esseintes felt incapable of moving his legs; a gentle, warm languor was flowing through his limbs [...] He kept telling himself: 'Come on now, on your feet, you must hurry'; but instantly there would be objections to gainsay his commands. What was the point of moving, when one could travel so splendidly just sitting in a chair? [...] After all, what kind of aberration was this, that I should be tempted to renounce long-held convictions, and disdain the compliant fantasies of my

mind, that I should, like some complete simpleton, have believed that a journey was necessary, or could hold novelty or interest?[24]

Of course, des Esseintes never makes it to London, and exhausted by his adventure, he returns home. For if it is indeed better to travel than to arrive, then des Esseintes has applied a logic of his own, suggesting that it is better to travel mentally than to leave home at all. Des Esseintes has been described as the 'Greta Garbo of the fictional universe'[25]; and his sedentary journey is a voyage to the furthest reaches of his own head, a virtual journey in which the imagination takes precedence over reality, creating a highly personal universe with only one inhabitant: for the imaginary traveller, by necessity, travels alone.

These twin themes of incarceration and isolation, ever present in this chapter, find their definitive expression in the work of one who, rather unexpectedly considering his predicament, produced what is certainly the most compelling account of how the act of walking can act as a bulwark against mental disintegration. At first glance, however, Albert Speer's *Spandau: The Secret Diaries* (1975) would appear an unlikely addition to the literature of walking. Yet on closer inspection, the contents page reveals that all is not quite as one might expect, hinting at an apparent degree of licence quite at odds with the historical fact of Speer's twenty–year imprisonment. Divided into twenty chapters to correspond to each of his years as a prisoner in Spandau, the summary of the ninth year, for example, contains, alongside the entries 'Pulmonary embolism' and 'My position on modern architecture', the intriguing 'Idea of circumambulating the globe'. More puzzling still are the entries, 'Arrive in Peking' (thirteenth year), 'Pass Seattle' (nineteenth year), and shortly before finishing his sentence, 'Crossing the Mexican Border' (twentieth year). The key, of course, to these entries lies in the fact that, during his long incarceration, Speer became an obsessive walker, who, by compiling a detailed study of his intended route and maintaining a rigorous daily routine of walking in the prison garden, managed to achieve what is surely the longest, most sustained and most sophisticated imaginary walk ever undertaken. He was not the first to apply this technique, however, for the writer John Finley, author of the essay 'Travelling afoot', was to pursue a similar regime in the 1930s:

> "You may be interested to know that I have a little game that I play alone: namely, that of walking in some other part of the world as many miles as I actually walk here day by day, with the result that I have walked nearly 20,000 miles here in the last six years, which means that I have covered the land part of the earth in a circuit of the globe. I finished last night 2,000 miles since the first of January 1934 and in doing so reached Vancouver from the north. My first year's walk was across the United States and I then started on the west coast of France. I will not bother you now with the rest of the itinerary but tell you only that I crossed Europe, southern Asia and then up through China and parts farther north to Bering Strait and from Alaska down to Vancouver."[26]

Finley's description appears in the introduction to *The Pleasures of Walking*, first published in 1934; it is hard to believe, however, that Speer, a voracious reader, would have come across this title in Spandau's prison library, unless its inclusion there was as an act of deliberate torment to him and his fellow inmates. Yet, while Finley's 'little game' clearly resembles the route chosen by Speer, and while he may have clocked up an undeniably impressive mileage, it represents little more than an imaginary stroll in comparison to the epic journey that Speer was to perform. For as the following entry, taken from Speer's diary in 1959 (thirteenth year of sentence; fifth year of walking tour) demonstrates, Speer regarded his journey as rather more than simply a game:

July 13, 1959 Arrived in Peking today. As I came to the Imperial Palace, some kind of demonstration was taking place in the great square outside it. Two, three, four hundred thousand people – who can say how many? In that constantly surging crowd I quickly lost all sense of direction; the uniformity of the people also frightened me. I left the city as quickly as I could.[27]

Of course, Speer was not in Peking that day. On July 13, 1959 he was, as every day, to be seen in the prison garden, which he designed himself, walking a well established route around its perimeter. The task he had set himself was to walk seven kilometres a day, every day, throughout a journey that would see him complete 2,296 circuits of this course. Distances covered, daily averages, shortfalls and ground to make up, all these were recorded in minute detail, a project he shared initially with his increasingly bemused fellow inmate Rudolf Hess.

Sentenced to twenty years imprisonment at the Nuremberg Trials of 1946, Speer was well aware of the psychological demands that awaited him during his long incarceration. Determined to maintain 'an even keel' mentally, Speer employed endless stratagems to keep himself occupied both physically and mentally.[28] His monumental history, *Inside the Third Reich* (1969), was written on toilet paper and other scraps and was smuggled out of the prison; while he maintained his interest in architecture, designing a house for one of his guards. But it was his 'Circumambulation of the World' which came to dominate his life, leading him and his fellow inmates to question his sanity. 'I insisted on my claim to have a screw loose', writes Speer, while his confidant Hess, seemingly unconcerned, was to respond: 'That just happens to be your pastime. Others have others.'[29]

Speer began his journey in September 1954, with the relatively modest goal of walking from his prison cell in Berlin to Heidelberg, a distance of some 620 kilometres. 'I have a new idea to make myself exercise regularly to the point of exhaustion,' he writes. 'For that purpose, I have marked out a circular course in the garden. Lacking a tape measure, I measured my shoe, paced off the distance step by step, and multiplied by the number of paces. Placing one foot ahead of the other 870 times, thirty-one centimetres to a step, yields 270 metres for a round [...] This project is a training of the will, a battle against the endless boredom; but it is also an expression of the last remnants of my urge toward status and activity.'[30] Speer planned his route meticulously, using the prison library to supplement his memory, allowing him to create an astonishingly detailed and deeply felt experience which momentarily dissolved the walls of Spandau. He reached Heidelberg on 19 March 1955, his fiftieth birthday, and in his diary entry for that day he records the following exchange with Hess:

"Now I am setting out for Munich", I said as I passed him on the next-to-last round. "Then on to Rome and down as far as Sicily. Sicily's in the Mediterranean, so I won't be able to walk any farther." When I had completed the last round, I stopped and sat down beside him.

"Why not by way of the Balkans to Asia?" Hess asked.

"Everything there is Communist," I replied. "But maybe I could go by way of Yugoslavia to Greece. And from there through Salonika, Constantinople, and Ankara to Persia."

Hess nodded, "That way you could reach China."

I shook my head, "Communist too."

"But then across the Himalayas to Tibet."

I turned that route down too. "Also Communist. But it would be possible to cross Afghanistan to India and Burma. The more interesting route would be through Aleppo, Beirut, Baghdad, and across the desert to Persepolis and Tehran. A long, hot tramp. Lots of desert. I hope I'll find oases. At any rate, I have a good program now. It should do me for the time being: it's a distance of more than four thousand kilometres. You've helped me out of an embarrassing predicament. Many, many thanks, Herr Hess."[31]

As the years passed and Hess's involvement diminished, so Speer's account was to become more detailed and descriptive, with his observations of the weather, wildlife and landscape all recorded:

February 24, 1963 In the immediate vicinity of Bering Strait, still craggy, hilly country, endless view of treeless rocky landscape [...] Sometimes I see creeping past me one of those arctic foxes whose habits I have recently looked into. But I have also encountered fur seals and the Kamchatka beaver known as *kalan* [...] if I arrive in time I might be able to cross Bering Strait. I would presumably be the first central European to reach America on foot.
September 5, 1965 Today I passed Los Angeles and tramped on southwest [...] Merciless sun on dusty roads. My soles burned on the hot ground, for months without rain. What a strange walking tour, from Europe across Asia to the Bering Strait and to America – with kilometre stones to mark my doleful passage.'[32]

So obsessive had Speer's imaginary pilgrimage become that it began to prove infectious, and by the time he reached Seattle in 1964, he noted that his tramping had infected several of the guards: 'Some days four or five persons can be seen on the track, with determined looks on their faces.' "I'll tell you the difference between you and me," Hess said to me today. "Your follies are contagious."[33]

By the time Speer was finally released in 1966, he had been on foot for almost twelve years. In what he described as the only tangible result of his time in Spandau, he carefully totted up his yearly totals, reaching a figure of 31,816 kilometres. On his final evening as an inmate he sent a telegram to an old friend that read: 'Please pick me up thirty-five kilometres south of Guadalajara,

Mexico.'[34] 'If anyone had told me, at the beginning of my walk to Heidelberg', wrote Speer, 'that my way would lead me into the Far East, I would have thought him crazy, or that I was going to be.'[35] Yet, as it turned out, the opposite was true. Speer's 'walking tour', both an extraordinary act of will and a monumental imaginative feat, had sustained him both physically and mentally during his long incarceration. He continued to feel the compulsion 'to tramp out my kilometres' after his release, even repeating his rounds of the prison garden in his dreams. But he had survived, and with the publication of his memoirs restoring his fortune, he died aged 76 in 1981.

Notes

[1] Zygmunt Bauman, 'Desert Spectacular' in *The Flâneur*, ed. by Keith Tester, London: Routledge, 1994, 138–157, p. 155

[2] Albert Speer, *Spandau: The Secret Diaries*, trans. by Richard & Clara Winston, London: Collins, 1976, p. 295

[3] Edwin Valentine Mitchell, ed., *The Pleasures of Walking* (1934), Bourne End, Bucks: Spurbooks, 1975, Introductory note, p. 7

[4] William Cowper, 6 October 1783, qtd. in Richard Holmes, *The Age of Wonder*, London: HarperCollins, 2008, pp. 51–52

[5] William Cowper, *The Task* (1784), Book 4, 'The Winter Evening', lines 107–119, qtd. in Holmes, *The Age of Wonder*, p. 52

[6] Xavier de Maistre, *A Journey Around my Room*, ed. & trans. by Andrew Brown, with a foreword by Alain de Botton, London: Hesperus, 2004, p. 7

[7] Alain de Botton, Xavier de Maistre, *A Journey Around my Room*, Foreword, p. viii

[8] de Maistre, pp. 8 & 13

[9] de Maistre, p. 14

[10] de Maistre, p. 7

[11] de Maistre, p. 41

[12] de Maistre, pp. 66–67

[13] de Maistre, p. 83

[14] de Maistre, p. 94

[15] de Maistre, p. 120

[16] Alain de Botton, *The Art of Travel*, London: Hamish Hamilton, 2002, p. 246

[17] de Botton, p. 246

[18] de Botton, p. 251

[19] Andrew Brown, ed., de Maistre, *A Journey Around my Room*, Introduction, pp. xi–xv

[20] John Sturrock, *Céline: Journey to the End of the Night*, Cambridge: Cambridge University Press, 1990, p. 37

[21] Arthur Rimbaud, *Rimbaud Complete*, ed. and trans. by Wyatt Mason, London: Scribner, 2003, p. 30

[22] For an account of Robinson's literary travels from Defoe to the present day, see Merlin Coverley, *Psychogeography*, Harpenden: Pocket Essentials, 2006, pp. 66–72

[23] Joris-Karl Huysmans, *Against Nature*, ed. by Nicholas White and trans. by Margaret Mauldon, Oxford: Oxford University Press, 1998, p. 110

[24] Huysmans, p. 114

[25] Nicholas White, ed., Huysmans, *Against Nature*, Introduction, p. xxvi

[26] Edwin Valentine Mitchell, ed., *The Pleasures of Walking*, Introductory note, p. 7

[27] Speer, p. 337

[28] Speer was not alone in employing the use of imaginary walking as a technique with which to combat the onset of mental illness. Indeed, walking has been used not only as a preventative measure but also as a means of alleviating the symptoms of mental disorder, with varying degrees of success. In *The Wild Places* (2007), for example, Robert Macfarlane discusses the case of the poet and musician Ivor Gurney who was committed to an asylum in Kent in the 1920s. It was here that he was visited by Helen Thomas, wife of Gurney's former friend and fellow poet, Edward Thomas. On her first visit she was barely able to communicate with Gurney, so severe was his illness. On her return visit, however, she came armed with one of her husband's maps of the

Gloucestershire countryside through which he and Gurney had walked, and together they traced out the routes they had taken: 'For an hour or more this dream-walking went on, Gurney seeing not the map, but looking through its prompts to see land itself. 'He spent that hour', Helen remembered, 'revisiting his beloved home [...] spotting [...] a track, a hill, or a wood, and seeing it all in his mind's eye, a mental vision sharper and more actual for its heightened intensity. He trod, in a way we who were sane could not emulate, the lanes and fields he knew and loved so well, his guide being his finger tracing the way on the map [...] He had Edward as his companion in this strange perambulation [...] I became for a while the element which brought Edward back to life for him and the country where the two could wander together.' Robert Macfarlane, *The Wild Places*, London: Granta, 2007, p. 110

[29] Speer, p. 255
[30] Speer, p. 255
[31] Speer, p. 268
[32] Speer, pp. 387 & 429
[33] Speer, p. 420
[34] Speer, pp. 445–7
[35] Speer, p. 338

The Walker as Vagrant

Va"grant, n. One who strolls from place to place; one who has no settled habitation; an idle wanderer; a sturdy beggar; an incorrigible rogue; a vagabond.[1]

There are some men born with a vagrant strain in the blood, an insatiable inquisitiveness about the world beyond their doors. Arthur Rickett[2]

According to the Vagrancy Act of 1824, 'every person wandering abroad and lodging in any barn or outhouse, or in any deserted or unoccupied building, or in the open air, or under a tent, or in any cart or waggon, not having any visible means of subsistence and not giving a good account of himself or herself [...] shall be deemed a rogue and vagabond.'[3] Punishable by a period of three months imprisonment, the act remains in force, albeit in an extensively amended form. In fact ever since the Peasants Revolt of 1381, and the subsequent statute of 1383, foot travellers, both urban and rural, who have been unable to provide evidence of their means of support, have been liable to arrest and imprisonment.[4]

In an article entitled 'Radical walking', Donna Landry writes: 'The ambiguity of walking can be traced to its association with vagrancy, the quintessential social crime in late sixteenth century Britain.' During this period, the unfortunate vagrant found himself trapped in a kind of legal Catch 22, having committed no crime except that of being a vagrant; it was not his actions that were found to be at fault but his very status, which was now that of the criminal. 'A similar suspicion attached to rural foot travellers in the eighteenth and nineteenth centuries', continues Landry, 'Enclosure and privatisation of common lands enlarged the possibility of trespass. Why perambulate the woods and fields without intent?'[5]

After the introduction of the Game Laws of 1671, the would-be wanderer would now have to contend with the suspicion of poaching too, effectively maintaining the landless individual within the confines of their immediate place of work, employment being the only measure of legitimacy for their movement. Hemmed in by the law, the act of walking inevitably acquired a political connotation, challenging those boundaries imposed by society, and increasingly aligned with 'a rebellious reclaiming of common rights, with the dream of liberal freedom, with the ideal of democracy.'[6] Thus the figure of the vagrant has developed a powerful symbolic charge, suggesting the existence of an individual at odds with our familiar sense of place, and questioning the enforced distinction between public and private space. It is for this reason, perhaps, that the vagrant has come to represent Romantic notions of freedom, both politically and aesthetically; an idea best articulated by the poet who gives voice to 'the strange half-absence of wandering and murmuring vagrancy.'[7]

The figure in whom these themes first coalesce, and in whose writing we find a powerful voice of protest against enclosure allied to a vagrant spirit, is the labouring poet John Clare. Born in 1793 in the Northamptonshire village of Helpston, Clare developed an extraordinary, even visionary, sense of place in which his very identity became grounded within the rural landscapes of his youth. Both enchanted by his immediate environment and drawn to explore beyond the horizon of his known world, Clare was later to recall his first attempt to transcend this boyhood perimeter when, at the age of five, he set off across neighbouring Emmonsales Heath:

I had imagind that the worlds end was at the edge of the orison and that a days journey was able to find it [...] so I went on [...] expecting when I got to the brink of the world that I coud [...] see into its secrets the same as I coud [...] see heaven by looking into the water so I eagerly wandered on and rambled along the furze [...] when I got home I found my parents in great distress and half the village about hunting me.[8]

It is exactly this sense of enchantment that was to characterise many of Clare's early poems of Helpston life, but these images of pastoral innocence were to be tempered by a growing awareness of the ways in which this landscape was being destroyed, as between 1809 and 1820 the old open-field parishes, such as Helpston, were subjected to Parliamentary enclosure. Much has been written about the effects of enclosure on the rural landscape, and in particular the emphatic role that these events played in Clare's life and work.[9] It is beyond the scope of this book to explore them in any detail here, but the consequences, at least as far as Clare would have experienced them, are clear:

Unbounded freedom ruled the wandering scene
Nor fence of ownership crept in between
To hide the prospect of the following eye
Its only bondage was the circling sky [...]
Inclosure came and trampled on the grave
Of labours rights and left the poor a slave
And memorys pride ere want to wealth did bow
Is both the shadow and the substance now [...]
These paths are stopt – the rude philistines thrall
Is laid upon them and destroyed them all
Each little tyrant with his little sign
Shows where man claims earth glows no more divine
On paths to freedom and to childhood dear
A board sticks up to notice 'no road here'
And on the tree with ivy overhung

The hated sign by vulgar taste is hung
As tho the very birds should learn to know
When they go there they must no further go
This with the poor scared freedom bade good bye
And much the[y] feel it in the smothered sigh
And birds and trees and flowers without a name
All sighed when lawless laws enclosure came
And dreams of plunder in such rebel schemes
Have found too truly that they were but dreams[10]

The sentiments expressed in *The Mores* are characteristic of many of the Helpston poems (c. 1812–1831) in which the walker finds himself increasingly hemmed in and redirected, his activities questioned and curtailed. This loss of pedestrian freedom is experienced by Clare as symptomatic of the slavery engendered by enclosure, for as the physical landscape was mapped and rights of ownership were apportioned, so Clare and his fellow foot-travellers would have found themselves increasingly liable to the charge of trespass:

I dreaded walking where there was no path
And pressed with cautious tread the meadow swath
And always turned to look with wary eye
And always feared the owner coming by;
Yet everything about where I had gone
Appeared so beautiful I ventured on
And when I gained the road where all are free
I fancied every stranger frowned at me
And every kinder look appeared to say
"You've been on trespass in your walk today."[11]

Clare belonged to a rural class to whom the act of walking was both an instrumental part of daily life as well as a means of ensuring social cohesion; but it was also an activity which Clare valued precisely because it signified a freedom from labour. For what distinguished Clare from his fellow Romantics, and Wordsworth in particular, is that, despite their shared reverence for the natural world and their acute awareness of the freedoms it engendered, Clare was also conscious of the fact that the land provided him and his contemporaries with their means of support. From an early age Clare was employed variously in ploughing, reaping, threshing, gardening, and herding cattle, activities to which he returned despite the success of his first volume of poetry, *Poems Descriptive of Rural Life and Scenery* (1820). Thus, the walking necessitated by his everyday work was sharply distinguished from those more restful and contemplative 'careless rambles' and 'stray walks' which occupied his days of leisure: 'A six days prisoner lifes support to earn/ From dusty cobwebs and the murky barn/ The weary thresher meets the rest thats given/ And thankfull sooths him in the boon of heaven/ And Sabbath walks enjoys along the fields'.[12]

If, then, walking purely for leisure was an activity viewed increasingly with suspicion, and regarded as a likely precursor to trespass or poaching, it was in Clare's case compounded by his poetic preoccupations.[13] For the success of Clare's early poems placed him in an increasingly precarious position, in which he found himself neither wholly accepted by the literary establishment in London, nor able to maintain his former relationship within his agricultural community. Finding himself increasingly isolated and distanced from his locality, Clare's poetic career developed in tandem with his own mental disorientation, a process which led inexorably towards the asylum. He was admitted to Dr Mathew Allen's private asylum at High Beach in Epping in 1837 where his 'lifelong solidarity with gypsies and other vagrants' deepened.[14] And it was here, almost four years later, on 20 July 1841, that John Clare escaped to embark upon one of the most celebrated of all English journeys. Both personally, and as a poet, 1841 was the most tumultuous year of his life; it was also his most productive period, a year in which he wrote more than 3,000 lines of verse. However, as far as his contribution to the literature of walking is concerned, it is his short prose account, *The Journey out of Essex* (1841) that remains his most significant work.[15]

Spanning more than ninety miles and taking some three and a half days to complete, Clare's walk home from High Beach to Northborough in Northamptonshire is, from the outset, a hallucinatory account of dislocation and despair. Having first been offered assistance in planning his escape by local gypsies, Clare sets out alone and in the wrong direction. Once redirected, however, and he is soon on the Great York Road, spending his first night sleeping in a shed outside Stevenage: 'I lay down with my head towards the north', writes Clare, 'to show myself the steering point in the morning.'[16] But the next day, as he progresses on through Bedfordshire, Clare's condition rapidly deteriorates. Crippled by gravel in his shoes, one of which has almost lost a sole, Clare has still not eaten, is unable to find a place to sleep, and is growing increasingly disorientated:

I then suddenly forgot which was North or South and though I narrowly examined both ways I could see no tree or bush or stone heap that I could reccolect I had passed so I went on mile after mile almost convinced I was going the same way I came and these thoug[h]ts were so strong upon me that doubt and hopelessness made me turn so feeble that I was scarcely able to walk yet I could not sit down or give up but shuffled along till I saw a lamp shining as bright as the moon.[17]

Having found a porch to sleep on, Clare continues on the following morning, accompanied some of the way by another gypsy he encounters on the road, a young woman who cautions him on his appearance, warning him that he'll be noticed. Yet visible or not, Clare is now oblivious to his surroundings, his mind dissociated from the legs that are carrying him homeward:

I have but a slight reccolection of my journey between here and Stilton for I was knocked up and noticed little or nothing – one night I lay in a dyke bottom from the wind and went sleep half an hour when I suddenly awoke and found one side wet through from the sock in the dyke bottom so I got out and went on [...] I then entered a town [...] I felt so weak here that I forced to sit down on the ground to rest myself and while I sat here a Coach that seemed to be heavy laden came rattling up and stopt in the hollow below me and I cannot reccolect its ever passing by me I then got up and pushed onward seeing little to notice for the road very often looked as stupid as myself and I was very often half asleep as I went.[18]

On the third day, Clare satisfied his hunger by eating the grass by the roadside, 'which seemed to taste something like bread I was hungry and eat heartily till I was satisfied and in fact the meal seemed to do me good.'[19] By the time he reached Stilton, however, he was 'compleatly foot foundered and broken down.'[20] Shortly before Peterborough he is passed by a cart carrying neighbours from Helpston, who, witnessing his condition, club together and throw him fivepence with which he buys some bread and cheese. By now only the shame of sitting down in the street is keeping him going, but on reaching Werrington, he meets a cart carrying a woman who urges him to get in: 'I refused and thought her either drunk or mad but when I was told it was my second wife Patty I got in and was soon in Northborough.'[21] Clare was soon home, where he was to discover that things were not quite as they appeared; for Patty was not his second wife but his first, and his journey had been in vain. Harbouring the fantasy that he was returning home to his first 'wife' Mary (in fact never his wife but the first love of his Helpston childhood), Clare was unaware that she had in fact died several years before, and on being confronted with the news he simply refused to believe it. It was Mary who had been his silent companion on his long walk home, the subject of his dreams and the object of his escape from

High Beach. The final entry in the *Journey out of Essex*, dated 24 July 1841, reads: 'Returned home out of Essex and found no Mary – her and her family are as nothing to me now though she herself was once the dearest of all – and how can I forget.'[22] Quite what Clare's newly demoted 'second' wife made of this is not recorded; but as soon as he reached home, Clare began the task of transcribing the notes he had made during his journey, after which he added the following letter to his wife ('Mary Clare', not Patty):

> My dear wife
> I have written an account of my journey or rather escape from Essex for your amusement and hope it may divert your leisure hours – I would have told you before now that I got here to Northborough last Friday night but not being able to see you or hear where you was I soon began to feel homeless at home and shall bye and bye feel nearly hopeless but not so lonely as I did in Essex [...] my home is no home to me my hopes are not entirely hopeless while even the memory of Mary lives so near me.[23]

'Homeless at home' is perhaps the perfect encapsulation of the vagrant spirit which animated Clare, and which propelled him on his compulsive homeward journey. In the prologue to his biography of Clare, Jonathan Bate retraces his journey home from Essex along the Great York Road, now the A1: 'Driving its dual carriageway today', writes Bate, 'it is impossible to imagine a man walking this route, tired, confused, cold at night and hungry by day.'[24] And yet in 2004 the writer and walker, Iain Sinclair, was to do exactly this, retracing Clare's footsteps from High Beach and in the process revealing a startlingly altered landscape:

> I set out from High Beach in Winter, logging the contour lines of lager cans, burger cartons, cigarette packets, bits of cars. Cargo-trash getting denser as I approached the roundabout

where four roads meet [...] An Enfield publican put Clare straight, pointing out the shortest way. The contemporary version is less certain of local topography. An instruction has gone out from the brewers enforcing a total embargo on courtesy. This was one of those 'High Beach, John? If I wanted fuckin' High Beach, I wouldn't start from here' scenarios. All we learn, from another lunchtime casual, one-eyed and three pints in, is: 'There used to be a road. I think. Once.'[25]

Political questions of land ownership and rights of access give Clare's walks an affinity with twentieth-century walkers; and perhaps it is this shared perception of a landscape threatened by erasure that helps to explain Iain Sinclair's acknowledgement that Clare's *Journey out of Essex* was 'one of my obsessions', a journey whose very existence acts as a 'provocation for future walkers.'[26] Sinclair describes Clare's walk as a 'revamped *Pilgrim's Progress*'; a 'frantic pilgrimage'; and a 'shamanic voyage to a more persuasive reality.'[27] In these remarks he echoes the words of an earlier walker and would-be vagrant, Stephen Graham, who wrote that 'Tramping and vagabondage is a short cut to reality.'[28] Certainly it seems clear that Clare's journey was more than merely an attempt to distance himself from uncongenial surroundings; for he was discarding both an unwanted identity and an inhospitable present, in favour of a re-imagined past unencumbered by awkward realities. But, of course, Clare's journey was unsuccessful, the longed-for object of his delusion long since dead, his sanity mislaid along the way. At first, his wife, Patty, believed him better, stating 'that she wished to try him for a while', but by December of 1841 Clare had once again been committed, this time to Northampton General Lunatic Asylum.[29] He wrote some of his finest poetry there, but his days of vagrancy were now passed and he never left, dying at the age of 70 in 1864.

If the Vagrancy Act of 1824 can be identified as the historical moment in which the vagrant was accorded formal recognition in the UK, then an equivalent date in the US is 1873, the year of the economic crisis out of which the tramp was born. As Christine Photinos indicates in *The Tramp in American Literature (1873–1939)*, the word 'tramp' had previously signified a journey taken on foot; but as a combination of railroad expansion and a series of economic crises from 1873 onwards resulted in the creation of a vast transient population of marginally employed men, so for the first time the tramp became a distinct social type.[30] It was the sheer scale of this new social class that led the figure of the tramp in late nineteenth-century America to become a subject of both trepidation and fascination for the middle classes, and this was soon reflected in a series of books which sought to reveal the true lifestyle of these mysterious figures. In the opening line of his novel *A Tight Squeeze* (1879), the author, George A. Baker, was to ask, 'What is a tramp?'; and both here and in novels such as Horatio Alger's *Tony, the Tramp* (1876), Lee O Harris's *The Man who Tramps* (1878) and, most influentially, Josiah Flynt's *Tramping with Tramps: Studies and Sketches of Vagabond Life* (1899), this question was debated. Depicting the tramp as either a victim of economic misfortune or as a willing participant in an adventurous lifestyle, it was, unsurprisingly, the picaresque view of the vagrant that won the day, and which was celebrated in Flynt's bestselling account. From this point on and despite dissenting voices, amongst them Jack London in his essay *The Tramp* (1903), the vagrant gradually attained a heroic, if not mythic, status as a figure who had seemingly rejected the strictures of the economic system in favour of a life of freedom; a figure later to be celebrated in the US by writers as diverse as Vachel Lindsay, Sinclair Lewis and John Dos Passos, as well as Kerouac, Ginsberg and the Beats.[31]

But in American literature, the romantic depiction of the vagrant has its own pioneering figure, the man who preached the gospel of the open road:

Afoot and light hearted I take to the open road,
Healthy, free, the world before me,
The long brown path before me leading wherever I choose.

Henceforth I ask not good-fortune, I myself am good-fortune
Henceforth I whimper no more, postpone no more, need nothing,
Done with indoor complaints, libraries, querulous criticisms,
Strong and content I travel the open road.[32]

Walt Whitman (1819–1892) was America's first significant urban poet. In his own words, 'Walt Whitman, a Kosmos, of Manhattan the son'[33], he bears the same relationship to the city of New York as does Baudelaire to Paris and Dickens to London, and like them he was to describe his city from street level and with a walker's perspective. Born in Long Island, Whitman lived and worked in some obscurity as a teacher and journalist, before self-publishing *Leaves of Grass* in 1855. Carrying Whitman's picture, but no name, and published in a first edition of only 795 copies, *Leaves of Grass* still managed to provoke one of the most celebrated responses in literary history, with Ralph Waldo Emerson praising it as 'the most extraordinary piece of wit and wisdom that America has yet contributed', adding, 'I greet you at the beginning of a brilliant career.'[34] In many ways, however, *Leaves of Grass* was to prove the beginning, middle and end of Whitman's career, for he was in fact to spend his entire life revising, enlarging and re-publishing the book through numerous editions, the last of which, the so-called 'Deathbed edition', appearing shortly before his death in 1892. By this time the original twelve poems had grown to almost four hundred.

The recurrent motif of Whitman's work is that of the open road, and in 1855 when *Leaves of Grass* first appeared, the road was still seen by most Americans as a symbol of opportunity. Indeed, as Paul Zweig has noted in his study of Whitman, at this point in America's history, the symbol of the road was rapidly becoming a concrete reality, as new routes sprung up from New England through to Ohio and on to the gold fields of California: 'The Yankee peddler, Johnny Appleseed, the Conestoga wagon, Horace Greeley's "Go West, young man", were on the road and defined the road.'[35] If, then, the road was the symbol, the preferred mode of transportation was on foot, and throughout Whitman's work, and especially in the most celebrated poems of the first edition of *Leaves of Grass*, the act of walking is ever present. Sauntering up and down Broadway, moving aimlessly through the city streets and beyond, Whitman remains the laureate of the American wandering tradition:

> Pleasantly and well-suited I walk,
> Whither I walk I cannot define, but I know it is good,
> The whole universe indicates that it is good,
> The past and the present indicate that it is good.[36]

> I tramp a perpetual journey, (come listen all!)
> My signs are a rain-proof coat and good shoes and a staff cut from the woods,
> No friend of mine takes his ease in my chair,
> I have no chair, no church, no philosophy,
> I lead no man to a dinner-table, library, exchange,
> But each man and each woman of you I lead upon a knoll,
> My left hand hooking you round the waist,
> My right hand pointing to landscapes of continents and the public road.[37]

Of course, Whitman's poems express more the spirit of vagrancy than the reality that such a lifestyle entails, and in his often highly sentimental evocation of a life of freedom on the open road he avoids altogether the depiction of suffering that Clare, for example, was to experience on his journey home from Essex. In this respect, Whitman belongs firmly within the Romantic tradition of walking literature that sees the vagrant, tramp or vagabond as a symbolic figure at odds with the orthodoxies of conventional society. This is an outlook which is mirrored, if not surpassed, in the work of Robert Louis Stevenson (1850–1894) whose own fervent celebration of vagrancy reaches its apotheosis in his poem *The Vagabond* (1896):

Give to me the life I love,
Let the lave go by me,
Give the jolly heaven above
And the byway nigh me.
Bed in the bush with stars to see,
Bread I dip in the river –
There's the life for a man like me,
There's the life for ever.
Let the blow fall soon or late,
Let what will be o'er me;
Give the face of earth around,
And the road before me.
Wealth I ask not, hope nor love,
Nor a friend to know me;
All I ask, the heaven above
And the road below me.[38]

During Stevenson's short but picaresque life, his walking was almost entirely confined to the period between 1874, the year of his recovery from a nervous breakdown, and his departure for California in 1879; and it was during this period that Stevenson's two major contributions to the literature of walking emerged: his essay 'Walking Tours' (1876), and his *Travels with a Donkey in the Cévennes* (1879). In the latter, Stevenson once again paints a highly romanticised picture of life on the open road, including a description of his pioneering use of a home-made sleeping bag, a landmark not so much in the literature of vagrancy, but that of camping, in which Stevenson's account must rank as the first.[39] 'For my part', writes Stevenson, 'I travel not to go anywhere, but to go. I travel for travel's sake. The great affair is to move; to feel the needs and hitches of our life more nearly; to come down off this feather-bed of civilisation, and find the globe granite underfoot and strewn with cutting flints.'[40] In this instance, however, Stephenson's need for movement was hindered severely by the pace of his reluctant companion, the donkey, Modestine:

'What that pace was, there is no word mean enough to describe; it was something as much slower than a walk as a walk is slower than a run; it kept me hanging on each foot for an incredible length of time; in five minutes it exhausted the spirit and set up a fever in all the muscles of the leg.'[41]

Stevenson formalises his philosophy of walking in 'Walking Tours'(1876), itself a response to Hazlitt's 'On Going a Journey' (1822), perhaps the best known essay in the entire walking canon, and it is here that Stevenson reaffirms Hazlitt's contention that walking should be a solitary occupation: 'A walking tour should be gone upon alone, because freedom is of the essence; because you should be able to stop and go on, and follow this way or that, as the freak takes you [...] And surely, of all possible moods, this, in which a man takes the road, is best.'[42] For Stevenson, however, like Whitman before him, the act of walking is never precipitated out of economic necessity, but is instead a means of temporarily breaking away from the confines of everyday existence. Thus, despite their evangelism for the open road and the vagrant's freedom, theirs is always a lifestyle and never quite the life itself. In short, having talked the talk, the question remains, did they really walk the walk? Perhaps by maintaining a twofold existence as writer and walker, the experiences on the road can never truly be more than episodes within the writer's life. But what if the life of the writer was itself merely a precursor to a life on the road, a life in which the writer was superseded by the vagrant?

Born in 1854; begins writing poetry as a teenager; 'retires' from poetry before reaching 21; travels through Europe, Indonesia and Africa; dies aged 37 in 1891. If Stevenson can be said to have lived a short, intense and exotic life, he is surpassed in each of these categories by his almost exact contemporary, the poet and vagrant *extraordinaire*, Arthur Rimbaud. Born in what he was later to describe as 'the most supremely idiotic of all little provincial towns'[43], Charleville in the Ardennes, the life of Arthur Rimbaud has been characterised as an elliptical series of escapes or desertions, punctuated by periodic returns to his childhood home, until, finally, he broke away for good, never to return.[44] Following a familiar template of adolescent development, Rimbaud's early academic success was soon to give way to full-blown teenage rebellion. In 1870, aged fifteen, his first poems were published in magazines, and the following year, after several earlier truancies (one of which resulted in a brief period of imprisonment in Paris), he headed off once again. Returning to Paris, he 'slept rough, ate out of dustbins, read pamphlets on the bookstalls',[45] before turning round again and, less than two weeks after arriving, walking home – a journey of some 150 miles:

> On the roads, through winter nights, without a home, without habits, without bread, a voice strangled my frozen heart: "Weakness or strength. These are your options, so strength it is. We know neither where you're going, nor why you're going, entering anywhere, answering anyone. You're no more likely to be killed than a corpse." By morning, I had developed such a lost, dead expression that those I met *may not have even seen me*.[46]

Within months he was off again, returning to Paris on foot to play his part, or so it is claimed, in the short-lived Paris Commune of 1871. Whether or not he was actually involved in the uprising is unclear, but he was certainly affected by these early experiences of life on the road. For, as Charles Nicholl has noted, this period marks the first of many transformations in Rimbaud's life, as the studious, introverted schoolboy became somebody else: 'a dirty, long-haired, loutish young man who "scandalizes" the locals with his new "romantic hairstyle coming halfway down his back", his workman's *brûle-gueule* or clay pipe, his obscenity-filled harangues against Church and State.'[47] Or as Jack Kerouac was later to intone in his paean to Rimbaud: 'The Vagrant is born/the deranged seer makes his first Manifesto [...] On foot Rimbaud walks.'[48] Vagrant, vagabond, or, in Rimbaud's parlance, *voyant*,[49] the poet was to be both walker and visionary: 'I tell you: the poet has to be a seer, to make himself a seer by a long, immense and systematic derangement of all the senses.'[50]

In Rimbaud's short life, 1871 was a turning point, for it was also the year in which he was to meet Paul Verlaine, the poet and lover with whom he was to continue both his derangement of the senses and his experience of the open road. In tandem with Verlaine, Rimbaud was to swap Paris for London, a chaotic period of 'walks, binges, and studies.'[51] The first of these preoccupations is captured in the poem 'Workers' in the *Illuminations* (1872–4), in which Rimbaud writes: 'We took a walk in the suburbs. It was overcast and the South wind stirred rank smells of ravaged gardens and starched fields [...] The city, its smoke and noise, pursued us down the roads.'[52] It is difficult to overstate the importance of walking to Rimbaud and Verlaine at this time as they explored London's outer perimeter, seeking to dispel the mysteries of the metropolis. In a letter to Émile Blémond, Verlaine was to write: 'Every day we take enormous walks in the suburbs and in the country round London [...] We've seen Kew, Woolwich, and many other places [...] Drury Lane, Whitechapel, Pimlico, the City, Hyde Park: all these have no longer any mystery for us.'[53]

In 'Vagabonds', also from the *Illuminations*, Rimbaud writes, 'We wandered, sustained by wine from cellars and the road's dry bread'[54]; and it is interesting to compare his harshly unsentimental account of life on the road with Stevenson's much more romantically inclined version. For while Whitman and Stevenson were to depict the walker as invariably well-fed and well-shod, as early as 1870 Rimbaud was describing, in his poem 'My Bohemia', his 'wounded shoes' and depicting a figure 'with fists thrust in the torn pockets of a coat held together by no more than its name.'[55]

In the years following his departure from London (and from Verlaine also), Rimbaud's travels become more erratic and consequently less well documented: Reading; Scarborough; Stuttgart; Milan; Marseilles; as the list of confirmed (and unconfirmed) destinations increases, so Rimbaud's poetic output comes to an abrupt end. Indeed, just as Rimbaud's final dateable poem appears in 1875, shortly before his 21st birthday, so he embarks upon the period of his most sustained and relentless travelling; for just as an earlier transformation was to see the schoolboy become the *voyant*, so 1875 appears to have marked another such reincarnation, as Rimbaud the poet becomes Rimbaud the vagrant, the pen set aside, finally and irrevocably, in favour of the wandering, often alone and usually on foot, which was to characterise so much of his later life.

From his earliest escapes from Charleville, it appears that Rimbaud had fallen upon the ideal method of travelling, a technique that was to stand him in good stead on future journeys. For complementing his predilection for marathon feats of long-distance pedestrianism, Rimbaud also discovered that legal expulsion was an economical way of getting around: by begging in the street until he was inevitably arrested, Rimbaud found himself repeatedly sent on to the next territory where he could begin the process again. In this way, notes Graham Robb, Rimbaud managed to get himself expelled through Europe, on one occasion being transported across Southern Germany before walking the 180 miles home to Charleville.[56]

But Rimbaud's walking was not simply a whim or a pose: he was undeniably in search of adventure; but he was also destitute. There are, for example, at least two recorded occasions where his walking very nearly proved fatal. In late 1877, already set upon reaching Africa, Rimbaud embarked, on foot, for Alexandria. By the time he reached Marseilles, however, he was so ill that he was forced to abandon the attempt. The cause, according to his friend Ernest Delahaye, was 'gastric fever and inflammation of the stomach-lining caused by rubbing of the sides against the abdomen in the course of excessive walking: this was, textually, the doctor's diagnosis.'[57] The following year, in a walk which was to foreshadow that of Hilaire Belloc some twenty years later, Rimbaud tried again, this time heading for Genoa, on a journey through the Vosges and on across the Alps via the Saint-Gothard pass: 'Now you're wading through snow more than a metre high. You can't see your knees any more. You're getting worked up now. Panting away, for in half an hour the blizzard could bury you without any trouble'.[58] It was not until 1880 that Rimbaud finally left Europe for good, only returning to Marseilles to die in 1891. He was going 'to traffick in the unknown', embarking on an African adventure so extraordinarily picaresque as to now read more as myth than history. In this final period of Rimbaud's life he was to transform himself for the final time, the vagrant and the wanderer giving way to the trader, the gun-runner, the explorer.[59]

As far as this account is concerned, however, Rimbaud remains, above all else, a walker. Verlaine had described Rimbaud as '*l'homme aux semelles de vent*' – his feet, or shoes, had 'soles of wind'; while another nickname was '*l'oestre*', the gad-fly.[60] But it was Ernest Delahaye, in 1876, who was to sketch the most enduring portrait of the vagrant, (ex-)poet, perpetually in transit, forever on the move:

> Rimbaud was then still robust. He had the strong, supple look of a resolute and patient walker, who is always setting off, his long legs moving calmly and very regularly, his body straight, his head straight, his beautiful eyes fixed on the distance, and his face entirely filled with a look of resigned defiance, an air of expectation – ready for everything, without anger, without fear.[61]

Notes

[1] *Webster's Revised Unabridged Dictionary*, ed. by Noah Porter, Springfield, MA: G&C Merriam, 1913, p. 1591
[2] Arthur Rickett, *The Vagabond in Literature*, London: Dent, 1906, p. 3. 'Sometimes the vagabond is a physical, sometimes only an intellectual wanderer', writes Rickett, who goes on to identify a 'spiritual brotherhood' of such figures, numbering amongst their

ranks: Hazlitt; De Quincey; Thoreau; Whitman and Stevenson.

[3] See Vagrancy Act (1824), The UK Statute Law Database, at http://www.statutelaw.gov.uk/

[4] Joseph A. Amato writes: 'Vagrancy, which had been proscribed since the early Middle Ages, unabatedly nagged at European society and continued to do so through modern European history. Trouble literally came on foot. Especially during bad times it came from the surrounding countryside in the form of straggling, destitute individuals and whole downtrodden families carrying all their worldly possessions on their backs. More terrifyingly, threat wore the face of independent armies, roving bands of peasants, and bandits intent on sacking the city.' Amato, p. 68

[5] Donna Landry, *Radical Walking* (2001) at http://www.opendemocracy.net/ecology-transport/article_465.jsp

[6] Landry, *Radical Walking* (2001)

[7] Celeste Langan, *Romantic Vagrancy: Wordsworth and the Simulation of Freedom*, Cambridge: Cambridge University Press, 1995, p. 223

[8] John Clare, 'Sketches in the Life of John Clare by Himself' in *John Clare: The Journal, Essays, The Journey from Essex*, ed. by Anne Tibble, Manchester: Carcanet New Press, 1980, pp. 9–10

[9] The definitive work on this subject is John Barrell's *The Idea of Landscape and the Sense of Place 1730–1840: An Approach to the Poetry of John Clare*, Cambridge: Cambridge University Press, 1972. Here, Barrell writes: 'To enclose an open-field parish means in the first place to think of the details of its topography as quite erased from the map. The hostile and mysterious road-system was tamed and made unmysterious by being destroyed.' (p. 94)

[10] John Clare, 'The Mores', in *Major Works*, ed. by Eric Robinson and David Powell, with an introduction by Tom Paulin, Oxford: Oxford University Press, 2004, pp. 167–9

[11] John Clare, 'Sonnet: I dreaded walking where there was no path' in *John Clare: Everyman's Poetry*, ed. by RKR Thornton, London: Phoenix, 1997, pp. 9–10

[12] Clare, 'Sunday Walks', in *Major Works*, p. 78

[13] Donna Landry writes: 'Going about the woods and fields writing poetry set John Clare sufficiently apart from his fellow villagers that he was the victim of speculation, with some believing him 'crazd', and others putting some more criminal interpretations to his rambles – that he was a 'night walking associate with the gipseys robbing the woods of the hares and pheasants.' Landry, *The Invention of the Countryside*, p. 83

[14] Robin Jarvis, *Romantic Writing and Pedestrian Travel*, Basingstoke: Macmillan, 1997, p. 178

[15] Although written in 1841, the *Journey from Essex* only reached a wider audience through its inclusion in Frederick Martin's biography of Clare, first published in 1865, which 'made known to the public for the first time the extremity of what Clare endured.' Jonathan Bate, *John Clare: A Biography*, London: Picador, 2003, p. 538

[16] Clare, 'Journey out of Essex', in *Major Works*, p. 433

[17] Clare, 'Journey out of Essex', p. 434

[18] Clare, 'Journey out of Essex', pp. 435–6

[19] Clare, 'Journey out of Essex', p. 436

[20] Clare, 'Journey out of Essex', p. 436

[21] Clare, 'Journey out of Essex', p. 437

[22] Clare, 'Journey out of Essex', p. 437

[23] Clare, *Major Works*, Notes, p. 496

[24] Bate, p. 3

[25] Iain Sinclair, *Edge of the Orison: In the Traces of John Clare's 'Journey out of Essex'*, London: Hamish Hamilton, 2005, pp. 126–7

[26] Sinclair, *Edge of the Orison*, pp. 15 & 31

[27] Sinclair, *Edge of the Orison*, pp. 11 & 122

[28] Stephen Graham, 'The Literature of Walking', in *The Tramp's Anthology*, p. x

[29] Tom Paulin, ed., Clare, *Major Works*, Introduction, p. xxiii

[30] Christine Photinos, *The Tramp in American Literature (1873–1939)* at http://ejournals.library.vanderbilt.edu/ameriquests/viewarticle.php?id=71&layout=html

[31] A significant addition to this list is the name of WH Davies,

author of *The Autobiography of a Super-Tramp* (1908) in which he describes his life as a vagrant in the US, Canada and the UK in the closing years of the nineteenth century. Despite losing a leg while riding the railroad in Canada, Davies continued to 'tramp' huge distances on his return to the UK, writing: 'I would rather take a free country walk, leaving the roads for the less trodden paths of the hills and the lanes, than ride in a yacht or a coach.' WH Davies, *Autobiography of a Super-Tramp* (1908), Oxford: Oxford University Press, 1980, p. 148.

In her account of Davies' life, Barbara Hooper has described the contrasting lifestyles of the American vagrant of Davies' era and his counterpart in the UK, noting that 'Begging in America was an almost legitimate lifestyle, far less despised than in England.' 'With a little rhetoric', she adds, 'a hobo's life could even be described as respectable.' This was certainly the view taken by Davies himself, who, on his arrival in America, soon gave up any idea of earning a living in favour of life on the road, 'seeking to improve my mind and body as a tramp.' Barbara Hooper, *Time to Stand and Stare: A Life of WH Davies, Poet and Super-Tramp*, London: Peter Owen, 2004, pp. 38–9

[32] Walt Whitman, 'Song of the Open Road' in Walt Whitman, *Leaves of Grass*, ed. by Jerome Loving, Oxford: Oxford University Press, 2008, pp. 120–1

[33] Whitman, 'Song of Myself' in *Leaves of Grass*, p. 48

[34] Letter from Emerson to Whitman, 21 July 1855, in *Leaves of Grass*, Appendix B, p. 463

[35] Paul Zweig, *Walt Whitman: The Making of the Poet*, Harmondsworth: Penguin, 1986, p. 243

[36] Whitman, 'To Think of Time' in *Leaves of Grass*, p. 337

[37] Whitman, 'Song of Myself' in *Leaves of Grass*, p. 73

[38] Robert Louis Stevenson, 'The Vagabond' (1896) in *The Magic of Walking*, ed. by Aaron Sussman & Ruth Goode, New York: Simon and Schuster, 1980, p. 347. In her biography of Stevenson, Claire Harman notes that Stevenson was deeply affected by the 'gospel' of Walt Whitman: 'Stevenson', she writes, 'admired, even

venerated, the poet's philosophy and hugely ambitious design. He later described Whitman as 'a teacher who at a crucial moment of his youthful life had helped him to discover the right line of conduct." Claire Harman, *Robert Louis Stevenson: A Biography*, London: HarperCollins, 2005, p. 73

[39] Marples, p. 152

[40] Robert Louis Stevenson, *Travels with a Donkey in the Cévennes and the Amateur Emigrant*, ed. by Christopher MacLachlan, London: Penguin, 2004, p. 35. In 1964, the biographer, Richard Holmes, then 18, was to retrace Stevenson's twelve-day journey across the Cévennes. Haunted by Stevenson and his account, Holmes' journey, conducted entirely on foot, 'was to become a kind of pursuit, a tracking of the physical trail of someone's path through the past, a following of footsteps.' See Richard Holmes, *Footsteps: Adventures of a Romantic Biographer*, London: Hodder & Stoughton, 1985, pp. 13–69

[41] Stevenson, *Travels with a Donkey*, p. 12

[42] Stevenson, 'Walking Tours' (1876), in *The Magic of Walking*, 234–40, p. 235

[43] Charles Nicholl, *Somebody Else: Arthur Rimbaud in Africa 1880–91*, London: Vintage, 1998, p. 21

[44] Graham Robb writes: 'It seemed as though every road was bound to return elliptically to the Ardennes until a certain escape velocity had been reached. Traced on a map, Rimbaud's wanderings take the same palindromic form as some of the *Illuminations* – repetitions around a non-existent centre.' See Robb, *Rimbaud*, London: Picador, 2000, p. 278

[45] Nicholl, p. 24

[46] Arthur Rimbaud, 'A Season in Hell' (1873), in *Rimbaud Complete*, ed. and trans. by Wyatt Mason, London: Scribner, 2003, p. 198

[47] Nicholl, p. 26

[48] Jack Kerouac, *Rimbaud*, San Francisco, CA: City Lights Books, 1960. According to his biographer, Graham Robb, Rimbaud displayed an interest in the figure of the vagrant from an early

age, habitually talking to 'strange men he met on the road – navvies, quarrymen and vagrants.' 'Even when they were drunk', he told his friend Ernest Delahaye, 'they were "closer to nature" and more truly intelligent than the educated hypocrites of his own class. These were men who, like Captain Rimbaud [Rimbaud's father], could set off down the road and never come back.' Robb, p. 40

[49] Rimbaud is employing a pun here between *voyou* and *voyant*, the former meaning 'a hooligan, a thug, a punk', the latter 'a prophet or visionary – literally a seer.' See Nicholl, p. 26

[50] Rimbaud in a letter to Paul Demeny, May 1871, in Nicholl, p. 26

[51] Nicholl, p. 54

[52] Rimbaud, 'Workers' in *Rimbaud Complete*, p. 239

[53] Letter from Verlaine to Émile Blémond, in Nicholl, p. 53

[54] Rimbaud, 'Vagabonds' in *Rimbaud Complete*, p. 244

[55] Rimbaud, 'My Bohemia: A Fantasy' (1870), in *Rimbaud Complete*, p. 49. 'For Rimbaud', writes Graham Robb, 'the point was to feel the regular thud of "rugged reality". In "Ma Bohème" he had written of his "wounded shoes" with the compassionate attachment that a long-distance walker feels for his equipment. These were the simple tools that turned the world into a moving spectacle. In less than three months, he hammered out more than 600 miles on some of the most gruelling terrain in Southern Europe. The usual result of these marathons – though this can hardly be attributed to a conscious plan – was that he reduced himself to a state of helpless destitution.' Robb, p. 269

[56] Robb, *Rimbaud,* p. 277

[57] Ernest Delahaye, qtd. in Nicholl, p.80. Graham Robb has questioned this diagnosis, however, suggesting that it might have been a product of Rimbaud's imagination: 'This unusual affliction might have been invented by Rimbaud. The idea that walking wears the stomach thin would be quite at home among the paradoxes of his *chansons*: even the arrangement of internal organs is self-defeating.' Robb, p. 292

[58] Nicholl, p. 81

[59] Rimbaud's years in Africa between 1880 and his death in 1891 remain largely undocumented. Even here, however, one finds further evidence of Rimbaud's prowess as a walker, with one friend from this period, Dimitri Righas, recalling: 'He was a great walker. Oh, an astonishing walker!' See Nicholl, p. 261

[60] Nicholl, p. 71

[61] Rimbaud described by Ernest Delahaye in Nicholl, pp. 74–5. Graham Robb, commenting on Delahaye's description, writes: 'By now, his body was tuned to long distances, though not always capable of covering them. Like verse or music, walking was a rhythmical skill, a combination of trance and productive activity. Delahaye's description of the athletic pedestrian suggests a special state of existence, a happy delegation of responsibility to blood and muscle.' (Robb, p. 277)

The Walker and the Natural World

When we walk, we naturally go to the fields and woods: what would become of us, if we walked only in a garden or a mall? Henry David Thoreau[1]

Being a leisurely walker in the so-called countryside is historically unusual behaviour [...] Those out walking in the countryside have been mostly regarded as poor, mad or criminal. John Urry[2]

In the final decades of the eighteenth century, popular attitudes to walking underwent a profound reversal. Within the space of a single generation, an activity previously regarded as little more than a consequence of economic necessity became something altogether different; walking became a pleasure not a chore, the preserve of the leisured classes and not merely the poor. This rediscovery of walking was partly the result of a newly evolving view of the traveller as a distinct type, itself a consequence of improvements in roads and transport, which allowed the kinds of touring previously enjoyed in Continental Europe to develop a domestic equivalent. These changes were to prove deep-rooted, for behind the superficial fluctuations of fashion, the common perception of nature itself was undergoing a transition, as landscapes hitherto regarded as unrewarding came to be viewed as spiritual and liberating.

The philosophical foundations underpinning this shift in visual awareness originated in the influence of Rousseau and were soon to find expression in the emergence of the Romantic Movement. But these sentiments were most clearly articulated by the then influential figure of the Reverend William Gilpin. It was Gilpin who, in the 1770s, had first developed the idea of the picturesque, popularising a new method of viewing our environment, through which the intrepid traveller was sent out into the wilds of the British countryside to engage in sublime communion with the rugged and untamed landscapes to be found there. Gilpin's work was itself part of a wider trend for travel narratives in the late eighteenth century that set about transforming our understanding of the British Isles in general, and Scotland, North Wales and the Lake District in particular. Soon the act of walking had given way to the walking-tour, and for the first time the figure of the pedestrian could be observed in his natural habitat.

> I regret much not having been made acquainted with your wish to have employed your vacation in a pedestrian tour, both on your own account – as it would have contributed greatly to exhilarate your spirits – and on mine, as we should have gained much from the addition of your society. Letter from William Wordsworth to William Mathews, Plas-yn-Llan, August 13, 1791[3]

This extract from Wordsworth's letter to his friend William Mathews in 1791 contains the first recorded usage of the word *pedestrian*, in its adjectival form, to capture the literal sense of being on foot. And few people, if any, before or since, have come close to Wordsworth in replicating the extent to which he was to become a living expression of this term. Wordsworth's dominant position within the canon of literary walkers is unchallenged; his crucial role in shaping our perceptions of the English landscape is unarguable. Indeed, so accustomed are we to associating Wordsworth's poetry with an idealised image of the English countryside, preserved through the increasingly symbolic representation of a landscape long since diminished, that he has been called the Patron Saint of the Natural Trust.[4] Yet if De Quincey's description is to be trusted, Wordsworth's stature as poet and walker was not reflected in his physical appearance:

> To begin with his figure: – Wordsworth was, upon the whole, not a well–made man. His legs were pointedly condemned by all the female connoisseurs in legs that I ever heard lecture on that topic; not that they were bad in any way which would force itself upon your notice – there was no absolute deformity about them; and undoubtedly they had been serviceable legs beyond the average standard of human requisition; for I calculate, upon good data, that with these identical legs Wordsworth must have traversed a distance of 175 to 180,000 English miles – a mode of exertion, which to him, stood in the stead of wine, spirits, and all other stimulants whatsoever to the animal spirits; to which he has been indebted for a life of unclouded happiness, and we for much of what is most excellent in his writings. But, useful as they have proved themselves, the Wordsworthian legs were certainly not ornamental; and it was really a pity, as I agreed with a lady in thinking, that he had not another pair for evening dress parties – when no boots lend their friendly aid to masque our imperfections from the eyes of female rigorists.[5]

If Wordsworth's extraordinary career as poet and pedestrian can be captured within a single work, then it is his prodigious feat of textual endurance, *The Prelude* (1850), which most faithfully records his twofold obsession with, what were for him, the indissoluble acts of walking and composition. First completed in 1805 and, like Whitman's *Leaves of Grass*, subsequently polished and revised over the course of his life, *The Prelude* was first published posthumously in 1850, the year of Wordsworth's death. In many ways a walker's autobiography, *The Prelude* offers a portrait of the walker as a young man, as Wordsworth recalls the nocturnal wanderings of his schooldays: 'twas my joy', he writes, 'To wander half the night among the Cliffs/ And the smooth

Hollows [...] For I would walk alone/ In storm and tempest, or in starlight nights/ Beneath the quiet heavens[6]; while later in the poem, he expresses his good fortune in having been close to nature from an early age: 'Happy in this, that I with nature walked/ Not having a too early intercourse/ With the deformities of crowded life.'[7] And it was the continuation of this childhood habit, along with his almost mystical rapport with the natural world, which was to provide the basis for his lifelong philosophy:

> I love a public road: few sights there are
> That please me more; such object hath had power
> O'er my imagination since the dawn
> Of childhood, when its disappearing line,
> Seen daily afar off, on one bare steep
> Beyond the limits which my feet had trod,
> Was like a guide in to eternity,
> At least to things unknown and without bound.[8]

The turning point in Wordsworth's life, or at least the first milestone in his career as poet and pedestrian, was to come in 1790 when, aged twenty, he embarked upon his first major walking-tour. Accompanied by his friend and fellow student, Robert Jones, such a tour would soon become a staple part of undergraduate life, but in 1790 such a journey was regarded as both 'mad and impracticable.'[9] Covering more than 350 miles in the first fortnight, the next two months saw Wordsworth and his companion cross Europe at a rate of some thirty miles a day, through France, Italy, Germany and Switzerland, an incursion through Continental Europe that was, once again, to be recalled in *The Prelude*:

> 'Tis not my present purpose to retrace
> That variegated journey step by step:
> A march it was of military speed,
> And earth did change her images and forms

Before us, fast as clouds are changed in Heaven.
Day after day, up early and down late,
From vale to vale, from hill to hill we went,
From Province on to Province did we pass,
Keen hunters in a chace of fourteen weeks[10]

The culmination of this tour was a visit to the Island of Sainte-Pierre in Switzerland, described by Rousseau in the fifth walk of his *Reveries* as something of a natural paradise. Indeed, Wordsworth appears to have been overcome by a similarly rapturous response himself, writing to his sister on his return: 'I am a perfect enthusiast in my admiration of Nature in all her various forms.'[11]

If, then, Wordsworth can be seen as a natural successor to Rousseau, he also inherits something of Rousseau's melancholic outlook; for despite the young man's reverie, the figure of the walker in Wordsworth's early work shares none of the intoxication with the natural world that he himself was to experience. On the contrary, the walker is invariably portrayed as a figure of social alienation, divorced both from his society and his surroundings. Hence, in place of the vigorous pedestrian, Wordsworth's early poems are peopled by the marginalised and dispossessed: the outlaw and the murderer, the abandoned woman, discharged soldiers, beggars and gypsies.[12]

Unlike John Clare, Wordsworth had little to fear from being mistaken for a gypsy poacher himself, or being prosecuted as a vagrant as he travelled along the public road; and yet his poetry displays both a fascination with these figures and an identification with their suffering. Indeed, it is precisely this awareness of the common ground between them that allows him to elevate walking to the status of a democratic act, a unifying practice through which the social divisions of the day may be challenged and overcome.[13] Yet Wordsworth's poetry also emphasises the distinction between the tourist and the traveller, the leisurely walker and the labourer, as he attempts to redefine the act of walking; establishing an entirely new kind of peripatetic verse in which the act of walking takes on the regular, repetitive metre not of the pedestrian but of the labourer. Here, the act of walking has become a metaphor for the working of the land, a restless, mechanical activity divorced from mental processes, an act of physical production whose output is measured in verse:

A length of open space where I might walk
Backwards and forwards long as I had liking
In easy and mechanic thoughtlessness[14]

Wordsworth's own walks soon came to reflect this new aesthetic, and after the age of thirty the epic touring of his youth gave way to an equally prodigious, yet more obsessive and metronomic form of movement, as he paced out his daily regimen. After 1799, when the Wordsworths had settled in Grasmere in the Lake District, famously he used to compose much of his work while striding up and down the straight gravel path in his garden. Along this small strip Wordsworth performed his pedestrian labours, the acts of walking and composition having finally become synonymous and indistinguishable.

Wordsworth went on walking for the rest of his long life and it was walking that sustained him. Friends came and departed as the radical politics of his youth gave way to the conservatism of old age; his reputation peaked only to suffer a prolonged decline. Yet throughout these fluctuations in fortune, he continued his astonishing pedestrian odyssey. Walking had become his natural state, the mode of being on foot the one which, above all others, allowed him (and those alongside him) to experience the natural world with an intensity alien to his predecessors.

As a pedestrian pure and simple Wordsworth could have held his own in an age of pedestrianism. He thought nothing of walking long distances in the ordinary course of his day-to-day affairs: seven miles out and seven miles back to fetch the post, fifteen miles across the mountains to have tea with a friend. Moreover he could walk for a long time at a great speed (as could his sister Dorothy in her youth). On one occasion in 1799 the two of them walked ten miles over a high mountain road, with a strong wind behind them, in 2.5 hours 'by the watch,' and then, after a rest of quarter of an hour in an inn, seven miles more in 1 hour 35 minutes – in all, seventeen miles in just over 4 hours: good going for a man, and remarkable for a woman at that time.[15]

While William Wordsworth's prodigious feats of pedestrianism have been the subject of endless commentary, those of his sister Dorothy have, like almost every aspect of her life, remained largely overshadowed. This does her a great disservice, for in fact she holds a pioneering position within the walking canon, not only for her startling achievements as a walker in her own right, but also as a result of her journals, in which she reveals the true extent to which the act of walking was to dominate the lives of herself and her brother.

Having drawn attention to the shortcomings of William's physique, De Quincey was to extend the same treatment to his sister, noting that Dorothy had a stooping attitude when walking, which he describes as ungraceful, lending 'an unsexual character to her appearance when out of doors.'[16] Yet if her gait was an unorthodox one it was also highly effective, for Dorothy was soon to display every sign of sharing her brother's congenital aptitude for walking, along with, it should be added, a character robust enough to ignore the criticisms of both her wider family and society at large, to whom her walking habits would not simply have been regarded as eccentric but disreputable.[17]

Dorothy Wordsworth would have developed the habit of walking during a childhood spent with her brother William, but her career as a long-distance walker can be dated from 1794 while staying on a farm belonging to William Calvert near Keswick in the Lake District. On her way there, as she was later to describe, she and her brother walked from Kendal to Grasmere, a distance of eighteen miles, and then from Grasmere to Keswick, another fifteen miles. As Morris Marples correctly observes, 'Not many women now would lightly walk thirty–three miles in a day.'[18]

Her first major 'walking–tour', and quite possibly the first such tour ever conducted by a woman, was taken alongside Wordsworth and Coleridge as they travelled from Alfoxden to Lynmouth and back in November 1797.[19] This was the famous journey that was to provide Coleridge with the inspiration to write 'The Rhyme of the Ancient Mariner', which was to appear as part of Wordsworth and Coleridge's *Lyrical Ballads* (1798), published the following year. Yet 1798 was also to produce another, much less celebrated work, this time not written for publication or for a wider audience, but one which illuminates this extraordinary period as Wordsworth, his sister and Coleridge walk their way into literary history.

Dorothy Wordsworth's *Alfoxden Journal* (1798) refers to the period between July 1797 and June 1798 when the Wordsworths rented 'Alfoxden', a large house three miles from Coleridge's cottage at Nether Stowey in Somerset. The journal covers only the four months from late January 1798 and contains both very little action and almost no authorial presence whatsoever. With its abrupt, pared down prose style in which brief descriptions of the landscape sit alongside daily walking routines, it has been described as reading like a 'pedestrian's log–book.'[20] Yet, this short and scantily written journal reveals both a fascination with the natural world as well as emphasising the bond between these three figures, who often appear to be in a state of perpetual motion.

From the opening entry, dated 20 January 1798, the author appears entranced by her environment, describing a garden 'gay with flowers' and the countryside bathed in sunbeams.[21] This reverie is gradually displaced, however, as the garden is left behind and she heads off on foot. Soon each entry is introduced with the same word: 'walked'; times and routes are given, as are observations of the weather, the sky and the landscape. The entries become shorter and more brisk as if the pace of the journal is itself replicating the walks it describes. At first alone, or with William, soon Coleridge is present too, and as the landscape changes with the season all extraneous information is cut back or omitted altogether, until only that which is essential remains:

> [March] 25th. Walked to Coleridge's after tea. Arrived at home at one o'clock. The night cloudy but not dark.
> 26th. Went to meet Wedgewood at Coleridge's after dinner. Reached home at half-past twelve, a fine moonlight night; half moon.
> 29th. Coleridge dined with us.
> 30th. Walked I know not where.
> 31st. Walked.[22]

This entry for the 31st, 'Walked', somehow seems a distillation of the entire journal, as if its principal activity is finally laid bare. We don't know where she walked, or why, and yet this seems unimportant; for the activity has finally gained a significance in and for itself, wholly divorced from its route or participants. And so it goes on, as the remaining days are passed in a welcome repetition of place and movement:

> April 1st. Walked by moonlight.
> 2nd. A very high wind. Coleridge came to avoid the smoke; stayed all night. We walked in the wood, and sat under the trees [...]
> 3rd. Walked to Crookham, with Coleridge and William [...]
> 4th. Walked to the sea-side in the afternoon [...][23]

The journal reaches a rather abrupt conclusion with its final entry, 'April 22nd [17th] *Thursday*. Walked to Cheddar. Slept at Cross.'[24] Once again, the day has been pared back to reveal its constituent parts – walking and sleeping – and the remainder is left unspoken.

The Alfoxden Journal has received little of the attention devoted towards Dorothy Wordsworth's much more substantial *Grasmere Journal* (1800–03) and from a purely literary point of view this is unsurprising. For the *Alfoxden Journal* shares none of the human interest, the exploration of character, and details of domestic daily life which characterise the *Grasmere Journal*, to which it is customarily seen as little more than an overture. Yet as far as the literature of walking is concerned, the *Alfoxden Journal* holds a much more significant position, for despite its brevity and almost skeletal form, or perhaps because of these, there is no other text which so clearly foregrounds the act of walking, or which affords this activity such a pre-eminent position within the process of literary composition.

If, then, 1798 is notable both for the publication of the *Lyrical Ballads* and for the events recorded in the *Alfoxden Journal*, it gains further significance from being the year in which Coleridge and Wordsworth were first introduced to William Hazlitt. Coleridge's own claims as a walker have been well documented, not least through his association with Wordsworth, and if De Quincey's description of Wordsworth's physique appears uncharitable, it is as nothing compared to Carlyle's description of Coleridge as 'a fat, flabby, incurvated personage, at once short, rotund, and relaxed [...] He never straightens his knee-joints. He stoops with his fat, ill-shapen shoulders, and in walking does not tread, but shovel and slide.'[25] As a young man Coleridge could match Wordsworth, step for step, and yet by the age of thirty, ill-health and depression had brought his walking career to a premature end. And while he often composed as he walked, his poetry does not express the overriding physical need for this activity to be found in Wordsworth's verse.

Hazlitt first met Coleridge during the course of a walk, escorting him on the first six miles of his journey home from Wem in Shropshire, where Hazlitt's father was a Unitarian

Minister and where Coleridge had been preaching.[26] This encounter resulted in an invitation for Hazlitt to visit Coleridge at his home in Nether Stowey, a journey of some 150 miles. Hazlitt completed this journey on foot and during the three weeks he was to spend with Coleridge he shared a pedestrian tour of the area with Coleridge and a local admirer named John Chester. Hazlitt evidently shared Coleridge's capacity for long-distance walking, the two covering more than thirty miles together on the day of Hazlitt's departure, but the 20-year old remained awe-struck in Coleridge's company and 'scarcely ever spoke himself, and never expressed an opinion.'[27] Hazlitt never made a direct record of these first steps in his walking career and his recollections of the itinerary can be unreliable, and yet it is he, and not his more celebrated Romantic contemporaries, who has bequeathed to us the most acclaimed distillation of the walker's philosophy:

> One of the pleasantest things in the world is going a journey; but I like to go by myself. I can enjoy society in a room; but out of doors, nature is company enough for me. I am then never less alone than when alone [...] I cannot see the wit of walking and talking at the same time. When I am in the country, I wish to vegetate like the country. I am not for criticizing hedge-rows and black cattle. I go out of town in order to forget the town and all that is in it. There are those who for this purpose go to watering-places, and carry the metropolis with them. I like more elbow-room, and fewer incumbrances [...] The soul of a journey is liberty, perfect liberty, to think, feel, do just as one pleases. We go a journey chiefly to be free of all impediments and of all inconveniences; to leave ourselves behind, much more to get rid of others [...] Give me the clear blue sky over my head, and the green turf beneath my feet, a winding road before me, and a three hours' march to dinner [...] I laugh, I run, I leap, I sing for joy.[28]

First published in the journal, *Table Talk*, in 1821, 'On Going a Journey' was the first essay to directly address the idea of walking as an activity in its own right, and despite the many successors and imitators which were to follow, amongst them Robert Louis Stevenson and Leslie Stephen, Hazlitt's essay remains the pre-eminent example of the genre. 'On Going a Journey' presents an idealized vision of both the walk and the walker, and sets out in prescriptive fashion the rules by which such an activity should be undertaken. The walk, as Hazlitt understands it, is purely a rural affair, a means of escaping the confines of the city to experience the unfettered freedom of the natural world, an experience to be enjoyed alone: 'I like to be either entirely to myself,' writes Hazlitt, 'or entirely at the disposal of others; to talk or be silent, to walk or sit still, to be sociable or solitary.'[29] However, later in the essay, he makes two exceptions to this rule: the first applies when travelling abroad, where, he informs us, a companion is a necessity – 'I should want at intervals to hear the sound of my own language.'[30]; the second concerns those walks which seek out specific locations – he gives the examples of 'ruins, aqueducts, pictures'; and in these instances a 'party of pleasure' is acceptable, for it seems that it is only when walking aimlessly that solitude becomes a prerequisite.

Hazlitt's essay is written in exactly the meandering, digressive style that he recommends for the walk itself, and it is adorned with numerous literary quotations from Shakespeare to Wordsworth.[31] In fact, so noble and elevated an activity does the act of walking seem to become, that it begins to resemble not so much an opportunity to experience nature as an attempt to replicate art. In practice, however, such an idealized and romantic formula seems difficult to follow, and despite his protestations to the contrary, it appears that Hazlitt himself was not averse to walking in company and generally tended to walk with a companion.[32] Hazlitt's essay, while outwardly upbeat, displays an ambiguity towards the countryside in which his apparent and oft-stated reverence for solitude remains unconvincing; for in retaining the viewpoint of the committed city-dweller, his ardent observations of rural purity are offset by the impression that he longs to return home to write up his notes.

Rebecca Solnit has been critical of the entire genre of the walking essay, arguing that rather than emphasising the freedom that walking represents, the essay tends to reduce the activity to little more than a display of pious sentiment, removing exactly that element which lends the walk its greatest appeal – the unexpected: 'The walking essay and the kind of walking described in it have much in common [...] both walk and essay are meant to be pleasant, even charming, and so no one ever gets lost and lives on grubs and rainwater in a trackless forest, has sex in a graveyard with a stranger, stumbles into a battle, or sees visions of another world. The walking tour was much associated with parsons and other Protestant clergymen, and the walking essay has something of their primness.'[33] To be fair to Hazlitt, however, the kinds of mishap that Solnit envisages were never likely to waylay the would-be walker in early nineteenth-century England, and between her depiction and his there remains sufficient leeway to encompass the entire literature of the subject.

Just as improvements in transportation and infrastructure facilitated the rise of the pedestrian in the late eighteenth century, so too did such changes see the act of walking ultimately superseded. In America, the development of the railroad swiftly eroded the supremacy of walking as the common mode of travel; and walking was soon relegated to the domestic sphere, a means of locomotion chiefly associated with women, the poor and infirm, and those who chose to wilfully reject the speed and clamour of metropolitan life. One such figure, who chose the pedestrian life in protest against the encroachments of the city and the erosion of the natural world, was Henry David Thoreau (1817–1862).

Thoreau, the quintessential American Romantic and greatest of all American walkers, is a figure whose transcendent, even mystical, appreciation of the natural world, makes him both a direct descendant of Wordsworth and Coleridge and, as we shall see, the progenitor of later walkers and naturalists, such as John Muir.

> I wish to speak a word for Nature, for absolute freedom and wildness, as contrasted with a freedom and culture merely civil – to regard man as an inhabitant, or a part and parcel of Nature, rather than a member of society.[34]

It is with these lines that Thoreau began his essay 'Walking', first published in the *Atlantic Monthly* of 1862 and originally called 'Walking and the Wild'; and it was here that Thoreau, naturalist, poet, and social critic, outlined his belief that the act of walking was an expression both of freedom and wildness, and as such stood in opposition to the expansion of urban society. In Thoreau's case, this threat came from the city of Boston, some eighteen miles from his home at Concord in Massachusetts, and it was here, through the preceding decades that he walked, endlessly crisscrossing Walden Woods and circumambulating Walden Pond. As a young man, Thoreau had walked from Concord to Boston and home again in a single evening in order to hear a lecture given by Ralph Waldo Emerson, and it was Emerson's message of solitude and self-reliance which was to inform Thoreau's own philosophy.[35] Emerson was a Transcendentalist – he believed that behind the empirical world of our everyday observation lay the world of the spiritual, a realm that could be accessed through living in harmony with the natural world. Thoreau was to transplant exactly this sense of mystical otherworldliness to his own surroundings, transforming his daily walks through the local countryside – an area which, far from being a virgin wilderness, had been settled for two hundred years – into a journey into the unknown:

> Two or three hours' walking will carry me to as strange a country as I expect ever to see. A single farmhouse which I had not seen before is sometimes as good as the dominions of

the Kings of Dahomey. There is in fact a sort of harmony discoverable between the capabilities of the landscape within a circle of ten miles' radius, or the limits of an afternoon walk, and the threescore years and ten of human life. It will never become quite familiar to you.[36]

Between July 1845 and September 1847 Thoreau was to put Emerson's philosophy into practice, living in a cabin at Walden Pond (on Emerson's property) and turning his back on modern society. The result was *Walden, or, Life in the Woods*, first published in 1854 and still regarded by many as one of the sacred texts of the Preservationist movement. Both here and in his essay, 'Walking', Thoreau was to espouse the idea of the reborn man, forged anew in the midst of a primordial America which could still be found beyond the margins of urban society. Such a man would be self-sufficient and solitary, pioneer and visionary; a representative of that rare order of men, the Walker:

> My companion and I [...] take pleasure in fancying ourselves knights of a new, or rather an old, order – not Equestrians or Chevaliers, not Ritters or Riders, but Walkers, a still more ancient and honourable class [...] He is a sort of fourth estate, outside of Church and State and People [...] It requires a direct dispensation from Heaven to become a walker. You must be born into the family of Walkers. *Ambulator nascitur, non fit.*[37]

Such men are, of course, a rare breed, and Thoreau acknowledges at the beginning of his essay only to have met 'but one or two persons in the course of my life who understood the art of walking, that is, of taking walks – who had a genius, so to speak, for *sauntering*.'[38] Emerson himself described Thoreau as a man who 'could not bear to hear the sound of his own steps, the grit of gravel; and therefore never willingly walked in the road, but in the grass, on the mountains and in the woods.'[39] For, like Hazlitt and his Romantic contemporaries, Thoreau saw the act of walking both as a means of escaping urban society and as an opportunity for solitude. Furthermore, just as Hazlitt's meandering essay replicates the act of walking it describes, so too does Thoreau avoid a straightforward narrative in favour of a series of circuitous paths around his subject, as if his essay were a reflection of his repeated encirclement of Walden Pond. Indeed, Thoreau has been described as having 'thought with his feet' in as far as the act of walking came to determine the form of all his books, which were structured not by logical argument but rather by the succession of observations that were presented to him while on foot.[40] Where Thoreau's attitude to walking differs from that of Hazlitt and his Romantic forbears, however, is in the degree to which he values the wild and the freedom it represents. For as an American in the early nineteenth century, Thoreau had direct access to a frontier which had long since been closed off to his European counterparts, an uncharted space into which a man, if he so chose, could walk and never return:

It is true, we are but faint-hearted crusaders, even the walkers, nowadays, who undertake no persevering, never-ending enterprises. Our expeditions are but tours, and come round again at evening to the old hearth-side from which we set out. Half the walk is but retracing our steps. We should go forth on the shortest walk, perchance, in the spirit of undying adventure, never to return – prepared to send back our embalmed hearts only as relics to our desolate kingdoms. If you are ready to leave father and mother, and brother and sister, and wife and child and friends, and never see them again – if you have paid your debts, and made your will, and settled all your affairs, and are a free man, then you are ready for a walk.[41]

In his awareness of the wilderness at his door and the possibility it afforded of a return to a primordial existence, whether real or imagined, Thoreau was consciously placing himself not within a tradition of contemporary walks and walkers, but within a much older lineage: 'I walk out into a Nature', he wrote, 'such as the old prophets and poets, Menu, Moses, Homer, Chaucer, walked in.'[42]

For Thoreau, the New World represented both the future and the growth of a new nation, but also a return to a past free from the taint of urban civilisation. 'Walking' is an essay that is, of course, about much more than its title suggests, and having identified the role that walking plays in his own life and the attributes that the walker requires, Thoreau's essay reaches a crossroads, the point at which the walker is faced with a choice: East or West? For Thoreau, the direction is clear:

> Eastward I go only by force; but westward I go free. Thither no business leads me. It is hard for me to believe that I shall find fair landscapes or sufficient wildness and freedom behind the eastern horizon. I am not excited by the prospect of a walk thither; but I believe that the forest which I see in the western horizon stretches uninterruptedly towards the setting sun, and there are no towns nor cities in it of enough consequence to disturb me [...] I must walk towards Oregon, and not towards Europe. And that way the nation is moving, and I may say that mankind progress from east to west [...] We go eastward to realize history and study the works of art and literature, retracing the steps of the race; we go westward as into the future, with a spirit of enterprise and adventure.[43]

'Front yards are not made to walk in, but, at most, through'[44] writes Thoreau, in direct contradiction of Wordsworth's daily routine; and Thoreau's essay, with its frontier spirit and visions of an untamed continent, can, by contrast, make its English counterparts appear quaintly domesticated and somewhat diminished in scope and ambition. Yet just as Thoreau was to celebrate the wild and the walker's place within it, so too was he writing against the inexorable encroachments at its borders; and while his essay represents the pinnacle of a literature which emphasises wildness and freedom, he appears also to foreshadow its end.[45] For a generation after his death in 1862, the frontier that he had eulogised was finally closed; the expansion of the railroad and the urban society that grew in its wake had finally eclipsed his vision of the wild, and the activity of walking was displaced successively by other forms of transportation. Yet while the landscapes he described were soon to be transformed, the spirit which animates his essay was to remain hugely influential. Indeed, within five years of his death, a figure whom Thoreau would no doubt have recognised as sharing, if not surpassing, his own genius for walking, was to embark upon his own epic journey into the wilderness.

Born in Scotland in 1838, John Muir and his family emigrated to the United States in 1849 where they started a farm near Portage, Wisconsin. A deeply religious man, Muir was also a keen, not to say obsessive, botanist and it is these twin passions for God and nature which inform his writing. Like Emerson and Thoreau before him, Muir was inspired by the pedestrian ordeals and botanical zeal of Alexander von Humboldt, who during a five-year (1799–1804) expedition through Central and South America had covered more than 6,000 miles, largely on foot, in search of new specimens.[46] Having recovered from a serious injury that almost cost him his sight, Muir finally decided to embark upon his long-held dream and follow in von Humboldt's footsteps, leaving Indianapolis in 1867 and heading south:

I had long been looking from the wild woods and gardens of the Northern States to those of the warm South, and at last, all drawbacks overcome, I set forth [from Indianapolis] on the first day of September, 1867, joyful and free, on a thousand-mile walk to the Gulf of Mexico [...] My plan was simply to push on in a general southward direction by the wildest, leafiest, and least trodden way I could find, promising the greatest extent of virgin forest. Folding my map, I shouldered my little bag and plant press and strode away among the old Kentucky oaks, rejoicing in splendid visions of pines and palms and tropic flowers in glorious array, not, however, without a few cold shadows of loneliness, although the great oaks seemed to spread their arms in welcome.[47]

Described as the 'first significant account of a long-distance walk for the sake of walking', Muir's *A Thousand-Mile Walk to the Gulf* (1914) was based upon the journal he kept throughout his epic walk, although it remained unpublished until Muir's death in 1914.[48] By this time Muir had gone on to become America's most celebrated naturalist; the author of a dozen books and a founder member of the Sierra Club; a renowned conservationist whose efforts had led to the formation of both Yosemite and Sequoia National Parks. In 1867, however, all this was to come as Muir, aged 29, set off on foot through Indiana and Kentucky, averaging some 25 miles a day as he walked on towards the Florida Keys. Walking through the Southern States, 'an open wound still festering from the Civil War', Muir has little to say about the aftermath of those events. Indeed he has little to say about anything except the wildlife he encounters. Avoiding towns and cities in favour of the mountains, forests and swampland of the American South, Muir's journal is in fact a surprisingly uneventful document in which we learn nothing of his attitude towards walking itself.[49] In part, Muir's journal can be read as an evangelical and more lushly descriptive, American counterpart to Dorothy Wordsworth's *Alfoxden Journal*, in which short episodic entries dwell on distances covered and wildlife observed: '*September 4* – Walked ten miles of forest. Met a strange oak with willow looking leaves [...] *September 30* – Traveled to-day more than forty miles without dinner or supper [...] *October 4* – New plants constantly appearing. All day in dense, wet, dark, mysterious forest of flat-topped taxodiums.'[50] But where the *Alfoxden Journal* remains sparse and restrained, Muir's prose is more frequently excited and overblown, as he struggles to relate, with biblical phraseology, the sheer exoticism of the landscapes he encounters:

I am now in the hot gardens of the sun, where the palm meets the vine, longed and prayed for and often visited in dreams, and, though lonely to–night amidst this multitude of strangers, strange plants, strange winds blowing gently, whispering, cooing, in a language I have never learned, and strange birds also, everything solid or spiritual full of influences that I never before felt, yet I thank the Lord with all my heart for his goodness in granting me admission to this magnificent realm.[51]

For Muir, one senses that the writing is always subordinate to the walking, which is itself simply a means to the botanical end he has set himself.[52] But although he lacks the style of Emerson and Thoreau, Muir achieves a degree of absolute identification with the natural world that is unparalleled in the literature of walking; for this is total immersion in one's surroundings to the point at which all extraneous material – society, politics, history – is stripped away to reveal the ecology that lies beneath.

Muir was not destined to reach South America on this occasion (he wasn't to make the journey until 1911), and considering that he was planning to float down the length of the Amazon on a raft, this was, as he later acknowledged, probably for the best.[53] Like von Humboldt before him, however, he did reach Cuba, but still weakened by the long period of illness he had suffered on reaching Florida, he changed course, eventually reaching California, the state with which he was to become most famously associated. Muir was to continue walking throughout his life, but it was his walk to the Gulf coast that remains his iconic journey. For in expressing his belief that it is the natural world which is man's true home, an environment superior to anything which human civilisation has to offer, he not only continued the work of Wordsworth and Thoreau, but also did much to inspire the preservation of our own wild places. In this way Muir's work has continued to influence contemporary walkers and writers of the natural world, such as Roger Deakin and Robert Macfarlane. Indeed, it is in the following observation, repeated as an epigraph to Macfarlane's *The Wild Places* (2007), that Muir provides us with both the perfect encapsulation of his philosophy and the expression of a sentiment which is shared, no doubt, by the generations of walkers who have followed in his footsteps: 'I only went out for a walk, and finally concluded to stay out till sundown, for going out, I found, was really going in.'[54]

Notes

[1] Thoreau, 'Walking', in *The Pleasures of Walking*, ed. by Edwin Valentine Mitchell, 129–172 , p. 135

[2] John Urry, *Mobilities*, Cambridge: Polity Press, 2007, p. 77

[3] William Knight, ed., *Letters of the Wordsworth Family: From 1787 to 1855; Vol. 1*, London: Ginn & Company, 1907, p. 31

[4] Landry, *The Invention of the Countryside*, p. 213

[5] Thomas De Quincey, *Recollections of the Lake Poets*, ed. by David Wright, Harmondsworth: Penguin, 1970, p. 135. It should be remembered that, at the time of De Quincey's estimate, Wordsworth was only 65 and had still another fifteen years of walking ahead of him.

[6] William Wordsworth, 'The Prelude' in *The Major Works*, ed. by Stephen Charles Gill, Oxford: Oxford University Press, 2008, Book II, Lines 313–323, pp. 383 & 400

[7] Wordsworth, 'The Prelude', Book XIII, Lines 463–465, p. 498

[8] Wordsworth, 'The Prelude', Book XII, Lines 145–152, p. 572. In these lines Wordsworth is expressing a sentiment which was later to be echoed both by Whitman ('Song of the Open Road') and Stevenson ('Roads'). It was to find its most emphatic confirmation, however, in the poetry of Edward Thomas (1878–1917), who writes: 'I love roads:/The goddesses that dwell/Far along invisible/Are my favourite gods.' See Edward Thomas, 'Roads' in *Collected Poems*, London: Faber, 1979, p. 163

[9] Marples, p. 34

[10] Wordsworth, 'The Prelude', Book VI, Lines 426–434, p. 461

[11] Letter to Dorothy Wordsworth, September 1790, in *The Letters of William and Dorothy Wordsworth: The Early Years, 1787–1805*, ed.

by Ernest de Selincourt, Oxford: Clarendon Press, 1967, p. 35

[12] Robinson, p. 25

[13] Solnit, p. 112

[14] Wordsworth, 'When First I Journeyed Hither' in *The Major Works*, Book VI, Lines 36–39, p. 221

[15] Marples, p. 37

[16] De Quincey, *Recollections of the Lake Poets*, p. 132

[17] It was in response to such criticisms of his sister's conduct that Wordsworth was to write his poem, 'To a Young Lady, Who Had Been Reproached for Taking Long Walks in the Country' (1802). See *The Collected Poems of William Wordsworth*, Ware, Hertfordshire: Wordsworth Editions, 1994, pp. 256–7

[18] Marples, p. 90

[19] Marples, p. 91

[20] Marples, p. 89. The brevity of the prose style may owe less to Dorothy Wordsworth than to the *Journal's* first editor, William Knight, who was responsible for omitting what he judged to be 'trivial detail'. Unfortunately for the modern reader, any such omissions can no longer be checked against the original MS, for as Pamela Woof notes in her introduction to *The Alfoxden Journal*, 'The teasing problem with the Alfoxden Journal is that there is no manuscript. Between Professor William Knight's readings of it in 1889, 1897, and possibly 1913, it has not been seen. We have to accept a reduced and somewhat unreliable text. See Dorothy Wordsworth, *The Grasmere and Alfoxden Journals*, ed. by Pamela Woof, Oxford: Oxford University Press, 2008, Introduction, p. xxviii

[21] Dorothy Wordsworth, p. 141

[22] Dorothy Wordsworth, p. 150

[23] Dorothy Wordsworth, p. 151

[24] Dorothy Wordsworth, p. 153

[25] Thomas Carlyle, 'Letter to John A Carlyle' (24 June 1824), qtd. in Gary Dexter, ed., *Poisoned Pens: Literary Invective from Amis to Zola*, London: Frances Lincoln, 2009, p. 64

[26] Marples, p. 47

[27] Marples, p. 48

[28] William Hazlitt, 'On Going a Journey', in *Selected Essays*, ed. by George Sampson, Cambridge: Cambridge University Press, 1917, 141–150, pp. 141–2

[29] Hazlitt, p. 142

[30] Hazlitt, p. 145

[31] As Anne D. Wallace has observed: 'Hazlitt's narrative, indeed, wanders, rambling from point to point along a line with little apparent attempt at unifying commentary or intentional shaping. It comes as something of a shock when he speaks of 'returning' to his main enquiry, for the unwary reader has been led down a bypath step by step.' Wallace, p. 178

[32] Marples, p. 53

[33] Solnit, p. 120

[34] Thoreau, p. 129

[35] Amato, p.142

[36] Thoreau, pp. 135–6

[37] Thoreau, pp. 130–1

[38] Thoreau, p. 129

[39] Amato, p. 142

[40] Amato, p. 143

[41] Thoreau, p. 130

[42] Thoreau, p. 138

[43] Thoreau, pp. 142–3

[44] Thoreau, p. 153

[45] Joseph A. Amato writes: 'Thoreau's life appears to stand at the end of American country walking. He witnessed walking – this first and principal way of American native and colonial locomotion – being displaced by horse, steamboat, train, and telegraph. Romantic walker, Thoreau circumambulated in ever tightening circles – like an archaic peasant around a church steeple – as vast systems of transportation, communication, commerce, and national power circumscribed the globe.' Amato, p. 151

[46] 'Humboldt did his science on foot', writes Amato, 'Humboldt

shaped the passionate intellect that directed the ever faithful foot toward nature on a pedestrian journey that took alternate steps between romantic awe and scientific knowledge.' Amato, p. 116

[47] John Muir, *A Thousand-Mile Walk to the Gulf*, New York: Mariner Books, 1998, pp. 1–2

[48] Solnit, p. 126. Miles Jebb, author of *Walkers*, has questioned Muir's choice of title, claiming that 'the name given to his walk is misleading: it was around 800 miles and done in two sections with a sea passage in between'. In his description of Muir himself, however, Jebb's tone is more reverential: 'As Abraham Lincoln was to the political world, so was John Muir to the natural world: a stern, dedicated, self-taught, 'log-cabined', middle-western prophet. Just as we owe the Union to Lincoln, to Muir we owe the national parks: as Lincoln was not afraid to be in the firing line, Muir led from the front in his discoveries of the wonders of Yosemite and his pedestrian penetration into the wilderness.' Jebb, p. 122

[49] Rebecca Solnit writes: 'An acute and often ecstatic observer of the natural world around him, he says nothing at all about why he is walking in *A Thousand-Mile Walk to the Gulf*, though it seems clear enough that it is because he is hardy, poor, and possessed of botanical passions best fulfilled on foot. But though he is one of history's great walkers, walking itself is seldom his subject. There is no well-defined border between the literature of walking and nature writing, but nature writers tend to make the walking implicit at best, a means for the encounters with nature which they describe, but seldom as a subject.' Solnit, p. 127

[50] Muir, pp. 6, 55 & 63

[51] Muir, p. 93

[52] Muir often expressed how little enjoyment he gained from the writing process, complaining that, 'This business of writing books is a long, tiresome, endless job.' Sally M. Miller & Daryl Morrison, *John Muir: Family, Friends and Adventure*, University of New Mexico Press, 2005, pp. 87–8

[53] Muir, p. 169

54 John Muir, *John of the Mountains: The Unpublished Journals of John Muir* (1938), ed. by LM Wolfe, Madison, WI: University of Wisconsin Press, 1979, p. 439, and qtd. in Robert MacFarlane, *The Wild Places*, London: Granta, 2007, epigraph

The Walker as Visionary

Blake is supposed to walk endlessly in London – he knows what he's doing. Iain Sinclair[1]

I am afraid that "wandering a little" is almost a hobby of mine. Arthur Machen[2]

Just as the transcendentalism of Emerson and Thoreau was to imbue their apprehension of the natural world with a sense of the otherworldly, so too was a similar shift in perception taking place on the streets of London. For while Wordsworth and his Romantic counterparts were to celebrate the sublime landscapes of rural Britain, they were also to depict the dark and alienating expanses of urban London, introducing an image of the city as labyrinthine and unknowable.[3] Here we are presented with an image of the city at night, and the figure of the night walker who reveals, with dreamlike intensity, his vision of the city's underworld.

The literary tradition of the city night walk originates almost a century earlier in John Gay's *Trivia; or, the Art of Walking the Streets of London* (1716), Book II of which is entitled, 'Of Walking the Streets by Night.' Gay's vision of the city is neither dreamlike nor visionary, however, instead depicting the city as an assault course, bristling with an array of physical and moral hazards with which to ensnare the unwary traveller:

Through Winter Streets to steer your Course aright,
How to walk clean by Day, and safe by Night,

How jostling Crowds, with Prudence, to decline,
When to assert the Wall, and when resign,
I sing: Thou *Trivia*, Goddess, aid my Song,
Thro' spacious Streets conduct thy Bard along;
By thee transported, I securely stray
Where winding Alleys lead the doubtful Way,
The silent Court, and op'ning Square explore,
And long perplexing Lanes untrod before.[4]

Gay's parody describes an art of urban walking which owes little to any aesthetic sentiment, instead revealing a carefully honed technique for navigating a hostile environment. Indeed, it is precisely the idea of a pedestrian–poet and the incongruity that such a figure would suggest which lends the poem its satiric force. For the middle–class readership for which Gay's poem was intended would certainly have looked upon the act of walking with some disdain, as befitting an activity largely associated with the likelihood of assault or some other indignity at the hands of the marauding urban poor.

Trivia reads, then, as a walker's handbook, a text directed not at the carefree wanderer but towards the resolute pedestrian and it offers no attempt to seek beneath the surface or to distance oneself from the crowd (except as a measure of self-protection). Neither does the poem attempt to map out a route in any recognisable manner, instead offering a series of discrete coordinates which do little to convey any sense of the city in its entirety.[5] Perhaps it is as a result of these deficiencies that Gay's poem is so little read today, and yet in the following passage he anticipates a wholly different chronicler of the city and its inhabitants:

But sometimes let me leave the noisie Roads,
And silent wander in the close Abodes
Where wheels ne'er shake the Ground; there pensive stray,
In studious Thought the long uncrowded Way.

Here I remark each Walker's diff'rent Face,
And in their Look their various Bus'ness trace.[6]

Towards the end of the eighteenth century, William Blake was to retrace Gay's steps, once again searching the faces of London's populace as they pass through the city's streets:

I wander thro' each charter'd street,
Near where the charter'd Thames does flow.
And mark in every face I meet
Marks of weakness, marks of woe.[7]

While Gay keeps his distance, however, and encourages his readers to do the same, Blake's work is bound up with his experience of the city to the extent that his own identity and that of London itself seem to become indivisible: 'My streets are my, Ideas of Imagination', he was to write.[8] For Blake too was a wanderer, a poet whose vision was born on foot as he walked the city streets:

From the beginning he was the child of the dream of London. As a boy he walked everywhere. He walked south from Soho towards Dulwich and Camberwell. He walked north as well as south. He crossed the Oxford Road towards Tottenham Court Road, where he turned left into St Giles High Street. He passed Hanway Street and Percy Street and Windmill Street before coming to the turnpike that marked the crossing of the New Road from Paddington to St Pancras. He had so much energy that he could not help but walk. Yet he was propelled by his own sense of destiny, inescapably caught up in his experience of London. He was chosen to understand the city.[9]

Born in London, the city in which he was to spend almost his entire life, William Blake (1757–1827) began his career as an apprentice engraver and student at the Royal Academy. His twofold passion for engraving and poetry was to result in a unique body of work – a series of illuminated books in which the battle between the anti-rational forces of the imagination and the repressive and systematic forces of authority is revealed. In his biography of Blake, Peter Ackroyd writes, 'It is characteristic of so lonely and separate a boy that Blake's principal childhood memory is of solitary walking [...] He had a very strong sense of place, and all his life he was profoundly and variously affected by specific areas of London.'[10] He is, declares Ackroyd, a 'Cockney Visionary', whose awareness of London's symbolic existence through time allowed him to perceive the unchanging reality of the city beneath the flux of the everyday; a transcendent image of 'the spiritual Four-fold London eternal.'[11] And it is through precisely this superimposition of his own highly individualistic worldview upon the topography of London's streets that Blake is able to create such startling juxtapositions between the familiar and the transcendent; thus was he to perceive angels in the unlikely environs of Peckham Rye and to provide precise coordinates for the New Jerusalem:

> The fields from Islington to Marybone,
> To Primrose Hill and Saint John's Wood:
> Were builded over with pillars of gold,
> And there Jerusalems pillars stood.[12]

While later in the same poem, *Jerusalem* (1804–20), Blake guides the reader (and walker) on an inward passage through London's eastern perimeter:

> He came down from Highgate thro Hackney & Holloway towards London / Till he came to old Stratford & thence to Stepney & the Isle / Of Leuthas Dogs, thence thro the narrows of the Rivers side / And saw every minute particular,
> the jewels of Albion, running down / The kennels of the streets & lanes as if they were abhorrd.[13]

Blake remaps the city as he walks its streets, leading Iain Sinclair to describe him as 'the godfather of all psychogeographers'; and it is through his emphasis upon the imaginative reconstruction of the city that Blake takes his place within a tradition of London writing that foreshadows many of the themes later to be gathered under this label.[14] It is the act of walking, however, which remains implicit to any such tradition, an activity that Blake was to imbue with a visionary power:

And all this Vegetable World appeard on my left Foot,
As a bright sandal formd immortal of precious stones & gold:
I stooped down & bound it on to walk forward thro' Eternity.[15]

Having been almost wholly neglected during his lifetime, it appears that Blake is still inspiring us to walk the city more than 150 years after his death[16]; yet in the pantheon of London visionaries, it is not Blake, but a later arrival to the city, who can perhaps claim the greatest credit for having established the image of the urban walker within the public imagination. Born in Manchester in 1785, Thomas De Quincey was never to attain quite the affinity with London which Blake was to achieve; but his depictions of the city reveal exactly that visionary intensity which was to animate Blake's work, creating a pioneering account of urban alienation in which the solitary walker comes to symbolise the modern city.

In 1802, De Quincey, aged sixteen, ran, or rather walked, away from Manchester Grammar School, covering thirty-eight miles in two days en route to Chester where his mother was staying. It was decided that a walking-tour would be good for De Quincey's health, and he was allowed to continue on into Wales where he soon settled into 'a tempo of no more than between 70 and 100 miles a week.'[17] It was here that De Quincey developed a passion for pedestrianism which would stay with him for life. 'Life on this model was but too delightful', he was to write, 'and to myself especially, that am never thoroughly in health unless when having pedestrian exercise to the extent of fifteen miles at the most, and eight to ten miles at the least.'[18] De Quincey was to feel no disgrace travelling through Wales as a pedestrian, as most of the Welsh travelled in the same manner at this time. Across the border in England, however, and this situation was reversed, with the would-be pedestrian viewed by English landlords, according to the admittedly sensitive De Quincey, as carrying 'the most awful shadow and shibboleth of the pariah.'[19] Indeed, De Quincey was deterred from walking on to London by precisely this fear of the humiliations he was likely to encounter. 'Happily the scandal of pedestrianism', he was to write, 'is in one respect more hopefully situated than that of scrofula or leprosy; it is not in any case written in your face.'[20]

Of course, De Quincey did make it to London, and it is his account of his time there, alongside his earlier adventures in Wales, that form the basis of his *Confessions of an English Opium Eater* (1821). De Quincey wrote the first draft of this work at the age of 36, returning to it with notes and amendments throughout his life; and so the experiences recounted there are not only coloured by his self consciously dramatic style, but must also be viewed through the distorting mirrors of both memory and the opium dream itself. Those wishing to find the harsh realism of the addict's spiral into despair and self-destruction will, therefore, be disappointed; for the *Confessions* are concerned only nominally with addiction, and it should be remembered that in De Quincey's day opium was both legal and cheaply acquired, having none of the edgy and alienated connotations that might be attributed to drugs today. Instead, the *Confessions* should be read principally as an account of the role of the imagination and the power of dreams to transmute the familiar nature of our surroundings into something strange and wonderful. It is here that De Quincey's true legacy lies, as a prototype for the obsessive wanderer, allowing his imagination to shape and direct the perception of his environment; his purposeless drifting at odds with the commercial traffic and allying him to the invisible underclass whose movements map the chaotic and labyrinthine aspects of the city:

> Some of these rambles led me to great distances: for an opium-eater is too happy to observe the motion of time. And sometimes in my attempts to steer homewards, upon nautical principles, by fixing my eye on the pole-star, and seeking ambitiously for a north-west passage, instead of circumnavigating all the capes and headlands I had doubled in my outward voyage, I came suddenly upon such knotty problems of alleys, such enigmatical entries, and such sphynx's riddles of streets without thoroughfares, as must, I conceive, baffle the audacity of porters, and confound the intellects of hackney-coachmen. I could almost have believed, at times, that I must be the first discoverer of some of these *terrae incognitae*, and doubted, whether they had yet been laid down in the modern charts of London. For all this, however, I paid a heavy price in distant years, when the human face tyrannized over my dreams, and the perplexities of my steps in London came back and haunted my sleep, with the feeling of perplexities moral or intellectual, that brought confusion to the reason, or anguish and remorse to the conscience.[21]

De Quincey's dreamlike vision of an unknown London awaiting discovery is particularly appealing to those who are all too familiar with its well-trodden streets[22]; and given that De Quincey's opium use seemingly resulted in little of the torpor usually associated with the drug, instead appearing to propel him through the city, his solitary and often nocturnal wandering would certainly have introduced him to a side of the city still invisible to many of its inhabitants. 'Being myself at that time of necessity a peripatetic, or a walker of the streets', writes De Quincey, 'I naturally fell in more frequently with those female peripatetics who are technically called Street-walkers. Many of these women had occasionally taken my part against watchmen who wished to drive me off the steps of houses where I was sitting.'[23] One such tragic figure was the young prostitute Ann, whose friendship and support De Quincey credited with keeping him alive, and whose loss he was to feel so keenly; for having briefly left London, De Quincey had arranged to meet Ann on Oxford Street on his return, but despite his prolonged attempts to find her they never saw each other again.

Another source of friendship to De Quincey in London at this time was the legendary walker, explorer and full-blown eccentric, John 'Walking' Stewart (1749–1822). Stewart was reputed to have wandered on foot throughout Europe, India and North America, and De Quincey was later to make him the subject of an affectionate essay.[24] Little is known about the facts of Stewart's life, however, as he wrote little about his travels and was a notoriously unreliable witness to the events of his own past. He did write, however, and amongst his many works of 'philosophy' are such intriguing titles as *The Apocalypse of Human Perfectibility* (1808) and *Roll of a Tennis Ball through the Moral World* (1812). Perhaps, it has been speculated, his amnesia regarding the details of his own life story was due to brain damage, since apparently 'the crown of his head was indented nearly an inch in depth by the blow of 'some warlike instrument.'[25] 'No region', wrote De Quincey, 'pervious to human feet except, I think, China and Japan, but had been visited by Mr. Stewart in this philosophical style; a style which compels a man to move slowly through a country, and to fall in continually with the natives of that country.'[26]

Having left London, De Quincey was never again able to fully disassociate the act of walking from his growing reliance on opium. He came to the view that walking could mitigate both the ill effects of the drug and the persistent digestive disorders which necessitated its use, and for this reason he habitually walked for three or four hours every evening.[27] In this way, De Quincey's health, at least as he regarded it, came to depend on walking, which became not merely a pleasure but a necessity. Walking to combat the melancholia induced by the drug, De Quincey's compulsion to keep moving reached the point at which he could only truly claim to be himself when on foot. Yet over the course of his long life, as his faith in the curative powers of pedestrianism increased, De Quincey struggled to remain one step ahead of his myriad ailments. This process reached a critical juncture in 1843 when De Quincey found himself stricken by a serious circulatory illness, as his biographer, Grevel Lindop, describes:

> He resolved on a policy of 'kill or cure.' Pacing out the tiny triangular cottage garden as soon as he was able to walk again, he found that one circuit of its perimeter measured forty-four yards, so that forty rounds were exactly required for one mile. He began to exercise there daily, doggedly walking round and round the garden, keeping count of his circuits by placing pebbles on the rungs in the back of a chair to form a primitive abacus. Before long he was averaging eleven or twelve miles a day so that, as he said proudly, 'I had within ninety days walked a thousand miles.'[28]

As an example of De Quincey's unswerving belief in the remedial power of walking, his thousand-mile walking cure is a triumph of the will that anticipates Albert Speer's similarly repetitive circling of Spandau's prison garden more than a century later. But De Quincey's most active years as a pedestrian were to come in his first few years at Dove Cottage in Grasmere, which he leased from Wordsworth in 1809; for as an admirer of Wordsworth, and as one who now lived in his former home, De Quincey no doubt felt more than usually inspired to walk during this period.[29] Whether motivated by concerns over his health or simply out of a Wordsworthian desire to keep in motion, De Quincey continued his often obsessive walking routine throughout his life. In 1855, at the age of seventy, he was still managing seven miles a day: 'Not much, certainly', he was to write, 'but as much as I can find spirits for.'[30]

In his recent novel, *The Unnamed* (2010), Joshua Ferris

describes a man suffering from a peculiar affliction: the inability to stop walking. Mercilessly propelled across America as his life disintegrates around him, Ferris portrays a man stuck in a permanent escape mode, a man whose feet have come to rule his head. Such a scenario is, of course, a highly imaginative literary conceit, but it is also one which is grounded in earlier accounts of, admittedly less extreme, but nevertheless acute, forms of peripatetic compulsion.

'If I couldn't walk fast and far', confided Charles Dickens in 1857, 'I should explode and perish.'[31] While elsewhere he was to claim, 'My only comfort is, in Motion.'[32] And of all the literary forbears to Ferris's novel, both real and imagined, it is surely Dickens himself who offers the most startling example of a man whose pedestrian endeavours came to dominate his life. Yet for such a prodigious walker, one struggles largely in vain to locate a major pedestrian episode within his fiction. There are, however, numerous walking scenes within the novels, which are often peopled by an array of footsore Londoners, whose principal function appears to be to reveal the city to the reader.[33] Of these, Miles Jebb has compiled the following selection: Oliver Twist's twenty-mile walk to rob a house in Chertsey; David Copperfield's twenty-three-mile walk from Blackheath to Chatham; the Pickwick Club's twenty-five mile walk at Dingley Dell; Nicholas Nickleby and Smike and their flight from Dotheboys Hall in Yorkshire to London; and finally Martin Chuzzlewit and Tom Pinch's invigorating walk to dinner in Salisbury, which leads them to exclaim: 'Better! A rare, strong, hearty, healthy walk – four statute miles an hour – preferable to that rumbling, tumbling, jolting, shaking, scraping, creaking, villainous old gig. Why, the two things will not admit of comparison. It is an insult to the walk, to set them side by side.'[34]

It is, however, *The Old Curiosity Shop* (1841) which remains the only one of Dickens' novels to provide the reader with a sustained walking episode crucial to the narrative structure of the book; in this instance, Nell Trent's long walk out of London with her grandfather. Indeed, *The Old Curiosity Shop* is also noteworthy for its opening passage, in which the narrator acts as a mouthpiece for Dickens' own attitude to walking:

> Night is generally my time for walking. In the summer I often leave home early in the morning, and roam about fields and lanes all day, or even escape for days or weeks together, but saving in the country I seldom go out until after dark, though, Heaven be thanked, I love its light and feel the cheerfulness it sheds upon the earth, as much as any creature living.
>
> I have fallen insensibly into this habit, both because it favours my infirmity and because it affords me greater opportunity of speculating on the characters and occupations of those who fill the streets. The glare and hurry of broad noon are not adapted to idle pursuits like mine; a glimpse of passing faces caught by the light of a street lamp or shop window is often better for my purpose than their full revelation in the daylight, and, if I must add the truth, night is kinder in this respect than day, which too often destroys an air-built castle at the moment of its completion, without the smallest ceremony or remorse.[35]

These remarks were later to find factual confirmation in Dickens' celebrated essay, 'Night Walks' (1859), and it is here, in his journalism, rather than in the novels, that Dickens' profound and often tortured relationship with walking is laid bare: 'Some years ago, a temporary inability to sleep, referable to a distressing impression, caused me to walk about the streets all night, for a series of several nights [...] In the course of those nights, I finished my education in a fair amateur experience of houselessness.'[36] Dickens assumes here the identity of 'houselessness' (today's homelessness), to explore the night-time city, depicting London as a never-ending panorama of empty streets concealing a population of the hopeless and the lost: 'Walking the streets under the pattering rain, Houselessness would walk and walk and walk, seeing nothing but the interminable tangle of streets.'[37] Dickens imbues his vision of the city with a lurking menace that recalls the darkest imaginings of De Quincey before him, but while De Quincey was able to view the city through the prism of the opium dream, Dickens' sense of heightened anxiety appears innate, or at least a consequence of his earliest memories of the streets.

Peter Ackroyd, in his biography of Dickens, imagines him as a small boy walking through the streets of London to his place of work and home again. 'Walking, and wandering,' he notes, 'seem to comprise a large part of Dickens's early years in London; but that was quite usual in the period [...] But by his own account Dickens's wanderings were of a more shiftless and dreamy nature.'[38] While in his essay 'Shy Neighbourhoods' (1860), the piece of writing in which he confronts most clearly the role of walking in his work, Dickens states:

> My walking is of two kinds: one straight on end to a definite goal at a sound pace; one, objectless, loitering, and purely vagabond. In the latter state, no gypsy on earth is a greater vagabond than myself; it is so natural to me, and strong with me, that I think I must be the descendant, at no great distance, of some irreclaimable tramp.[39]

It is the latter, 'objectless' drifting which Dickens employs to such great effect in his descriptions of London's labyrinthine topography, his aimless motion allowing to him to capture the city in all its immeasurable complexity. And yet, it is the former, obsessive and relentless movement which came to define Dickens' own life, as increasingly, and through displays of astonishing athleticism, he sought to escape from his difficulties, on foot, and at speed:

> So much of my travelling is done on foot, that if I cherished betting propensities, I should probably be found registered in sporting newspapers under some such title as the Elastic

Novice, challenging all eleven stone mankind to competition
in walking. My last special feat was turning out of bed at two,
after a hard day, pedestrian and otherwise, and walking thirty
miles into the country to breakfast. The road was so lonely in
the night, that I fell asleep to the monotonous sound of my
own feet, doing their regular four miles an hour. Mile after
mile I walked, without the slightest sense of exertion, dozing
heavily and dreaming constantly.[40]

Dickens was by no means unique in his desire to pace the streets
at high speed. Indeed, along with Ruskin, another speed-walker,
Dickens was merely one of many such figures whose activities
may be compared to the joggers of today.[41] Where Dickens stands
apart from his contemporaries, however, is in the degree of
significance with which he was to endow his pedestrian
endeavours. In his essay, 'On an Amateur Beat' (1860), Dickens
compares the role of the walker to that of a policeman, in which
even the most idle stroll is attributed a higher purpose: 'On such
an occasion,' he writes, 'it is my habit to regard my work as my
beat, and myself as a higher sort of police-constable doing duty
on the same.'[42] Here, Dickens, like Wordsworth before him, likens
the act of walking to that of work, a labour to be performed
rather than a diversion to be enjoyed. Indeed, as he became older
and his walking routines became increasingly arduous, both for
himself and his companions,[43] so did his relationship to walking
change; as what had begun as an escape, a diversion from the
pressures of life, gradually became a necessity and, finally, an
obligation that he felt compelled to discharge:

These "daily constitutionals", as he sometimes called them, in
fact turned into something of an obsession and it came to be
his settled opinion that it was important for him to spend as
many hours walking as he did working. It became what he
described as a "moral obligation." His steady pace was some
four and a half miles per hour, and it was quite common for

him to walk twenty or even thirty miles at a stretch. The covering of such distances was not an uncommon feat in those early nineteenth-century years [...] But what was different about Dickens was the speed and the determination of his perambulation. In later life it was to be the means of warding off melancholy or a way of fighting off the worries which beset him but, in those early years, it can be fruitfully seen as the blowing off of superfluous energy.[44]

As an antidote to the growing anxieties of his everyday existence, however, ever greater distances were required to achieve a state of equilibrium. Dickens' walks were soon to be characterised by a persistent state of fervour as he fought to outpace his lurking and ever-present fears, and in this sense his growing mania for long-distance walking came to assume the form of a disease.[45] Such an obsession was to prove highly destructive, both to him and to those of his companions who were lamed in the process. But whether, as some have speculated, these ferocious pedestrian routines were to prove a contributory factor in his death, it is impossible to verify. In the end, however, in a curious reflection of De Quincey's addiction to opium, which had propelled him through his phantasmagoric visions of night-time London, so did this very act of propulsion become Dickens' own addiction, and one which he too came to depend on to fulfil his creative needs.

While Blake, De Quincey and Dickens each holds a prominent place within the canon of literary walkers, the figure of Arthur Machen is one which is routinely overlooked; his name is absent from all the major histories of the subject, and his works remain largely neglected. Of course, his absence here simply reflects his marginal position within wider literary history, yet while he is unlikely ever to be elevated to a dominant position within the literary canon, his significance as a literary walker is at least as great as that of his more celebrated forbears. For no other figure has ever walked London's streets in quite the way that Machen did, nor has anyone else ever described them with such a mixture of reverence and awe:

> London is a bus that no one has ever caught. It is an ocean that no one has voyaged all over, whether in body or in spirit [...] I do not think that there are any more awful concepts presented to the human mind than the eternities and infinitudes of time and space [...] And the sight of a map of London always leaves me with a sense of a kind of lesser infinitude if the phrase may be allowed. Here are marked streets and alleys and squares and bye-ways, which strike the eye as past numbering. They were all here, in undoubted brick and stone and marble and mortar, and yet one feels that no living man has trodden them all; that to the most energetic and leisured explorer there must ever be myriads of streets that he will never enter. And, extending the notion, how many houses must remain unvisited; secrets throughout all ages to all but a very few?
>
> Thus does London make for us a concrete image of the eternal things of space and time and thought.[46]

Born in 1863 in Caerleon on Usk, in Gwent, South Wales, Arthur Machen[47] was the son of an Anglican vicar and was raised in the rectory of Llandewi church. The Gwent countryside had a profound impact on him, and it was the enchanted landscapes of his youth which were to provoke the sense of mystic wonder which later came to inform his work. Machen described his life until the age of seventeen as all 'solitude and woods and deep lanes and wonder' and he adopted early the habit of wandering on long walks in the countryside around his home.[48]

Unable to afford a place at Oxford, and having failed the exams for medical school in London, Machen was soon to leave Gwent permanently for London, and it was here, while enduring a lonely and impecunious existence, that he was to begin the series of long rambling walks across the city that were to form the backdrop to so much of his future writing. Avoiding the centre and striking out for the vast and desolate expanses of the suburban city, Machen came to imbue these overlooked outer limits, with their endless streets of Victorian villas, with exactly that sense of otherworldly enchantment that had coloured his experiences of the Gwent countryside. For 'the unknown world', he wrote, 'is about us everywhere, everywhere near to our feet; the thinnest veil separates us from it, the door in the wall or the next street communicates with it.'[49] It was a message that he was to repeat throughout his work:

> Here, then, is the pattern in my carpet, the sense of the eternal mysteries, the eternal beauty hidden beneath the crust of common and commonplace things; hidden and yet burning and glowing continually if you care to look with purged eyes [...] I think it is easier to discern the secret beauty and wonder and mystery in humble and common things than in the splendid and noble and storied things.[50]

Machen's first major success was to come in 1894 with *The Great God Pan*, a tale of pagan horror with a powerful and barely concealed sexual undertow; and the following year he was to publish a novel of interwoven tales, *The Three Impostors*, an equally shocking work of decadent horror. But in the climate of *fin de siècle* excess that was to scandalise London in the 1890s, Machen's work quickly became associated with the aestheticism of Oscar Wilde, and he was to suffer as a result: the backlash against Wilde that followed his trial in 1895 ensured that many of Machen's finest works written in the latter part of that decade were to remain unpublished until well into the next century. The most notable of these, and Machen's acknowledged masterpiece, was *The Hill of Dreams* (1907), a largely autobiographical tale of a young man's struggle to become a writer in London. Machen himself experienced real hardship as a fledgling writer, a period he was later to recall as one of intense loneliness and endless wandering:

I lived a life of such desperate loneliness that I might almost have been Robinson Crusoe on his Island [...] though I walked daily amidst myriads I was yet alone [...] I think I see the young man with the moustache slouching along the roads, always alone [...] Day after day I wandered about in this fashion.[51]

It was in the early 1890s, however, while living in Soho Street and later, between 1893 and 1895, while living on Great Russell Street, in Bloomsbury, that Machen's daily walks outward through London's unknown and unloved hinterlands began to develop a more systematic tenor. For what had previously been little more than a flight from loneliness and desperation had gradually become something quite different, a deliberate and sustained attempt to access the eternal and ineffable which, he believed, lay behind the everyday reality of London's streets. Setting out to lose himself, willingly, amidst those 'raw, red places all around the walls of London', Machen embarked on a journey whose sole guidance was the need to 'utterly shun the familiar.'[52] So Machen's 'London Science' was born:

I will listen to no objections or criticisms as to the Ars Magna of London, of which I claim to be the inventor, the professor and the whole school. Here I am artist and judge at once, and possess the whole matter of the art within myself. For, let it be quite clearly understood, the Great Art of London has nothing to do with any map or guide-book or antiquarian knowledge, admirable as these are [...] But the Great Art is a matter of quite another sphere; and as to maps, for example, if known they must be forgotten [...] Of all this the follower of the London Art must purge himself when he sets out on his adventures. For the essence of this art is that it must be an adventure into the unknown, and perhaps it may be found that this, at last, is the matter of all the arts.[53]

'Sometimes', writes Machen, 'I took a friend with me on my journeys, but not often. The secret of it all was hidden from them, and they were apt to become violent.'[54] Machen was later to move to the Verulam Buildings off the Gray's Inn Road, and it was here, while taking his customary midday stroll, that he was to experience a sudden sense of disorientation: 'I got home somehow by complicated and dubious calculations,' recalled Machen, 'and in a somewhat confused and alarmed frame of mind. And odd as it may seem, this perplexity has never wholly left me.[55] Indeed, it was exactly this sense of perplexity that was to characterise Machen's best writing about London, a city he came to view with both wonder and dread:

> And it is utterly true that he who cannot find wonder, mystery, awe, the sense of a new world and an undiscovered realm in the places by the Gray's Inn Road will never find those secrets elsewhere, not in the heart of Africa, not in the fabled hidden cities of Tibet. "The matter of our work is everywhere present," wrote the old alchemists, and that is the truth. All the wonders lie within a stone's-throw of King's Cross Station.[56]

Towards the end of his third and final volume of autobiography, entitled *The London Adventure, or, the Art of Wandering* (1924), the text which inspired the title for this book, Machen returns once again to the sense of perplexity that always accompanied him on his travels across London: 'So, here was the notion.' he writes, 'What about a tale of a man who "lost his way"; who became so entangled in some maze of imagination and speculation that the common, material ways of the world became of no significance to him?'[57] It is something of an understatement to describe *The London Adventure* as a digressive or meandering work, for it is in fact little more than a sustained attempt to avoid the task he has set himself, an attempt, in literary form, to capture the aimlessness which defined his urban wandering. For throughout much of Machen's work, but especially here and in his previous volumes of autobiography, *Far Off Things* (1922) and *Things Near and Far* (1923), his prose seems to direct the reader in one direction, only to veer off at an unexpected tangent; his most insightful comments often appear in an oblique form, seemingly mentioned only in passing, remaining always in the shadow of other objectives, themselves never clearly articulated. In this way, and in the manner of so many of the writers and walkers gathered here, Machen's work can closely resemble the nature of the walks he describes. So, for example, the sensational fiction from the late nineteenth century, on which Machen's reputation, as it is, now largely rests, repeatedly depicts the dandified and slightly disreputable character of the *flâneur* as he strolls his way through the occult puzzle of London's streets[58]; while in later works, Machen's wanderings anticipate the overtly aimless yet curiously regimented walks soon to be conducted by the Surrealists, and later the Situationists, on the streets of Paris. Yet, ultimately, Machen's London Science, while anticipating, at least in part, the activities of these later avant-garde groups, remains unique and unclassifiable, a project peculiar to Machen himself.

Where Machen's outlook diverges so dramatically from that of both his contemporaries and his would-be successors, however, is in the sheer ambivalence of his reaction to the city he took such painstaking efforts to describe. For while he was, on the one hand, to celebrate London in all its immensity and to revel in the occult preoccupations of his fiction, his own response to the endless horizon of streets within which he found himself, was that of an overwhelming sense of awe, bordering upon outright terror.[59] Indeed, much of Machen's work can be viewed as a means of combating precisely this sense of dread; an attempt to gain mastery over London's streets by walking them, and through this knowledge a means of countering their menace. This, of course, as Machen knew only too well, was the work of many lifetimes, a gargantuan and never-ending project whose goal was to come to terms with a city whose perimeter was always out of sight and whose perpetual growth seemed always to outstrip the attempts of those who sought to capture it in its entirety. And it is this image, which remains the abiding symbol of his work, that of the solitary walker seeking an escape from the labyrinth, yet fated to spend a lifetime in doing so:

> Years ago, I remember, I used to wander, by day and night, about the western limits and outposts of this most vast London. I would go out and pass from street to street with the purpose of escaping from London and attaining the true country. The streets at last faded into open fields, and I would say 'I am free at last from this mighty and stony wilderness.' And then suddenly, as I turned a corner the raw red rows of houses would confront me, and I knew that I was still in the labyrinth [...] This was thirty years ago or more, and since then London has swollen like a flood. Its extent is mighty almost beyond the power of imagination, huge in a way that no mileage and figures can express.[60]

Notes

[1] Iain Sinclair, *Blake's London: The Topographic Sublime*, London: Swedenborg Society, 2011, p. 25

[2] Arthur Machen, *The London Adventure, or the Art of Wandering*, London: Martin Secker, 1924, p. 69

[3] This urban metaphor is most powerfully conveyed by De Quincey and Dickens, but is prefigured by Wordsworth in his account of his 'London Residence' in Book VII of the *Prelude*, in which he writes: 'Private Courts,/ Gloomy as coffins, and unsightly lanes,/[...] May then entangle us awhile,/Conducted through those labyrinths unawares.' Wordsworth, 'The Prelude', in *Major Works*, p. 473

[4] John Gay, 'Trivia; or, the Art of Walking the Streets of London' in Clare Brant & Susan Whyman, eds., *Walking the Streets of Eighteenth-Century London: John Gay's* Trivia (1716), Oxford: Oxford University Press, 2007, 169–219, p. 170

[5] For this reason, those attempting to follow in Gay's footsteps

across London today are likely to be disappointed: 'In my attempt to walk some of the spaces represented in *Trivia*, it was abundantly clear that using the poem like a map was impossible because places are not represented in an orderly or logical way – the journey is more like sticking a pin in a map, than following a linear route.' Alison Stenton, 'Spatial Stories: Movement in the City and Cultural Geography', in *Walking the Streets of Eighteenth-Century London: John Gay's* Trivia (1716), 62–74, p. 70

[6] Gay, 'Trivia', p. 185

[7] William Blake, 'London', in *The Complete Poems*, ed. by Alicia Ostriker, London: Penguin, 2004, p. 128

[8] Blake, 'Jerusalem', in *The Complete Poems*, p. 700

[9] Peter Ackroyd, 'The London that Became Jerusalem', in *The Times*, March 3, 2007 and at http://entertainment. timesonline.co.uk/tol/arts_and_entertainment/books/non-fiction/article1461686.ece

[10] Peter Ackroyd, *Blake*, London: Sinclair–Stevenson, 1995, pp. 30–1

[11] Blake, 'Milton', in *The Complete Poems*, p. 521

[12] Blake, 'Jerusalem', in *The Complete Poems*, p. 686

[13] Blake, 'Jerusalem', in *The Complete Poems*, p. 725. 'So here was a very interesting series of instructions', writes Iain Sinclair, describing this passage, 'a particular kind of walk, and quite an eccentric journey laid out, a trajectory which is both spiritual and physical'. See Sinclair, *Blake's London*, p. 17

[14] Iain Sinclair, *Lights Out for the Territory*, London: Granta, 1997, p. 208. Blake has proved crucial in moulding Sinclair's own perception of the city: 'The triangle of concentration. A sense of this and of all the other triangulations of the city: Blake, Bunyan, Defoe, the dissenting monuments in Bunhill Fields. Everything I believe in, everything that London can do to you, starts there.' Sinclair, *Lights Out*, p. 34

[15] Blake, 'Milton', in *The Complete Poems*, p. 554

[16] For a practical example of Blake's influence upon contemporary London walking, see 'Blakewalking' by Thomas

Wright at http://www.timwright.typepad.com/L_O_S/. Here Blakewalking is described as 'a new way of conversing, participating, publishing, performing and creating on the hoof. The aim of Blakewalking is to transform an everyday walk into a Visionary Experience. We want you to join us out on the streets, on the web and on your mobile – making notes, recording thoughts and feelings, responding to the world we walk through – and the world within.'

[17] Marples, p. 59

[18] Marples, p. 60

[19] Marples, p. 63

[20] Marples, p. 63

[21] Thomas De Quincey, *Confessions of an English Opium-Eater and Other Writings*, ed. by Barry Milligan, London: Penguin, 2003, pp. 53–4. Just as Blake stands as a symbolic representative of a retrospective psychogeographic tradition, so may De Quincey be described as psychogeography's first actual practitioner. For the drug-fuelled journeys through the London of De Quincey's youth seem to capture exactly that state of aimless drift and detached observation which were to become the hallmarks of the Situationist *dérive* some 150 years later; and as Phil Baker has claimed: 'Classic urban psychogeography could almost be said to begin – retrospectively, and from a Situationist influenced perspective – with Thomas De Quincey.' See Baker, p. 326

[22] Geoff Nicholson writes: 'De Quincey's fantasy of an unknown London is an attractive one, since London is, in every sense I can think of, exceptionally well-trodden territory: a place of walkers, with a two-thousand-year-old history of pedestrianism [...] No part of London is genuinely unknown. However obscure or hidden the place and its history, somebody has already discovered it, walked it, staked a claim to it. Nicholson, *The Lost Art of Walking*, p. 41

[23] De Quincey, *Confessions*, p. 24

[24] 'Walking Stewart' was to appear in two essays written by De Quincey, the first published in *The London Magazine* (September,

1823) and the second in *Tait's Magazine* (October, 1840). The former can be accessed at http://www.readbookonline.net/readOnLine/47766/

[25] Jebb, p. 127

[26] De Quincey, 'Sketches of Life & Manners' (October, 1840) in *The Works of Thomas De Quincey*, ed. by Grevel Lindop, London: Chatto & Pickering, 2000–2003, vol. 11, 245–260, p. 246, and qtd. in Solnit, p. 108–9

[27] Grevel Lindop, *The Opium-Eater: A Life of Thomas De Quincey*, London: Dent, 1981, p. 246

[28] Lindop, p. 349

[29] Marples, p. 63

[30] Marples, p. 66

[31] Charles Dickens, letter to John Forster (1857), qtd. in Michael Slater, *Charles Dickens*, London: Yale University Press, 2009, p. 382

[32] Charles Dickens, in a letter to his wife, 8 November, 1844, and qtd. in Peter Ackroyd, *Dickens*, London: Sinclair-Stevenson, 1990, p. 444

[33] Describing him as an urban counterpart to Thoreau, Joseph A. Amato claims that Dickens wanted to illustrate London from the walker's perspective, 'to explain the half that walks to the half that rides.' 'In more than one work', he writes, Dickens 'explained dark, grimy, ashen, toil-laden, hunger-filled, and foot-weary London to the glittering and glamorous world of carriages and boulevards, of selective ambling and ostentatious strolling.' Amato, pp. 176–7

[34] Charles Dickens, *Martin Chuzzlewit*, ed. by Patricia Ingham, London: Penguin, 2004, p. 194, qtd. alongside other examples of walking in Dickens, in Jebb, pp. 91–92

[35] Charles Dickens, *The Old Curiosity Shop: A Tale*, ed. by Norman Page, London: Penguin, 2000, p. 9

[36] Charles Dickens, 'Night Walks', in *The Uncommercial Traveller*, Stroud: Nonsuch Publishing, 2007, Chapter XIII, p. 138

[37] Dickens, 'Night Walks', p. 139

[38] Ackroyd, *Dickens*, p. 87. In making this observation Ackroyd

echoes the words of GK Chesterton, perhaps Dickens' most astute critic, who notes that the realism employed by Dickens is born of exactly this mode of dreamlike motion: 'And this kind of realism can only be gained by walking dreamily in a place; it cannot be gained by walking observantly.' Warming to his theme, Chesterton continues: 'Few of us understand the street. Even when we step into it, we step into it doubtfully, as into a house or room of strangers. Few of us see through the shining riddle of the street, the strange folk that belong to the street only – the street-walker or the street arab, the nomads who, generation after generation have kept their ancient secret in the full blaze of the sun. Of the street at night many of us know less. The street at night is a great house locked up. But Dickens had, if ever man had, the key of the street; his stars were the lamps of the street; his hero was the man in the street. He could open the inmost door of his house – the door that leads into that secret passage which is lined with houses and roofed with stars.' GK Chesterton, *Charles Dickens*, London: Wordsworth Editions, 2007, pp. 24–5

[39] Dickens, 'Shy Neighbourhoods', in *The Uncommercial Traveller*, Chapter X, p. 106

[40] Dickens, 'Shy Neighbourhoods', p. 105

[41] Jebb, p. 89

[42] Dickens, 'On an Amateur Beat', in *The Uncommercial Traveller*, Chapter X, p. 75

[43] Peter Ackroyd has described how Dickens's guests were frequently subjected to a punishing walk of twelve miles in two and a half hours, with only a five-minute break. An ordeal often endured in complete silence. Ackroyd, *Dickens*, p. 930

[44] Ackroyd, *Dickens*, pp. 291–2

[45] Wallace, p. 232

[46] Arthur Machen, 'The Joy of London' (1914) in *The Secret of the Sangraal and Other Writings*, Leyburn: Tartarus Press, 2007, p. 78

[47] Christened Arthur Llewellyn Jones, the correct pronunciation of Machen's (mækən) adopted surname (his mother's maiden name) has long since been the subject of debate, perhaps to his

detriment. Such confusion prompted the novelist and critic, Cyril Connolly, to suggest that 'If I had been Arthur Machen, I would have added "rhymes with bracken" to my signature by deed-poll, for nothing harms an author's sales like an ambiguity in the pronunciation of his name.' See Gary Lachman, *The Dedalus Book of the Occult: A Dark Muse*, Sawtry: Dedalus, 2003, p. 220 (n. 28)

[48] Mark Valentine, *Arthur Machen*, Bridgend: Seren, 1995, p. 9. 'Journeying was important for Machen', notes Valentine, 'from the long solitary rambles of his youth to the explorations of remotest London and his days as a "strolling player." Quoting from Machen's *The Secret Glory* (1922), he adds: 'We came very near to the ideal life which man was meant to lead. Who can measure the excellent effects of vagabondage, of the continual rolling which keeps the stone clean of moss and lichen?' Valentine, p. 66

[49] Arthur Machen, *The London Adventure, or the Art of Wandering*, London: Martin Secker, 1924, p. 100. The 'door in the wall' that Machen describes here recalls the short story of the same name by HG Wells, in which the protagonist, having as a schoolboy located a door leading to an enchanted realm, spends the remainder of his life attempting to rediscover it. Wells' story, first published in 1906, also has strong affinities with Machen's later story 'N', published in 1936, which concerns the search to rediscover a similarly enchanted domain. See HG Wells, 'The Door in the Wall' (1906) in *The Country of the Blind and Other Selected Stories*, ed. by Patrick Parrinder, London: Penguin, 2007, pp. 365–381, and Arthur Machen, *N*, Leyburn: Tartarus Press, 2010

[50] Arthur Machen, *The London Adventure*, p. 75. Machen's highly idiosyncratic worldview has much in common with that of another equally neglected writer, John Cowper Powys. Powys, like Machen, was also alert to the connection between walking and creativity, and used himself to walk prodigious distances in search of inspiration. For an analysis of the role of walking in his work, see Mark Boseley, *Walking in the Creative Life of John Cowper Powys: The Triumph of the Peripatetic Mode*, Västeras, Sweden:

Mälardalens Högskola, 2001

[51] Machen, 'When I was Young in London' (1913) in *The Secret of the Sangraal and Other Writings*, p. 66

[52] Machen, *The London Adventure*, p. 49

[53] Machen, *Things Near and Far*, London: Martin Secker, 1923, pp. 62–3

[54] Machen, *Things Near and Far*, p. 63

[55] Machen, *The London Adventure*, p. 141

[56] Machen, *Things Near and Far*, p. 59

[57] Machen, *The London Adventure*, p. 141

[58] Machen was certainly familiar with the figure of the *flâneur*, as he reveals in the following extract from his novella *A Fragment of Life* (1906): 'And he reflected with sorrow on the innumerable evenings on which he had rejected his landlady's plain fried chop, and had gone out to *flaner* among the Italian restaurants in Upper Street, Islington.' Arthur Machen, 'A Fragment of Life', in *The Collected Arthur Machen*, ed. by Christopher Palmer, London: Duckworth, 1988, 23–88, p. 36

[59] A view of Machen endorsed by Philip Van Doren Stern, who was to write: 'He seems never to have fitted into the life of the huge metropolis. He explored London endlessly and came to know it well, but it evidently terrified him.' Arthur Machen, *Tales of Horror and the Supernatural*, ed. by Philip Van Doren Stern, London: Richards Press, 1949, Introduction, p. ix

[60] Arthur Machen, 'The Re-Discovery of London' (1914) in *The Secret of the Sangraal and Other Writings*, p. 80

The *Flâneur*

Around 1840 it was briefly fashionable to take turtles for a walk in the arcades. The flâneurs *liked to have the turtles set the pace for them. If they had had their way, progress would have been obliged to accommodate itself to this pace.* Walter Benjamin[1]

But one realizes to be sure to satiety that he loves to walk as well as he loves to write; the latter of course perhaps just a shade less than the former. Robert Walser[2]

There is no direct equivalent in English for the French verb *flâner*: to stroll, saunter, drift, dawdle, loiter, linger – one can identify an entire vocabulary that approaches, but which fails to capture, its meaning. Larousse provides us with the following definition: '*Flâner: Errer sans bout, en s'arrêtant pour regarder*', which has been translated as 'wandering without aim, stopping once in a while to look around.'[3] The term has only been in common usage since the nineteenth century, although its derivation has been traced back both to the Old Scandinavian, *flana* ('to run giddily here and there'), and to the Irish term for libertine.[4] It is precisely this elusive quality, and a resistance to easy classification, which is so apparent in the identity of the *flâneur* himself (for he is invariably seen as male), a character who has managed to establish a literary history for himself without having ever fully disclosed his origins.

Today the *flâneur* has become a somewhat overworked figure, beloved of academics and cultural commentators who have staked out competing claims both for his literary antecedents and the cities in which his activities were first observed. Hence, the earliest sightings of the fledgling *flâneur* have been credited to London, Berlin and Vienna, while figures such as Victor Fournel, Heinrich von Kleist and Heinrich Heine have all been identified as possible progenitors of this tradition.[5] Yet none of these suggestions, however plausible, can disguise the fact that the figure of the *flâneur* remains inextricably linked with the streets of Paris and the poetry of Charles Baudelaire (1821–1867); and it is in his essay, 'The Painter of Modern Life' (1863), that Baudelaire provides us with what remains the closest we have to a definitive account of the *flâneur's* often contradictory nature:

> The crowd is his element, as the air is that of the birds and water of fishes. His passion and his profession are to become one flesh with the crowd. For the perfect *flâneur*, for a passionate spectator, it is an immense joy to set up house in the heat of the multitude, amid the ebb and flow of movement, in the midst of the fugitive and the infinite. To be away from home and yet to find oneself everywhere at home; to see the world, to be at the centre of the world, and yet remain hidden from the world – such are a few of the slightest pleasures of these independent, passionate, impartial natures which the tongue can but clumsily define.[6]

For Baudelaire, Paris becomes a book to be read by walking her streets; but as a result of Haussmann's wholesale reconfiguration of the city, this labyrinthine and essentially medieval topography was soon to be destroyed. In such an environment the *flâneur* is under threat and Baudelaire responds by creating an idealised figure, and an idealised city, in which everyone conforms to some degree to the figure of the *flâneur* but no one actually attains his elusive status; for as Rebecca Solnit has noted: 'The only problem with the *flâneur* is that he did not exist, except as a type, an ideal, and a character in literature [...] no one quite fulfilled the idea of the *flâneur*, but everyone engaged in some version of flâneury.'[7]

The *flâneur* is elusive to the point that he cannot be located at all, the search for this figure itself taking on the characteristics of *flânerie,* and offering new ways of experiencing the city.[8] Like London before it, Paris in the nineteenth century had expanded to the point where it could no longer be comprehended in its entirety. It had become increasingly alien to its own inhabitants, a strange and newly exotic place to be experienced more as a tourist than as a resident. Soon the city becomes characterised as a jungle, uncharted and unexplored, a virgin wilderness populated by savages demonstrating strange customs and practices. The navigation of this city becomes a skill, a secret knowledge available only to an elect few, and in this environment the stroller is transformed into an explorer, or even a detective solving the mystery of the city streets.[9] As these streets are gradually destroyed and reordered, however, so this wilderness is tamed and domesticated and the walker's arcane knowledge is rendered obsolete. As public spaces become private ones and the streets become choked with traffic, so walking is reduced to mere promenading, explorers becoming little more than window-shoppers. In the modern city the man of the crowd must adapt or perish.

Towards the end of his *Intimate Journals* (1909), Baudelaire writes, 'Lost in this vile world, elbowed by the crowd, I am like a worn-out man.'[10] Can this really be the voice of the *flâneur,* the man of the crowd? It seems that in many ways Baudelaire's own life reflects the trajectory of the *flâneur* as he battles against modernity, as the streets become more hostile to the stroller whose insistence upon a walker's pace questions the need for speed and circulation that the modern city promotes (yet seldom achieves). For even as he was describing the *flâneur,* Baudelaire was to act as a witness to his demise; his is not a portrait of the future but rather a nostalgic depiction of a way of life about to be swept away forever. The *flâneur* is, then, not so much a man of his time as a man out of time, a symbol of a bygone age. And while Baudelaire may have been the first to offer an explicit portrait of the *flâneur*, he was to credit the flâneur's literary conception to Edgar Allan Poe, whose short story, 'The Man of the Crowd' (1840) is one of the earliest examples of the use of the crowd as a symbol for the emerging modern city, exploring the role of the detached observer who becomes intoxicated by its movement.

Born in Boston in 1809 and briefly a schoolboy in Stoke Newington in London (1815–20), Edgar Allan Poe spent the remainder of his life on the east coast of the USA. It is tempting, therefore, to see Poe as the pioneer of American *flânerie*, but in reality Poe is less at home within an American tradition than he is within a European one.[11] He was largely dismissed during his lifetime, in the Anglophone world, as a highly disreputable figure, 'a mad loner who wandered the city streets night and day'; it was Baudelaire, through his translations of Poe's work, who was almost single-handedly responsible for rebuilding Poe's reputation and disseminating his work to a wider audience.[12]

Baudelaire was specifically to cite Poe's story as inaugurating a new urban type, an isolated and estranged figure who is both a man of the crowd and a detached observer of it, and as such, the avatar of the modern city. Describing 'The Man of the Crowd' as a picture, 'painted – or rather written by the most powerful pen of our age', Baudelaire sketches the following outline of the plot:

In the window of a coffee-house there sits a convalescent, pleasurably absorbed in gazing at the crowd, and mingling, through the medium of thought, in the turmoil of thought that surrounds him. But lately returned from the valley of the shadow of death, he is rapturously breathing in all the odours and essences of life; as he has been on the brink of total oblivion, he remembers, and fervently desires to remember, everything. Finally he hurls himself headlong into the midst of the throng, in pursuit of an unknown, half-glimpsed countenance that has, on an instant, bewitched him. Curiosity has become a fatal, irresistible passion.[13]

Having set off in pursuit, our narrator is led on a seemingly aimless and haphazard journey across the city. Night follows day and this pursuit continues until finally, feeling that the journey will never end, he approaches his quarry. The man barely notices him, however, and simply continues on his way: "This old man', I said at length, 'is the type and the genius of deep crime. He refuses to be alone. *He is the man of the crowd*. It will be vain to follow; for I shall learn no more of him, nor his deeds."[14] In these few pages, then, we witness the emergence of the *flâneur*, the wanderer in the modern city, both immersed in the crowd but isolated by it, an outsider (even a criminal) yet ultimately a man impossible to fathom and one whose motives remain unclear.

Of course, the reason that the figure of the *flâneur* has come to gain such prominence in recent years is not through a reappraisal of the work of Baudelaire or Poe, but rather through that of Baudelaire's most insightful critic, Walter Benjamin (1892–1940). Best known today for his fragmentary and incomplete account of nineteenth-century Paris, *The Arcades Project* (*Das Passagen-Werk*; 1982), Benjamin was to publish his first major essay on Baudelaire in 1938, although this, like much of his work, was to remain unpublished in English until the 1970s. Recalling the glass-covered arcades that were the natural habitat of the *flâneur* in early nineteenth-century Paris, Benjamin was to move beyond Baudelaire's account of this archetypal stroller, in offering an analysis of the city street in which the *flâneur* was to make his home:

The leisurely quality [...] fits the style of the *flâneur* who goes botanizing on the asphalt. But even in those days it was not possible to stroll about everywhere in the city. Before Haussmann wide pavements were rare, and the narrow ones afforded little protection from vehicles. Strolling could hardly have assumed the importance it did without the arcades. 'The arcades, a rather recent invention of industrial luxury', so says an illustrated guide to Paris of 1852, 'are glass-covered, marble-panelled passageways through entire complexes of houses whose proprietors have combined for such speculations. Both sides of these passageways, which are lighted from above, are lined with the most elegant shops, so that such an arcade is a city, even a world, in miniature.' It is in this world that the *flâneur* is at home [...] The arcades were a cross between a street and an *intérieur* [...] The street becomes a dwelling for the *flâneur*, he is as much at home among the façades of houses as a citizen is in his four walls. To him the shiny, enamelled signs of businesses are at least as good a wall ornament as an oil painting is to a bourgeois in his salon. The walls are the desk against which he presses his notebooks; news–stands are his libraries and the terraces of cafés are the balconies from which he looks down on his household after his work is done.[15]

'The *flâneur*', writes Benjamin, 'is someone who does not feel comfortable in his own company. That is why he seeks out the crowd'; 'Baudelaire loved solitude,' he adds, 'but he wanted it in a crowd.'[16] But Benjamin cautions against viewing the *flâneur* as a self–portrait of Baudelaire himself, arguing that there is a key difference between the two: absentmindedness. For while the *flâneur* is a keen observant of his surroundings, Baudelaire, claims Benjamin, was nothing of the sort; and instead he compares him to Dickens, a man who, in Chesterton's words, 'roams about the big city lost in thought.'[17]

In fact, Benjamin's portrait of Baudelaire reveals a deeply tragic figure, one who is both attracted and at the same time alienated by the crowd in which he has sought out a home. Indeed, as early as 1853, Baudelaire, harassed by his many creditors and in increasing ill–health, had been brought almost to a standstill: 'I must admit', he writes, 'that I have reached the point where I don't make any sudden movements or walk a lot because I fear that I might tear my clothes even more.'[18] The London that Poe depicts in 1840 is shown already to be inimical to the stroller; and this was a situation soon to be replicated across metropolitan

Europe. Visiting Brussels towards the end of his life, Baudelaire was to write: 'No shop-windows. Strolling, something that nations with imagination love, is not possible in Brussels. There is nothing to see, and the streets are unusable.'[19] Retreating to Paris, Baudelaire's short, unhappy existence finally saw him turn against the crowd which had so enthralled him:

> Of all the experiences which made his life what it was, Baudelaire singled out his having been jostled by the crowd as the decisive, unique experience. The lustre of the crowd with a motion and a soul of its own, the glitter that had bedazzled the *flâneur*, had dimmed for him [...] Baudelaire battled the crowd – with the impotent rage of someone fighting the rain or the wind.[20]

Yet what of Benjamin himself? Can we find in him too some trace of the *flâneur*? 'I don't think I ever saw him walk with his head erect', recalled his friend, Gershom Sholem. 'His gait had something unmistakable about it, something pensive and tentative, which was probably due to his shortsightedness.'[21] Elsewhere, Susan Sontag has described his twofold nature: on the one hand, forever on the move, a wanderer, a walker; yet on the other, a collector, 'weighed down by things; that is, passions.'[22] His own stature as a great walker of the streets is confirmed through his work, in his descriptions of strolls through Marseilles, Moscow and the Berlin of his childhood, alongside, of course, his account of Paris, the city which was to teach him the art of wandering:

> Not to find one's way in a city may well be uninteresting and banal. It requires ignorance – nothing more. But to lose oneself in a city – as one loses oneself in a forest – that calls for quite a different schooling. Then signboards and street names, passers-by, roofs, kiosks, or bars must speak to the wanderer like a cracking twig under his feet in the forest, like the startling call

of a bittern in the distance, like the sudden stillness of a clearing with a lily standing erect at its centre. Paris taught me this art of straying.[23]

A much later visitor to Paris, Edmund White, noted that to be a successful *flâneur* required time – the kind of freedom enjoyed by those unencumbered by the need to work, those 'who can take off a morning or an afternoon for undirected ambling.'[24] And here again, Benjamin certainly fits the bill. Born into a wealthy middle-class family and bankrolled by his father, he was able to take not merely the morning or afternoon off, but his entire adult life, much of which was devoted to ambling. Indeed, if anything, Benjamin was to become the *flâneur's flâneur*, not merely the observer of the crowd but the observer of the *flâneur* himself, the passionate spectator who attains one further degree of insight into his quarry.

The history of the *flâneur*, as Benjamin was to demonstrate, is one in which the city he inhabits is shown to grow increasingly hostile towards him, as ultimately he is evicted from the street and forced to seek a new environment elsewhere. Benjamin was to describe Paris as a city 'which had long since ceased to be home to the *flâneur*', and so, in the end, it was to prove for him.[25] For when war broke out in 1939, Benjamin was rounded up along with other German men and marched to a camp in Nevers, some 100 miles south of Paris, where he was to spend the next three months. Having obtained his release through the intercession of the writers' group PEN, Benjamin was to return briefly to Paris before the Nazi occupation of France led him to return southwards once again in an attempt to cross the Pyrenees into Spain. Needless to say, his strolls through the streets of Paris could have done little to prepare him for this, his final flight, as he fled across France and upwards through the mountains, frequently overcome by exhaustion and increasingly reliant on the support of his companions. His tragic end is well documented; but it is a savage irony that his death should have come about as a consequence of an enforced walk. For having reached the Spanish border and been refused entry, he took his own life rather than face the return journey across the mountains into occupied France.

In an essay written in 1929, Benjamin was to describe a fellow writer and walker in the following words: 'No sooner has he taken up his pen than he is overpowered by the urges of a desperado: everything seems lost; a surge of words gushes forth in which each sentence only has the task of obliterating the previous one.'[26] The subject of Benjamin's description was the then little known Swiss writer, Robert Walser (1878–1956), a figure who was to share with Benjamin both a passion for wandering and a tragic fate. Like Benjamin, Walser was to be largely overlooked during his lifetime, only to experience a gradual reappraisal once his works began to be translated into English in the 1960s. Since then, however, Walser's work has come to be recognised as a major addition both to European literature as a whole and to the literature of walking in particular.

Born in Biel in 1878, the life of Robert Walser is a tale of four cities: Zurich (1896–1905); Berlin (1905–13); Biel (1913–21) and Bern (1921–29).[27] These four cities were to provide fixed co-ordinates in a life of constant motion, periods of relative stability punctuating a largely nomadic existence characterised by long treks through the Swiss countryside. Moving from lodging to lodging and job to job, 'Walser's life', writes Susan Sontag, 'illustrates the restlessness of one kind of depressive temperament: he had the depressive's fascination with stasis, and with the way time distends, is consumed; and spent much of his life obsessively turning time into space: his walks.'[28] Walser was to write several novels, amongst them *The Tanners* (1907), *The Assistant* (1908) and *Jakob von Gunten* (1909), but it was his shorter fiction that gained him what reputation he was to earn during his lifetime. Walser published numerous short stories in newspapers and magazines, often character sketches drawn with a surreal sense of the absurd, which depicted the everyday lives and occupations of those who seemed, like Walser himself, to pass through life devoid of any particular sense of purpose or destination. In many of these stories, and in the absence of any recognisable plot, Walser simply used the device of describing a short walk, in which the themes of wandering and the imagination become linked, the one acting as a catalyst for the other.[29] Sontag has described these stories as 'portraits of consciousness walking about in the world'[30]; but for Walser, what distinguishes the true walker, the *flâneur*, from the crowd he passes amongst is not so much a heightened awareness of one's surroundings as a sense of bemused detachment:

> I am one of the multitude, and that is what I find so strange. I find the multitude strange and always wonder: "What on earth are they all doing, what are they up to?" I disappear, yes, disappear in the mass. When I hurry home at midday, as twelve o'clock strikes, from the bank where I am employed, they are all hurrying with me: this one is trying to overtake another, that one is taking longer strides than another; yet, still one thinks, "They will all reach home," and they do reach home, for among them there is not a single extraordinary person who could happen not to find his way home.[31]

Just as Poe was to outline the fate of the walker in the modern city, so too is Walser alert to the vertigo–inducing power of the crowd; and aware also of the aimless, undirected energy which can benumb the senses, leaving the walker disorientated and overwhelmed:

> I had taken some steps, useless they had been, and now I went out into the street, agitated, numb [...] A shiver passed through me; I hardly dared to walk on. One impression after another seized hold of me. I was swaying, everything was swaying. All the people walking here had plans in mind, business [...] The crowds were seething with energy. Everybody thought himself out in front. Men, women floated by. All seemed to be making

for the same goal. Where did they come from, where were they going?

One of them was this, another that, a third nothing. Many were driven, lived with purpose, let themselves be flung every which way. Any sense for the good was set aside, not used; intelligence was groping in emptiness; fine faculties and plenty bore meagre fruit.[32]

Throughout his work Walser returns obsessively to the motif of the walk – it provides not only a structuring device, but also informs the opinions of his characters, who often appear as little more than mouthpieces for Walser's frequently gnomic utterances, cumulatively articulating a pedestrian philosophy: 'Things in motion are always most just.'; 'Wandering, what a brilliant, light blue joy you are.'; 'Aimlessness leads to the aim, while firm intentions often miss.'; 'Walking, I observed others storking along on adjacent paths; pedestrians, after all, walk for seconds at a time on a single leg.'; 'Couldn't he take a walk without fantasizing, dreaming up poetry? But that's what made these walks of his so rich, so pleasurable time and again.'[33]

If there is a single, predominant Walserian characteristic that defines his work, then it is his fondness for digression, an unceasing resistance to any overriding aim, direction or resolution; a characteristic which finds its natural expression through the act of walking. Furthermore, if there is any single stylistic trademark emblematic of Walser's work, then it is his extraordinary loquaciousness, or what Benjamin describes as *'geschwätzigkeit'*, or garrulousness.[34] For Walser's work is peppered by episodes of extraordinary verbosity, occasions in which the author's reserve momentarily gives way to an outpouring of quite striking intensity. One critic has described such moments as a 'blurt', an opportunity for Walser to speak directly to his readership about a particular issue.[35] One such moment, perhaps the most pronounced 'blurt' of his career, appears in his story 'The Walk' (1917) and describes the topic closest to his heart, that of walking itself.

'The Walk', as the title suggests, is exactly that, a description of a stroll taken by the narrator over the course of a single day, as he wanders through an unnamed town and on into the countryside. It is also one of the most peculiar and unclassifiable contributions to the literature of walking ever written, in which modernism meets the fairy tale while taking a stroll: 'I have to report', begins Walser, 'that one fine morning [...] as the desire to take a walk came over me, I put on my hat, left my writing room, or room of phantoms, and ran down the stairs to hurry out into the street [...] I found myself, as I walked into the open, bright, and cheerful street, in a romantically adventurous state of mind.'[36] As he walks through the town, the narrator enters a bookshop and then a bank, passes children playing and converses with strangers; outwardly normal, a heightened sense of unreality pervades every exchange, every meeting. Leaving the town behind him he passes a giant on the road before entering a forest; he has a lunch appointment – a very sinister experience; he posts a letter and visits a tailor. Finally, he reaches the office of the tax inspector, with whom he pleads (as a poor writer) to pay a lower rate of tax. 'But you're always to be seen out for a walk!' responds the official, to which our narrator replies:

"Walk," was my answer. "I definitely must, to invigorate myself and to maintain contact with the living world, without perceiving which I could not write the half of one more single word, or produce the tiniest poem in verse or prose. Without walking, I would be dead, and my profession, which I love passionately, would be destroyed. Also, without walking and gathering reports, I would not be able to render one single further report, or the tiniest of essays, let alone a real, long story. Without walking, I would not be able to make any observations or studies at all [...] On a lovely and far-wandering walk a thousand usable and useful thoughts occur to me. Shut in at home, I would miserably decay and dry up. Walking is for me not only healthy and lovely, it is also of service and useful. A walk advances me professionally and provides me at the same time also with amusement and joy; it refreshes and comforts and delights me, is a pleasure for me, and simultaneously, it has the peculiarity that it allures me and spurs me on to further creation, since it offers me as material numerous small and large objectivities upon which I later work at home, diligently and industriously. A walk is always filled with significant phenomena, which are valuable to see and to feel. A pleasant walk most often teems with imageries and living poems, with enchantments and natural beauties, be they ever so small. The lore of nature and the lore of the country are revealed, charming and graceful, to the sense and eyes of the observant walker, who must of course walk not with downcast but with open and unclouded eyes, if the lovely significance and the gay, noble idea of the walk are to dawn on him [...] Without walking and the contemplation of nature which is connected with it, without this equally delicious and admonishing search, I deem myself lost, and I am lost. With the utmost love and attention the man who walks must study and observe every smallest living thing [...] If he does not, then he walks only half attentive, and that is worth nothing [...] Spirit, devotion, and faithfulness bless him and raise him high up above his own inconspicuous walking self, which has only too often a name and evil reputation for vagabondage and vagrancy [...] Mysterious and secretly there prowl at the walker's heels all kinds of beautiful subtle walker's thoughts [...] There accompanies the walker always something remarkable, some food for thought, something fantastic, and he would be foolish if he did not notice this spiritual side, or even thrust it away; rather, he welcomes all curious and peculiar phenomena, becomes their friend and brother, because they delight him; he makes them into formed and substantial bodies, gives them structure and soul just as they for their part instruct and inspire him. In a word, by thinking, pondering, drilling, digging, speculating, writing, investigating, researching, and walking, I earn my daily bread with as much sweat on my brow as anybody."[37]

The arrival of this speech is, of course, wholly unexpected; and yet in retrospect the whole story appears to revolve around this astonishing proclamation. The walk continues on, as does the mood of understated surreality, and as darkness falls the story finishes. Here, then, as nowhere else, we are offered an impassioned justification for the role of the writer as walker, alongside an explicit expression of the ways in which these two activities intersect. For both here and throughout his work, Walser is compiling a manifesto of sorts for the would-be *flâneur*, his characters setting down the accumulated wisdom of the walker and delivering a robust defence of the peripatetic existence: 'A life of observant idling, city strolling, mountain hikes, and woodland walks, a life lived on the edges of lakes, on the margins of meadows, on the verges of things, a life in slow but constant motion, at a gawker's pace.'[38]

Sadly for Walser, however, this was a life that he was unable to sustain, and in 1929, the year in which Walter Benjamin was to make him the subject of his essay, Walser voluntarily entered a psychiatric clinic. Four years later he was moved to the asylum at Herisau where he was to spend the next 23 years. In 1936, Walser was visited by the Swiss writer Carl Seelig, who was to become a close friend; for many years they were to take walks together and the ensuing conversations between them were to be published by Seelig in 1957.[39] The diagnosis of Walser's schizophrenia has since been questioned but, while he continued to walk, his writing career ended at Herisau: 'I'm not here to write', he was to say, 'but to be mad.' He died on Christmas Day, 1956, while out for a walk on his own.

If Poe and Baudelaire, Benjamin and Walser, trace out the trajectory of the *flâneur* as he walks the streets of Europe, what of his female counterpart, the *flâneuse*?[40] The dandy, the stroller, the *flâneur*, these are invariably male figures, dominating the street life and public spaces of cities in which solitary women are largely absent figures. In nineteenth-century Paris and elsewhere, the *flâneur* represented freedom; a kind of freedom which was, however, one largely denied to women, to whom the streets were to remain the site of prohibition and exclusion. Yet such a situation pertained principally to the bourgeois woman, for there was, of course, an entire population of solitary women walking the streets at this time, that of the prostitute. But as modernity transformed the city, it was not only the built environment that was subjected to radical change, but also the gender relations of its inhabitants. Could the revolutionary change that Baudelaire and later Benjamin were to identify as sounding the death knell of the *flâneur* itself herald the emergence of his successor, the *flâneuse*?

In recent years, numerous names have been put forward to fill the role of the prototypical *flâneuse*, from George Sand and Frances Trollope, to Kate Chopin and Djuna Barnes. Such suggestions, however, manage curiously to overlook the single outstanding candidate, Virginia Woolf (1882–1941). Perhaps because she returns the stroller to the streets of London, more possibly because she represents an upper-middle class outlook unacceptable to some, Virginia Woolf remains a divisive figure, albeit one with an unerring ability to articulate the walker's vision of the street:

> In London she was known, social, much invited and inviting: a focus and a participant of London life. That was indoors. Outdoors, she walked about anonymously, looking, collecting, absorbing – 'seeing life', reading the street. She often called the noise of the streets a kind of language: 'I shop in London sometimes and hear feet shuffling. That's the language, I think, that's the phrase I should like to catch' [...] But her pleasure in walking through the city alone never diminished. The more violent and strange the sights, the better pleased she was.[41]

Amongst her novels it is *Mrs Dalloway* (1925) that is regarded, by some, as one of the great London walking novels.[42] Set on a single day in London on 13 June 1923, *Mrs Dalloway* is one of the highpoints of literary Modernism, taking its place alongside Joyce's account of another such June day in the life of Leopold Bloom in *Ulysses* (1922). Yet amidst the impressionistic style, interior monologue and other, by now familiar, modernist devices, *Mrs Dalloway* records in precise topographical detail the morning walk through central London untaken by Clarissa Dalloway as she goes out to buy some flowers for the party she is to host with her husband that evening. And however one might regard this modest pedestrian ambition, there can be no doubting her enthusiasm for walking, as with an ecstatic 'What a lark! What a plunge!' she positively leaps into the street.[43] Indeed, only a couple of pages later and she is exclaiming: 'I love walking in London [...] Really, it's better than walking in the country.'[44] Perhaps Clarissa Dalloway, as a fifty-two year old woman walking alone in London, is simply experiencing the joy that Woolf herself was to experience at being able to escape, however briefly, from the stifling confines of a middle-class life in which even such a short journey would be regarded as an act of eccentricity. For in June 1923, a lady of Mrs Dalloway's social standing would still be expected to rely on her servants for such a task, at a time when the constraints of Edwardian life were only yet beginning to loosen. As she approaches Bond Street, however, Mrs Dalloway begins to experience a sensation that Woolf was to describe many times in her work, as engulfed by the crowd, her sense of self appears to subside, leaving her an anonymous spectator to her surroundings: 'She had the oddest sense of being herself invisible; unseen; unknown.'[45] Needless to say, Mrs Dalloway regains her diminishing sense of self sufficiently to complete her return journey. But this sense of slippage, as one's identity is blurred with that of the crowd, is exactly that modernist moment celebrated by the *flâneur*.

One consequence of demarcating a walk so clearly within the

pages of a fictional account, however, as Bloomsday walkers in Dublin will testify, is that the reader can then follow in one's footsteps. One such walker who has retraced Mrs Dalloway's route is the critic John Sutherland, with surprising results. For using the chimes of Big Ben and St Margaret's, the House of Commons parish church, which punctuate Woolf's text, Sutherland was able not only to retrace Clarissa's steps but also to gauge how long her journey took her. And as the title of his essay, 'Clarissa's Invisible Taxi', would appear to suggest, he was to find a puzzling discrepancy between her experience and his own. In short, even if one discounts the modest pace a lady of Clarissa's age and health (she suffers from a heart complaint) is likely to achieve, Sutherland found that she could not possibly have made it home, on foot, in the allotted time: 'Unless those feet are very swift indeed', he concludes, 'a taxi there must be.'[46] Rather than suggesting that Woolf is complicit in some unexplained attempt to defraud her readers, a sort of Bloomsbury equivalent to Ffyona Campbell[47], Sutherland argues that, for a woman such as Clarissa, dependent as she no doubt is upon a retinue of household servants, the act of taking a taxi is in fact as, if not more, natural than walking. In such an environment, claims Sutherland, Clarissa would simply see no need to mention it.[48]

The jumbled recollections expressed in *Mrs Dalloway* are presented as the natural companion to walking, an act in which the digressions and improvisations of associative thinking find an outlet. Yet beyond the formal experimentation of the novel, it is the essay in which Woolf's credentials as *flâneuse* can best be appreciated. In *The London Scene*, for example, a series of five essays on London life, written for *Good Housekeeping* magazine in 1931, Woolf returns to the idea of her identity as something malleable and transient, the act of walking precipitating a process by which the observer becomes a screen on to which impressions of London's streets may then be recorded: 'The mind becomes a glutinous slab that takes impressions and Oxford Street rolls off upon it a perpetual ribbon of changing sights, sounds and movement.'[49] Throughout her writing on London one is struck by Woolf's sense of the fleeting and contingent, the idea that London, like Baudelaire's Paris, is the site of perpetual change and transition, as the city seemingly reinvents itself before one's eyes. For Woolf, nowhere is this process more apparent than on Oxford Street, a 'gaudy, bustling, vulgar street', which 'reminds us that life is a struggle; that all building is perishable; that all display is vanity.'[50]

In allowing her to escape the solitude and introspection of the writer's life, as well as the confinements of class and gender, the act of walking was for Woolf both an act of recollection, as the streets evoked memories of earlier walks, and also an act of creativity, as, like so many writers, she carried out much of her creative thinking, planning and 'scene-making' as she walked.[51] Woolf described this process of recreating the streets, fictionalising the life she witnessed there as she passed through it, as 'street-haunting', a lifelong habit which, according to her biographer, Hermione Lee, began in 1904, when Woolf first moved to Gordon Square in Bloomsbury.[52] Here, Woolf was to embark upon her London odyssey, as she roamed through the streets, recording her impressions, her memories, and becoming the detached observer, the *flâneuse*: 'London was her past, which she traced and retraced, meeting her previous selves as she went. It was her key to the culture. It unsettled identity, turned her from a writer, wife, sister, aunt, friend, woman, into an unobserved observer.'[53]

Ostensibly a light-hearted account of one woman's walk through London in search of a pencil, and often invoked by feminist critics as documentary evidence of the female experience of walking in the early twentieth-century city, the culmination of Woolf's pedestrian endeavours is her short essay, 'Street Haunting', first published in 1927. Subtitled 'A London Adventure', Woolf's essay invokes Machen's own 'London Adventure' written three years earlier, and both texts share not only a digressive form, but also a sense of the profound and intrinsic strangeness of London street life.

'When the desire comes upon us to go street rambling', Woolf begins, 'the pencil does as a pretext [...] as if under cover of this excuse we could indulge safely in the greatest pleasure of town life in winter – rambling the streets of London.'[54] Escaping from the solitude of her room Woolf celebrates the chance to enter into 'that vast anonymous army of anonymous trampers'; in doing so, however, 'we are no longer quite ourselves', she writes, for in escaping from our room we have also 'shed the self our friends know' in favour of the anonymity of the crowd.[55]

Transformed by our entry into the crowd and stripped of our customary defences, Woolf likens the newly immersed walker to an oyster broken from its shell, vulnerable yet incredibly receptive to its surroundings: 'a central oyster of perceptiveness, an enormous eye.' The primary function, indeed the only function, of this all-seeing eye, this hyper-perceptive pedestrian, is to record, instinctively, those sensations that flash across its retina: 'We are only gliding smoothly on the surface. The eye is not a miner, not a diver, not a seeker after buried treasure. It floats us smoothly down a stream, resting, pausing, the brain sleeps perhaps as it looks.'[56] Here, then, is the ultimate detached observer; so detached it seems, that its eyes and, no doubt, its legs are working independently of its brain.

On one level, Woolf's essay simply records the observations of a walker on a late afternoon stroll through London in winter; but it is about many other things too: the fleeting beauty of the city street; and the ways in which the imagination moulds the image that the eye records. It is, however, principally concerned with the ways in which identity can be easily mislaid in the crowd, and how having been lost, however momentarily, one can see the world anew: 'Am I here, or am I there?', asks Woolf, 'Or is the true self neither this nor that, neither here nor there, but something so varied and wandering that it is only when we give the rein to its wishes and let it take its way unimpeded that we are indeed ourselves?'[57] This sense of self as something fragile and free-floating, lends Woolf's essay a disconcerting sense of unreality, as if she cannot wholly rely upon the evidence of her own eyes. The dreamlike intensity of her prose recalls Poe's 'Man of the Crowd' and an earlier London street-scene; for here too we see 'the velocity and abundance of life', that Poe's narrator witnessed, alongside that sense of the crowd as a sentient being wholly impervious to its surroundings: 'But the main stream of walkers at this hour sweeps too fast to let us ask such questions. They are wrapt, in this short passage from work to home, in some narcotic dream [...] Dreaming, gesticulating, often muttering a few words aloud, they sweep over the Strand and across Waterloo Bridge.'[58] Having accomplished her mission and purchased her pencil, Woolf returns home to 'enclose the self which has been blown about at so many street corners, which has battered like a moth at the flame of so many inaccessible lanterns, sheltered and enclosed.'[59]

If, then, London has its *flâneuse*, and a tradition of literary wandering to set alongside that of Baudelaire's Paris, what of that other great city of walkers and writers, New York? In his book, *The Flâneur: A Stroll through the Paradoxes of Paris*, Edmund White claims that 'Americans are particularly ill-suited to be *flâneurs*', arguing that his countrymen are inhibited both by an excessive work ethic and an urge towards self-improvement, traits which place them at odds with the decidedly leisurely ethos of the *flâneur*.[60] But can White's observation really be correct?

As we have seen, it is Walt Whitman who is usually identified as the foremost poet of the New York street; but while Whitman celebrates the city in his work, substituting the crowd for nature as a subject worthy of poetic expression, he remains just as easily associated, in the public imagination at least, not with the crowded boulevard but with the open road, and with the freedom of the solitary walker.[61] Whitman is, or at least likens himself to, the vagabond rather than the casual stroller, and it is to a later figure, much indebted to Whitman, to whom we must turn in our search for the true American *flâneur*.

Light and sassy. With a slight twist and a slight bounce. With the top half of his body slightly thrust forward. Head back. It was a beautiful walk. Casual. Confident.[62]

He walked on his toes, stretched his neck, and angled his head, all to add an inch or two to his height. I never walked the same after I met him.[63]

These remarks describe the distinctive walk of Frank O'Hara (1926–1966), the poet whose daily strolls formed the backdrop to his casual and inconsequential portraits of New York City in the 1950s and 1960s. 'It's my lunch hour,' writes O'Hara, 'so I go/ for a walk among the hum-colored/ cabs. First, down the sidewalk/ where labourers feed their dirty/ glistening torsos sandwiches/ and Coca-cola, with yellow helmets/ on [...]'[64] Immediately, we find ourselves immersed amidst the sights and sounds of the city; not a grandiose vision of the city, however, but rather an everyday city of the marginal and the incidental, a meandering vision captured at street level.

Born in Baltimore and educated in Massachusetts, O'Hara didn't move to New York until 1951, where he soon began work at the Museum of Modern Art. It was here that he began to write in earnest, his poems appearing, almost effortlessly, to capture the vitality of the city around him. Largely influenced by Surrealism and the French Symbolists, in particular Rimbaud, as well as Whitman and William Carlos Williams, O'Hara instinctively took New York as his subject, the canvas on to which he transposed his autobiographical sketches of city life. Freewheeling through the city on his lunch break, O'Hara was not the Baudelairian *flâneur* of seemingly limitless leisure, but rather a hyperactive stroller juggling work with an epic social life, yet still able to access the fabric of the city at will. 'Unlike his nineteenth-century predecessor', writes one critic, 'the twentieth-century remake of the Baudelairian *flâneur* takes cabs, swings in hammocks and chews over gossip. But he actively *participates* in the city, and rubs shoulders with the crowd.'[65]

The result of O'Hara's peripatetic lunchtime excursions from the Museum of Modern Art was *Lunch Poems* (1964), a collection which displays O'Hara's preference for what he calls the 'elbow of noon walks', as he loses himself amidst the crowds of lunchtime workers.[66] Elsewhere, in poems such as 'The Day Lady Died', O'Hara, like Woolf before him, maps out the city in precise topographical detail, outlining walks for future readers: 'It is 12:20 in New York a Friday/ three days after Bastille day, yes/ it is 1959 and I go get a shoeshine/ because I will get off the 4:19 in Easthampton/ at 7:15 [...] I just stroll into the PARK LANE/ Liquor Store and ask for a bottle of Strega and/ then I go back where I came from to 6th Avenue/ and the tobacconist in the Ziegfeld Theatre [...]'[67]

New York was, for O'Hara, a completely self–contained universe. He travelled widely, particularly in Europe, yet even in poems such as 'Rhapsody' in which O'Hara recalls the world outside New York, his memories are transposed upon familiar New York streets; while in 'Meditations in an Emergency', O'Hara contrasts the immediacy of city life with what he sees as the emptiness which lies beyond its borders: 'One need never leave the confines of New York to get all the greenery one wishes – I can't even enjoy a blade of grass unless I know there's a subway handy, or a record store or some other sign that people do not totally *regret* life.'[68] 'I love this hairy city', he exclaims in 'To the Mountains in New York', 'I walk watching, tripping, alleys/ open and fall around me like footsteps.'[69]

O'Hara reveals a city in motion, defined by endless speed and circulation, its streets clogged with traffic and pedestrians battling for mastery of the sidewalks. New York demonstrates the evolution the *flâneur* has undergone in order to face up to the demands of twentieth–century urban life. Walking in New York is not, as O'Hara suggests dismissively, comparable to 'the poet's walk in San Francisco.'[70] Instead it is something altogether more vigorous and demanding, a hectic, headlong rush through the unforgiving streets, the brutal repetition of foot against asphalt:

'the shape of the toe as/ it describes the pain/ of the ball of the foot, / walking on/ asphalt/ the strange embrace of the ankle's/ lock/ on the pavement/ squared like mausoleums/ but cheerful/ moved over and stamped on/ slapped by winds.'[71]

Frank O'Hara died in 1966, aged 40, fatally injured by a dune buggy on Fire Island. By this time he was, of all the members of the New York School (which included Ashbery, Schuyler, Guest and Koch), the poet most closely identified with the city. Indeed, his celebrity was such that he was frequently followed and accosted during his lunchtime strolls by would-be poets and admirers eager to catch a glimpse of him. Since his death, his work has been endlessly revived and anthologised but perhaps the most heartfelt, and certainly the most apt, epitaph to his work is the artist Jasper Johns' *Memory Piece (Frank O'Hara)*, completed in 1970, some four years after O'Hara's death. Comprising a rubber cast of O'Hara's foot (taken in 1961) mounted on the inside flap of a lid hinged to the top of a wooden box, *Memory Piece* is the ultimate walker's memorial. For when the lid is closed, the foot presses down upon a layer of sand, and when opened one can see the mould of O'Hara's foot alongside its footprint. 'With the completed sculpture', writes Timothy Gray, 'viewers can continue to have O'Hara's peripatetic foot, or at least a mould of it, make its mark. Long after the poet's death, we can continue to see the paths he walks.'[72]

Notes
[1] Walter Benjamin, *Charles Baudelaire: A Lyric Poet in the Era of High Capitalism*, trans. by Harry Zohn, London: New Left Books, p. 54. According to Rebecca Solnit, Benjamin's claim is apocryphal: 'No one has named an individual who took a tortoise for a walk, and all who refer to this practice use Benjamin as their source.' Solnit, p. 200. The impact of such a practice would surely have been eclipsed, however, by the writer Gérard de Nerval who used famously to take a lobster for a walk, attached to a silk ribbon as a leash. See Richard Holmes, *Footsteps,* pp. 212–216

2 Robert Walser, 'The Walk' in *The Walk*, London: Serpent's Tail, 1992, 54–104, p. 65

3 Zygmunt Bauman, 'Desert Spectacular', in Keith Tester, ed., *The Flâneur*, London: Routledge, 1994, 138–157, p. 138. While the English language fails to provide a direct translation of *flânerie*, there does appear to be an Italian equivalent: '*andare a Zonzo*', meaning 'to waste time wandering aimlessly.' 'It's an idiomatic expression,' writes Francesco Careri, 'whose origins have been forgotten, but it fits perfectly into the context of the city wandered by the *flâneurs*.' Careri, p. 185

4 Solnit, p. 198

5 See James V. Werner, *American Flâneur: The Cosmic Physiognomy of Edgar Allan Poe*, London: Routledge, 2004, p. 7, and Anke Gleber, *The Art of Taking a Walk: Flânerie, Literature, and Film in Weimar Culture*, Princeton, NJ: Princeton University Press, 1999, p. 6

6 Charles Baudelaire, 'The Painter of Modern Life' in *The Painter of Modern Life & Other Essays*, ed. and trans. by Jonathan Mayne, London: Phaidon, 1995, 1–41, p. 9

7 Solnit, p. 200

8 Or in other words: 'The aimless stroll *is* the aim [...] The *flâneur* wanders in search of the aim of his wandering.' Bauman, 'Desert Spectacular', p. 139

9 'If the *flâneur* is thus turned into an unwilling detective', writes Walter Benjamin, 'it does him a lot of good socially, for it accredits his idleness. He only seems to be indolent, for behind this indolence there is the watchfulness of an observer who does not take his eyes off a miscreant.' Benjamin, *Charles Baudelaire*, pp. 40–1

10 Charles Baudelaire, *Intimate Journals*, trans. by Christopher Isherwood, London: Picador, 1990, p. 23

11 The writer, Rémy de Gourmont, declared that Poe in fact belonged to French rather than to American literature. Peter Ackroyd, *Poe: A Life Cut Short*, London: Chatto & Windus, 2008, p. 160

[12] Kevin J Hayes, *Edgar Allan Poe*, London: Reaktion, 2009, p. 7. Poe and Baudelaire shared a remarkable affinity: reading Poe for the first time, Baudelaire was to discover 'not simply certain subjects, which I had dreamed of, but *sentences* which I had thought out, written by him twenty years before.' Ackroyd, *Poe*, p. 159

[13] Baudelaire, 'The Painter of Modern Life', p. 7

[14] Edgar Allan Poe, 'The Man of the Crowd', in *The Fall of the House of Usher and Other Tales*, ed. by David Galloway, London: Penguin: 2003, 131–140, p. 139

[15] Benjamin, *Charles Baudelaire*, pp. 36–7

[16] Benjamin, *Charles Baudelaire*, pp. 48 & 50

[17] Benjamin, *Charles Baudelaire*, p. 69

[18] Benjamin, *Charles Baudelaire*, p. 72

[19] Benjamin, *Charles Baudelaire*, p.50

[20] Benjamin, *Charles Baudelaire*, p.154

[21] Gershom Sholem, qtd. in Solnit, p. 198

[22] Susan Sontag, ed., Walter Benjamin, *One-Way Street and Other Writings*, trans. by K. Shorter & E. Jephcott, London: Verso, 1979, Introduction, p. 19

[23] Walter Benjamin, 'A Berlin Chronicle' in *Reflections: Essays, Aphorisms, Autobiographical Writings*, ed. by Peter Demetz, New York: Schocken, 1986, p. 9

[24] Edmund White, *The Flâneur: A Stroll through the Paradoxes of Paris*, London: Bloomsbury, 2001, p. 39

[25] Benjamin, *Charles Baudelaire*, p. 47

[26] Walter Benjamin, 'Robert Walser' (1929), in *Robert Walser Rediscovered: Stories, Fairy-Tale Plays, and Critical Responses*, ed. and trans. by Mark Harman, Hanover, NE: University Press of New England, 1985, pp. 144–7

[27] Mark Harman, ed., *Robert Walser Rediscovered*, Introduction, p. 2

[28] Susan Sontag, 'Walser's Voice' (1982) in Robert Walser, *The Walk*, Foreword, p. viii

[29] George C. Avery, *Inquiry and Testament: A Study of the Novels*

and Short Prose of Robert Walser, Philadelphia: University of Pennsylvania Press, 1968, p. 204. Avery claims that Walser was to write more than fifty such 'walks' (p. 227)

[30] Susan Sontag, 'Walser's Voice', in Walser, *The Walk*, p. ix

[31] Robert Walser, 'Helbling's Story' (1914) in *The Walk*, 32–43, p. 32

[32] Robert Walser, 'The Street (1)' (1919) in *The Walk*, pp. 123–4

[33] Robert Walser, *Masquerade and Other Stories*, ed. by William H. Gass & trans. by Susan Bernofsky, London: Quartet, 1993: 'Market' (1908), p. 36; 'The Aunt' (1918), p. 105; 'Energetic' (1924), p. 123; 'A Lump of Sugar' (1925), p. 154; 'Sunday Walk (1)' (1925), p. 159

[34] Samuel Frederick, 'Stealing the Story: Robert Walser's *Robber-Novel*', in *Digressions in European Literature: From Cervantes to Sebald*, ed., Alexis Grohmann & Caragh Wells, Basingstoke: Palgrave Macmillan, 2011, 130–142, p. 138

[35] William H. Gass, ed., Robert Walser, *Masquerade and Other Stories*, Introduction, p. xv

[36] Walser, 'The Walk', p. 54

[37] Walser, 'The Walk' pp. 85–8

[38] William H. Gass, ed., Robert Walser, *Masquerade and Other Stories*, Introduction, p. ix

[39] For an ongoing English translation of Seelig's book, *Wanderungun mit Robert Walser* (1957), see 'Wandering with Robert Walser' at http://goldenrulejones.com/walser/. Seelig was responsible for maintaining an interest in Walser's work after his death, an interest which has blossomed in recent years, culminating with the English translation of Walser's *Microscripts* (2010). As early as 1917, Walser began writing in a miniaturised script barely a millimetre in height, and many pages of these microscripts were discovered after his death. Initially dismissed as undecipherable, they were later found to be written in a form of shorthand and were painstakingly transcribed. See Robert Walser, *Microscripts*, ed. and trans. by Susan Bernofsky, New York: New Directions, 2010

[40] The critic Janet Wolff is credited with coining this term in an article entitled 'The Invisible *Flâneuse*: Women and the Literature of Modernity' (1985). Here, she argues that faced with the sexual division of public space in the late nineteenth century, a time in which women were often confined to the home and prohibited from strolling alone, the *flâneuse* did not, could not, exist. This article can be viewed at http://www.fll.vt.edu/Johnson/431405paristexts/wolff.pdf

[41] Hermione Lee, *Virginia Woolf*, London: Chatto & Windus, London, 1996, p. 552

[42] Amongst the dissenting voices to this view is that of Geoff Nicholson, whose comments are a perfect illustration of the violent response that Woolf's work can provoke in some readers. Nicholson questions whether *Mrs Dalloway* is, in fact, a walking novel at all, claiming that its heroine 'is so little a walker that the very idea of having to walk to the florist is an incredible excitement that sets her off thinking, "What a lark! What a plunge!" 'You'd slap her, wouldn't you?' concludes Nicholson, pp. 65–6

[43] Virginia Woolf, *Mrs Dalloway*, ed. by Elaine Showalter, London: Penguin, p. 3

[44] Woolf, *Mrs Dalloway*, p. 6

[45] Woolf, *Mrs Dalloway*, p. 11

[46] John Sutherland, 'Clarissa's Invisible Taxi', in *Can Jane Eyre be Happy? More Puzzles in Classic Fiction*, Oxford: OUP, 1997, 215–224, p. 222

[47] Campbell was a once well-known long-distance walker, accounts of whose record breaking feats can be found in books entitled *Feet of Clay* (1991) and *On Foot through Africa* (1994). She is best remembered today, however, for her third book, *The Whole Story* (1996), a walker's *mea culpa* in which she owns up (unwisely it would seem, judging by the savaging that she received subsequently from the media) to having spent much of her journey across America not on foot but in a truck, largely as a consequence of having fallen pregnant en route with one of her

support team. See Nicholson, pp. 253–6

[48] Sutherland, p. 223

[49] Virginia Woolf, 'Oxford Street Tide', in *The London Scene: Five Essays by Virginia Woolf,* London: Hogarth Press, 1982, 16–22, p. 17

[50] Woolf, 'Oxford Street Tide', in *The London Scene,* p. 21

[51] Julia Briggs, *Virginia Woolf: An Inner Life,* London: Penguin, 2005, p. 278

[52] Lee, p. 206

[53] Lee, p. 553

[54] Virginia Woolf, 'Street Haunting: A London Adventure', in *Selected Essays,* ed. by David Bradshaw, Oxford: OUP, 2008, 177–187, p. 177

[55] Woolf, 'Street Haunting', p. 177

[56] Woolf, 'Street Haunting', p. 178

[57] Woolf, 'Street Haunting', p. 182

[58] Woolf, 'Street Haunting', p. 185

[59] Woolf, 'Street Haunting', p. 187

[60] White, *The Flâneur,* p. 40

[61] Phillip Lopate writes of Whitman: 'His positive love of crowds was unusual for the nineteenth century, when many American intellectuals were expressing a fastidious scorn for the "mob." [...] Whitman saw no contradiction between joining a crowd and being alone. His solitary, essential self was not threatened by the masses; rather, he took energy and comfort from their surrounding bodies.' Phillip Lopate, 'On the Aesthetics of Urban Walking and Writing' at http://mrbellersneighborhood.com/2004/03/on-the-aesthetics-of-urban-walking-and-writing

[62] Joe Brainard describing Frank O'Hara and qtd. in David Herd, 'Stepping Out with Frank O'Hara', in *Frank O'Hara: New Essays on the New York Poet,* ed. by Robert Hampson & Will Montgomery, Liverpool: Liverpool University Press, 2010, 70–85, p. 83

[63] Larry Rivers describing O'Hara and qtd. in Timothy Gray, *Urban Pastoral: Natural Currents in the New York School,* Iowa City, IA: University of Iowa Press, 2010, p. 25

[64] Frank O'Hara, 'A Step Away from Them', in *The Selected Poems of Frank O'Hara*, ed. by Donald Allen, New York: Vintage, 1974, p. 110

[65] Hazel Smith, *Hyperscapes in the Poetry of Frank O'Hara: Difference/Homosexuality/Topography*, Liverpool: Liverpool University Press, 2000, pp. 65–6

[66] Frank O'Hara, 'Pistachio Tree at Chateau Noir', *Lunch Poems*, San Francisco, CA: City Lights Books, 1964, p. 53

[67] O'Hara, 'The Day Lady Died', *Selected Poems*, p. 146

[68] Frank O'Hara, 'Meditations in an Emergency', *The Collected Poems of Frank O'Hara*, ed. by Donald Allen, New York: Alfred A. Knopf, 1972, pp. 197–8

[69] O'Hara, 'To the Mountains in New York', *Collected Poems*, p. 198

[70] O'Hara, 'Personal Poem', *Selected Poems*, p. 157

[71] O'Hara, 'Walking', *Collected Poems*, p. 476

[72] Gray, p. 36

Experimental Walking

*We are doubtless about to witness a complete upheaval of the
established fashions in casual strolling and prostitution.* Louis Aragon[1]

*Dérive was a continuous flow in which protagonists embarked upon a
Surrealist trip, a dreamy trek through varied Parisian passageways,
forever on foot, wandering for hours, usually at night, identifying subtle
moods and nuances of neighbourhoods [...] Through these real and
imagined perambulations, Situationists became latter-day flâneurs,
aimless urban strollers who weren't quite so aimless.* Andy Merrifield[2]

In his book *Walkscapes: Walking as an Aesthetic Practice*, Francesco
Careri identifies the period of transition from Dada to Surrealism
(1921–1924) as the first of 'three important moments of passage
in art history [...] in which an experience linked to walking
represented a turning point'; the second is the emergence of the
Situationist Movement from the Letterist International (1956–
1957); and the third, the movement from Minimal Art to Land
Art (1966–1967).[3] According to Careri, the link between walking
and art is such that 'for the entire first part of the 20th century',
walking was experienced as 'a form of anti-art.'[4] For having
rejected the hitherto constrained and circumscribed nature of art,
the act of walking was propelled into the realm of aesthetic
practice, in an, admittedly unsuccessful, attempt to reclaim urban
space. This process, by which an everyday action was transformed
into an experimental one, was inaugurated (and, for the Dadaists
at least, largely concluded) in a single event on a single day: 14
April 1921. For it was on this date, in Paris, at three in the

afternoon, in the rain, that eleven individuals, amongst them André Breton, Louis Aragon and Philippe Soupault, conducted a 'lay pilgrimage' to the church of Saint-Julien-le-Pauvre. This was the Dada Movement and their meeting was planned as the first in a series of urban excursions to the 'banal places' of the city, a serious aesthetic undertaking supported by press releases, photographs, numerous proclamations, and the following flyer, outlining their aims:

> The Dadaists passing through Paris, as a remedy for the incompetence of guides and dubious pedants, have decided to undertake a series of visits to selected places, in particular to those places that do not truly have any reason to exist. It is incorrect to insist upon the picturesque, historical interest and sentimental value. The game has not yet been lost, but we must act quickly. Participation in this first visit means answering for human progress, for possible destructions and responding to the need to pursue our action, which you will attempt to encourage by any means possible.[5]

Upgrading the role of the *flâneur* from disinterested observer to participant in an aesthetic experiment, the Dadaists hoped to attribute a symbolism to the act of walking which would transfer artistic value away from the realm of objects, towards space and performance. Rather than merely drawing attention to the city that surrounded them, the Dadaists hoped to actively encourage its habitation, in the process transforming the perception of those overlooked quarters of the city, of which Saint Julien was emblematic. These were bold plans outlining a new vision for the city, but in the event expectations rather outstripped reality, as the assembled crowd of fifty or so journalists and spectators were subjected to a dismal series of performances, the highlight of which was a random recitation of words from the Larousse dictionary. 'After an hour and a half', writes Mark Polizzotti, 'the already thinning crowd, soaked by the rain and bored by the speeches, went home. The Dadaists themselves repaired to a nearby café to take stock. The bottom line: they had bombed.'[6]

Unsurprisingly, given the calamitous nature of the event, the Dadaists chose not to repeat the experience of April 14, which remains the sole example of their planned series of excursions. In a more charitable interpretation of the event and its aftermath, Francesco Careri argues that 'the work lies in having thought of the action to perform, rather than in the action itself', adding that 'the project was not taken to its conclusion because it was already finished. Having performed the action in that particular place was the equivalent of having performed it on the entire city.'[7] This troubling gap between thought and action, plan and performance, was to remain, however, and three years later, with the Dadaists now having merged with the Surrealists, another such excursion was to end in farce: on this occasion, in May 1924, André Breton, Louis Aragon, Max Morise and Roger Vitrac, decided to leave Paris for a more prolonged stroll through the countryside. By this time, the Dadaist search for the banal had given way to the Surrealist belief in chance, as Breton's biographer, Mark Polizzotti, once again describes:

> The four men caught a train to Blois, a town they had picked at random on the map, then set off haphazardly on foot; their only planned detours would be for eating and sleeping. Their goal was an absence of goals, an attempt to transpose the chance findings of psychic automation onto the open road [...] During rest stops they composed automatic texts, many of which contained reflections of their momentary surroundings. But for the most part, they wandered aimlessly throughout the French countryside, conversing all the while, resolutely following their lack of itinerary.[8]

As before, the idea seemed plausible, but almost from the start the random element of the stroll and the absence of any fixed goal proved to have a detrimental effect on Breton's sanity.

Bedevilled by 'increasingly numerous and disturbing phantoms', matters reached crisis point in the bathroom of a small inn where Breton suddenly noticed an enormous white cockroach crawling towards him: 'Now everyone knows there's no such thing as a white cockroach!', exclaimed Breton, before fleeing the bathroom in panic.[9] Shortly afterwards a fight broke out between Aragon and Vitrac, the former having grown increasingly exasperated by Vitrac's 'insistence on seeing every minor coincidence as a major revelation.' Walking without direction or purpose had, in this instance at least, resulted in mental disturbance and violence. Ten days after having set out, Breton put an end to the debacle and the four Surrealists returned to Paris by train.[10]

Despite, or perhaps because of, its unexpected results, the practical value of this trip was by no means dismissed by Breton, who was to describe it as a 'quartet deambulation', or an example of automatic writing in real space, in which the act of walking was directly imprinted upon the map of a mental territory.[11] *Deambulation*, the Surrealist term for this 'automatic' form of walking, has been defined as 'the achievement of a state of hypnosis by walking, a disorientating loss of control. It is a medium through which to enter into contact with the unconscious part of the territory.'[12] The characteristic 'loss of control' is certainly evident in the description of the walk above, albeit not quite in the manner that Breton might have hoped for, and just as the excursions planned by the Dadaists were never completed, so too was this rural foray never to be repeated. Deambulation, however, was to remain a much practised element of Surrealist activity in Paris itself, where the city's outskirts were the site for what the Surrealist poet, Jacques Baron, was later to describe, with questionable enthusiasm, as an 'interminable stroll.'[13]

Later in 1924 Breton was to publish his first *Manifesto of Surrealism* in which he was to define the term for the first time, proclaiming: 'I believe in the future resolution of these two states, dream and reality, which are seemingly so contradictory, into a kind of absolute reality, a *surreality*, if one may so speak.'[14] But the Surrealist contribution to the literature of walking is not to be found here, nor does it rest upon the hapless adventures of its principal adherents outlined above. Instead, the concept of random or automatic walking first espoused by Breton, and the search for the banal places of the city described by their Dadaist forbears, find its most eloquent expression in a trio of 'novels' published in the late 1920s, all of which take Paris as their subject. André Breton, Louis Aragon and Philippe Soupault first met in 1918 and soon after they were to launch the review, *Littérature*; but it was later in the following decade that Aragon's *Le Paysan de Paris* (*Paris Peasant*, 1926), Breton's *Nadja* (1928) and Soupault's *Les Dernières Nuits de Paris* (*The Last Nights of Paris*, 1928) were published, providing us with an extraordinary triptych of pre-war Parisian street life, structured around the series of walks which they describe.

Unlike *Nadja* and *The Last Nights of Paris*, both of which are principally dictated by sexual desire and the search for the 'eternal female', Aragon's *Paris Peasant* is largely polemic in tone, displaying a hostility against what he sees as an attack on the very fabric of the city. *Paris Peasant* outlines two walks undertaken in Paris between 1924 and 1926, in which Aragon, while acknowledging the erotic aspects of the street (and describing the customary visit to a brothel), also bears witness to a city disappearing before his eyes:

The covered arcades which abound in Paris in the vicinity of the main boulevards and which are rather disturbingly named *passages*, as though no one had the right to linger for more than an instant in these sunless corridors [...] The great American passion for city planning [...] now being applied to the task of redrawing the map of our capital in straight lines, will soon spell the doom of these human aquariums.[15]

In fact, the 'human aquarium' which was to be the principal focus of Aragon's attention, the Passage de l'Opéra, was already under threat of destruction when he began writing the book, and by the time it was published it had been destroyed.[16] As Aragon walks through the Passage de l'Opéra and later takes a night–time stroll through the park at Buttes–Chaumont (accompanied by André Breton and Marcel Noll), his meanderings reveal what he describes as 'a charming multiplicity of appearances and provocations [...] a mobile human tapestry, continually fraying, continually being repaired.'[17] Neither purely experimental in form, nor straightforwardly a documentary account of his experiences, *Paris Peasant* remains an unclassifiable work whose attempts to directly transpose the 'surreality' of everyday life on to paper is never wholly convincing.[18] Indeed, Aragon's 'novel' reads less like an example of avant–garde experimentalism and more as an ethnographical account of Parisian street life, an attempt to document what one critic has described as the 'mythology' of a society through an analysis of its behaviour and customs.[19] In this respect, Aragon's text may be seen as a precursor to the work of Walter Benjamin, and it was in fact *Paris Peasant* that first drew Benjamin's attention to the significance of the arcades and to the role of walking as a cultural act, leading him to comment on the impact of Aragon's book: 'Each evening in bed I could not read more than a few words of it before my heartbeat got so strong I had to put the book down.'[20] *Paris Peasant* is unlikely to provoke quite the same reaction in the contemporary reader, although with its digressive style and its preoccupation with the overlooked and neglected aspects of the city, Aragon's book does bear a strong resemblance to many of today's psychogeographical accounts of urban life.

Looking back on his friendship with Aragon some twenty years later, André Breton was to write: "I still recall the extraordinary role that Aragon played in our daily strolls through Paris. The localities that we passed through in his company, even the most colourless ones, were positively transformed by a spellbinding romantic inventiveness that never faltered and that needed only a street-turning or a shop-window to inspire a fresh outpouring.'[21] Of course, Breton's comments can be applied equally to his own work, and not least to *Nadja*, his attempt to transcribe the Surrealist ethos to the novel. 'Nothing is imagined in *Nadja*', writes Maurice Nadeau, 'everything is utterly, rigorously true.'[22] Yet within the works of Breton and his contemporaries nothing is as it seems, and Breton's biographer Mark Polizzotti has claimed the opposite, noting that 'the first thing is, this is not a novel. The second: it's not strictly factual, either.'[23] Truth or fiction, *Nadja*, more than any other Surrealist text, foregrounds the city street as the site of the uncanny, the coincidental and the unexpected. It is here that Breton outlines the freedom to be gained by following one's feet wherever they might lead you, the random stroll acting as the catalyst, transforming the mundane and the everyday into the marvellous:

> Meanwhile, you can be sure of meeting me in Paris, of not spending more than three days without seeing me pass, toward the end of the afternoon, along the Boulevard Bonne-Nouvelle between the *Matin* printing office and the Boulevard de Strasbourg. I don't know why it should be precisely here that my feet take me, here that I almost invariably go without specific purpose, without anything to induce me but this obscure clue: namely that it (?) will happen here. I cannot see, as I hurry along, what could constitute for me, even without my knowing it, a magnetic pole in either space or time.[24]

It was as the result of one such stroll on an October afternoon, 'one of those idle, gloomy afternoons I know so well how to spend', that Breton had exactly the type of chance encounter that the Surrealist stroll was supposed to facilitate: 'She carried her head high, unlike everyone else on the sidewalk. And she looked so delicate she scarcely seemed to touch the ground as she walked. A faint smile may have been wandering across her face.'[25]

Nadja, the mysterious heroine of Breton's book, was inspired by one of the writer's actual lovers, who, in true surrealist fashion, ended her days in an asylum. Written in the misleadingly objective tone of a medical case-study, *Nadja* is a surrealist romance filled with those correspondences, coincidences and uncanny juxtapositions that characterised the movement, and Breton's account is dominated by the spontaneous and unexpected, reflecting an outlook in which chance governs all. As we follow Breton and Nadja through Paris, on foot, it becomes clear that the act of walking has become the central metaphor of the text. For *Nadja* is encoded in the language of walking, idling, and wandering; movement is meaning and the journey is what supplies both a form to the text and a structure to the lives of its protagonists. 'If you desired it,' says Nadja to Breton, 'I would be nothing, or merely a footprint.'[26] And as Nadja sleepwalks through the text like a ghost haunting the streets, it is only the record of her movement, the trace of her footsteps, that gives her identity any substance. She has become symbolic of Paris itself, and it is only as long as she continues to move through the street – 'the only region of valid experience for her' – that she can be said to exist at all.[27]

Published in the same year as *Nadja*, and as a consequence somewhat overshadowed by it, Philippe Soupault's *The Last Nights of Paris* has much in common with Breton's work, also detailing a series of randomly motivated strolls through Paris, in search of an equally elusive quarry. Like Nadja, Soupault's heroine, Georgette, is also the subject of a series of involuntary meetings and occult episodes as she is pursued through the Parisian night; and just as Nadja comes to symbolise the city, so too does Georgette, transforming herself and her surroundings as she passes through them:

Georgette resumed her stroll about Paris, through the mazes of the night. She went on, dispelling sorrow, solitude or tribulation. Then more than ever did she display her strange power: that of transfiguring the night. Thanks to her, who was no more than one of the hundred thousands, the Parisian night became a mysterious domain, a great and marvellous country [...] That night, as we were pursuing or, more exactly, tracking Georgette, I saw Paris for the first time. It was surely not the same city [...] As I looked at it, it contracted. And Georgette herself became a city.[28]

'I know, we know', writes Soupault, 'that in Paris death alone has power to quench that pointless thirst, to bring to a close an aimless walk.'[29] For Soupault, as for Breton and Aragon before him, walking had become a way of life, an instinctive reflex which cannot be restrained.

The Surrealist movement promised much in its numerous *Manifestoes*; but reality was to prove stubbornly mundane, while the realm of divine enchantment was to remain tantalisingly out of reach. Automatism turned out to provide distinctly uninspired results, and as far as walking was concerned, a lot of legwork was expended with little obvious result. The surrealist engagement with communism had a rather desultory effect on those members more used to the spirit of playful abandon from which the movement had arisen, and in a foretaste of the problems that were to beset Guy Debord a generation later, Breton managed to alienate almost all his former allies as Surrealism collapsed under the weight of personal vendetta and infighting. *Paris Peasant*, however, remains, alongside *Nadja* and *The Last Nights of Paris*, as a memorial to a way of life under threat. For as the ill-fated dalliance with communism was to demonstrate, the day of the apolitical and dispassionate stroller was at an end. What surrealism in general, and these books in particular, were to emphasise is the fact that the idle stroller can no longer stand at the wayside or retreat to his armchair, but must now face up to the destruction of his city. In the aftermath of the war, the streets were radicalised as never before and revolutionary change was in the air. If the urban wanderer was to continue his aimless strolling then the very act of walking had to become subversive, a means of reclaiming the streets for the pedestrian.

By the end of the Second World War the Surrealist movement was effectively over and the publication of Maurice Nadeau's *History of Surrealism* (1944) was to provide its epitaph. The tension between aesthetic and political impulses within the movement had inevitably resulted in splits and counter-movements, and it was as a response to a perceived lack of political radicalism that many of the avant-garde collectives of post-war Europe were formed. Movements as diverse and ephemeral as Cobra, the Lettrist International and the Imaginist Bauhaus formed a new avant-garde fuelled by new revolutionary sentiments; but they were hampered both by a lack of direction and, more crucially, members.[30] Acknowledging their debt to the playful subversion of Dada and Surrealism, these movements continued to proclaim the need for a new society, free from the homogenising effects of capitalist development; but it was only with the emergence of the Situationist International in 1957, under the firm, if not tyrannical, grip of Guy Debord that a momentum for change began to appear. Debord, however, like Breton before him, was soon to display exactly those dictatorial tendencies that had reduced the Surrealists to an exhausting round of infighting and expulsions, and in a similar vein, he was equally disinclined to acknowledge the clear debt the Situationists owed, both to Surrealism and to earlier traditions of urban exploration.

The term with which Debord has become most closely associated and which has since come wholly to dominate any discussion of walking as an aesthetic or political practice finds its first, and oft-repeated, definition in his 'Introduction to a Critique of Urban Geography', written in September 1955 and later published in the Belgian journal *Les Lèvres Nues*:

The word *psychogeography*, suggested by an illiterate Kabyle as a general term for the phenomena a few of us were investigating around the summer of 1953, is not too inappropriate. It does not contradict the materialist perspective of the conditioning of life and thought by objective nature. Geography, for example, deals with the determinant action of general natural forces, such as soil composition or climatic conditions, on the economic structures of a society, and thus on the corresponding conception that such a society can have of the world. *Psychogeography* could set for itself the study of the precise laws and specific effects of the geographical environment, consciously organized or not, on the emotions and behaviour of individuals. The adjective *psychogeographical*, retaining a rather pleasing vagueness, can thus be applied to the findings arrived at by this type of investigation, to their influence on human feelings, and even more generally to any situation or conduct that seems to reflect the same spirit of discovery.[31]

Of course, it is precisely this 'pleasing vagueness' which has since allowed so many writers to identify themselves and their work with this movement. Psychogeography becomes for Debord the point where psychology and geography intersect. Gone are the romantic notions of an artistic practice; here we have an experiment to be conducted under scientific conditions and whose results are to be rigorously analysed. The emotional and behavioural impact of urban space upon individual consciousness is to be carefully monitored and recorded; its results are to be used to promote the construction of a new urban environment that both reflects and facilitates the desires of its inhabitants; and its transformation is to be conducted by those people skilled in psychogeographical techniques. The principal tool at the psychogeographer's disposal, claims Debord, is the aimless drift, or *dérive*, which enables its practitioner to ascertain the true nature of the urban environment as he passes through it. Hence, emotional zones that cannot be determined simply by architectural or economic conditions must be revealed by the *dérive*; the results of which may then form the basis of a new cartography characterised by a complete disregard for the traditional and habitual practices of the tourist:

> The production of psychogeographical maps, or even the introduction of alterations such as more or less arbitrarily transposing maps of two different regions, can contribute to clarifying certain wanderings that express not subordination to randomness but complete *insubordination* to habitual influences [...] A friend recently told me that he had just wandered through the Harz region of Germany while blindly following the directions of a map of London. This sort of game is obviously only a mediocre beginning in comparison to the complete construction of architecture and urbanism that will someday be within the power of everyone.[32]

Written in 1956, but first published in the *Internationale Situationniste* #2 in December 1958, Guy Debord's 'Theory of the Dérive' describes 'a technique of transient passage through varied ambiances', involving 'playful-constructive behaviour and awareness of psychogeographical effects; which completely distinguishes it from the classical notions of the journey and the stroll.'[33] Of course, this statement is a highly contentious one, for it seems hard to think of the *dérive* in terms other than of those strolls undertaken by the Surrealists a generation earlier. Yet, on closer inspection, although both appear to involve an element of chance and lack a pre-ordained direction, the *dérive* does not demonstrate the pure submission to unconscious desire that characterised the surrealist wanderings or the journeys of the strolling *flâneur*.[34] For although the *dérive* may lack a clear destination, it is not without purpose; on the contrary, the *dériveur* is conducting a psychogeographical investigation and is expected to return home having noted the ways in which the areas traversed resonate with particular moods and ambiences. In fact, it has been claimed that far from being the aimless, empty-headed drifting of the casual stroller, Debord's principle is nearer to a military strategy and has its roots, not in earlier avant-garde experimentation, but in military tactics, where drifting is defined as 'a calculated action determined by the absence of a proper locus.' In this light, the *dérive* becomes a strategic device for reconnoitring the city, 'a reconnaissance for the day when the city would be seized for real.'[35] In short, the *dérive* takes the wanderer out of the realm of the disinterested spectator and places him in a subversive position as a revolutionary following a political agenda; the *dériveur* is a foot soldier in a Situationist militia, an advance guard sent out to observe enemy territory.

Debord balances his theoretical concerns with more practical information, suggesting that the *dérive* should be conducted in small groups of two or three people and noting that its average duration is a single day, although acknowledging that one sequence of *dérives* lasted for around two months. Indeed, as Ralph Rumney was later to admit, for some the *dérive* could become the work of a lifetime:

I began to understand what it was through Debord, not so much because he talked about it, but because he practised it. And ever since I have never, or hardly ever, done anything else. My whole life became a *dérive*. I was gripped, fascinated by the idea [...] In Paris we wandered from café to café – we went where our feet and our inclinations carried us. We had to make do with very little money. I still wonder how we managed. We did *dérives* in Paris in an extremely limited zone. We discovered routes to go from one place to another that were more like detours [...] You discover certain places in a city that you start to appreciate, because you are welcomed in a bar or because suddenly you feel better [...] if you set off on a *dérive* in a good state of mind, you'll end up finding a good place. Yes, that's what it is, and I'd even say if you put me in an unknown town I will find the place where I should be.[36]

Storms and other types of precipitation, continues Debord, are apparently favourable, but prolonged rains can render such activities almost impossible; the use of taxis is not forbidden but can alter the nature of the *dérive*. In conclusion, Debord writes: 'The lessons drawn from the *dérive* permit the drawing up of the first surveys of the psychogeographical articulations of the modern city. Beyond the discovery of unities of ambiance, of their main components and their spatial localization, one comes to perceive their principal axes of passage, their exits and their defences. One arrives at the central hypothesis of the existence of psychogeographical pivotal points.'[37]

So, the stage has been set. Debord has provided us with our theoretical underpinning as well as furnishing us with practical advice. It is 1958, Paris is ripe for revolutionary change and, armed with the *dérive*, we are sent into the field. It is at this point, however, that one cannot help but notice that while the theoretical and instructive elements of psychogeography are manifest, the actual results of all these experiments are strangely absent. Trawling through the extensive literature on psychogeography and situationism, one is hard pressed to find any concrete examples of the results of such psychogeographical activity. 'Perhaps not surprisingly', one commentator has observed, 'the Situationists didn't do much in the way of travel – they were too busy talking, fighting, writing manifestos and being expelled to get much travelling done.'[38]

By 1962, the Situationist movement had split, as tensions between artistic and political priorities resurfaced once again. The Second Situationist International was now separated from the Specto–Situationist International, the latter group, under Debord and Vaneigem, now free to pursue an increasingly overt political agenda; and thanks to the translation of their works into English, situationism is today much better known for its emphasis on revolutionary politics than it is for its cultural component. Considered solely on its merits as a practical tool at the vanguard of a revolutionary movement, psychogeography must be considered an abject failure. For the meagre results of prolonged theorising reveal such a paucity of useful material that it is barely surprising that psychogeography fell from favour. In this respect, as in so many others, the fate of psychogeography resembles that of Surrealist automatism, where a prominent theoretical position at the outset was quickly followed by a realisation of its obvious limitations and its quiet demotion.

Looking back upon his former friendship with Debord (a period culminating in his inevitable expulsion from the Situationist movement), Scottish beat writer, pornographer and junkie Alexander Trocchi was to write: 'I remember long, wonderful psychogeographical walks in London with Guy [...] he took me to places in London I didn't know, that he didn't know, that he sensed that I'd never have been to if it hadn't been with him. He was a man who could discover a city.'[39] This search for De Quincey's 'Northwest Passage', a metaphor for that concealed entrance to the magical realm which had been at the forefront of early Situationist ideas, was soon to be forgotten, however, as Debord became increasingly preoccupied with a Marxist revisionism that had little time for the unfettered romanticism that Trocchi had so fondly recalled. But ultimately Debord came to recognise the essentially personal nature of the relationship between the individual and the city, sensing that this subjective realm was always going to remain at odds with the objective mechanisms of the psychogeographical methodology that sought to expose it: 'The secrets of the city are, at a certain level, decipherable,' he wrote, 'but the personal meaning they have for us is incommunicable.'[40]

Resisting the subjective and mysterious currents that the *dérive* promoted, Debord became increasingly dogmatic in his insistence upon a rigorous examination of the spectacular society – a society whose seductive surface belied the repressive realities of capitalist consumption. Debord's *Society of the Spectacle* was published in 1967 and its allusive and often ambiguous series of *apercus* proved tailor-made in providing the slogans that would adorn Paris during the uprising the following year. Debord's iconic work may not mention psychogeography by name yet, in its depiction of the ways in which the essential emptiness of modern life is obscured behind an elaborate and spectacular array of commodities, Debord has much to say to the urban wanderer. For amidst our immersion in this world of rampant consumerism and regimented monotony, street life has been suppressed, and the hostility towards the pedestrian that drove the *flâneur* from the streets of nineteenth-century Paris continues unabated today. The urban wanderer has been subordinated to the 'dictatorship of the automobile' as a new urban landscape emerges, a non-place dominated by technology and advertising whose endless reflective surfaces are devoid of individuality.[41] This is the future which Debord had attempted to avert.

In his biography of Debord, Andy Merrifield positions his subject outside the tradition of his avant-garde predecessors, Baudelaire, Benjamin and Breton; and instead, in emphasising his political agenda, he places Debord and his comrades from the 1968 uprising alongside their revolutionary forbears from 1848. Indeed, in his search for what he regards as Debord's true antecedents, he travels even further back through France's revolutionary past, for it is not the figure of the *flâneur* who is invoked here, but instead his more militant ancestor, the *frondeur.*

Debord idolized Retz [Cardinal de Retz, Jean François Paul de Gondi], the master of deception, the folk hero and trusted patron of Paris's poor and dangerous classes, who between 1648 and 1652 helped incite the street protests against Louis XIV, revolts that became known as 'The Fronde'. Retz welcomed the name *frondeur,* a term originally applied to rampaging gangs of street ruffians who brandished slings (*frondes*) and ran riot across medieval France. Seventeenth-century *frondeurs* took pride in wearing this once pejorative appellation; Retz and his coterie of aristocratic dissidents appropriated it in their risky revolt. Debord was a particularly distant cousin of Retz, as it were, many times removed; he was the cardinal's twentieth-century alter ego [...] both men would lead, in exile, a fugitive and vagabond existence. Together they'd become aesthetes of subversion and Debord the *frondeur* of our spectacular age.[42]

If, then, Debord is to be viewed within a politically more radical tradition than many, if not all, of his counterparts in this account, his role within the admittedly less militant (and more pedestrian) tradition of the walker remains less clear. Yet Merrifield helps us to clarify this position by identifying Debord as a 'passive adventurer' who, despite his very active role in the politics of his day, has paved the way for an equally radical assault upon the 'urban unconscious':

Passive adventurers [...] are more sensitive explorers, more cerebral, more studious and solitary, reading a lot and dreaming often. Passive adventuring [...] is an art form, 'a question of intellectual gymnastics, understanding everyday exercises and practising the methodology of the imagination' [...] Voyages here are more commonplace, more carefully chosen: cities and cabarets, burlesque and books, wine and song, love and hate, intimacy and death [...] studying Debord's life and following his trail, one could justifiably wonder: what kind of adventurer was Guy Debord? In a way, it's obvious, but only now can we state it: he was a pre-eminent passive adventurer [...] Debord's life was an active voyage of discovery – engaging in covert activities here, disturbing the peace there; and yet, for all that, his enduring legacy is perhaps how he tapped the mysteries of the urban unconscious, unearthed the sentimental city, opening up its everyday heights and illuminated its nocturnal depths.[43]

In this light, Debord and the Situationists may be judged finally as unable to wholly divorce themselves from their avant-garde heritage; for just as Debord must be seen within a revolutionary context, so too must he and the Situationists be regarded within the more playful and experimental tradition of urban wandering. Furthermore, by characterising Debord as a voyager in the urban unconscious, Merrifield recalls the visionary tradition of Blake and De Quincey. Of course, the Situationists' moment came and passed and the ultimate failure of 1968 was to be followed by the movement's dissolution in 1972. Yet it was during this brief passage of time in Paris that *flâneur* and *frondeur* were to meet for the first, and to date, only time, a meeting which was to inspire a new and more politically active role for the next generation of urban walkers.

Notes

[1] Louis Aragon, *Paris Peasant*, trans. by Simon Watson–Taylor, London: Jonathan Cape, 1971, p. 29

[2] Andy Merrifield, *Guy Debord*, London: Reaktion, 2005, pp. 30–31

[3] Careri, p. 21. While this chapter is concerned with the first and second 'passages' in Careri's schema, the third and final of these, that which accounts for the emergence of Land Art, lies beyond the scope of this book. However, those looking for a discussion of this movement and its principal practitioners, amongst them Richard Long, Hamish Fulton and Robert Smithson, should read Careri's account (pp. 119–175) or visit the Walkart blog at http://walkart.wordpress.com/

[4] Careri, p. 21

[5] Careri, p. 75

[6] Mark Polizzotti, *Revolution of the Mind: The Life of André Breton*, London: Bloomsbury, 1995, p. 153

[7] Careri, p. 78

[8] Polizzotti, pp. 201–2

[9] Polizzotti, p. 202

[10] Polizzotti, p. 202

[11] Careri, p. 79

[12] Careri, p. 82. 'The Surrealists,' writes Careri, 'believed that urban

space could be crossed like our mind, that a non–visible reality can reveal itself in the city [...] Surrealism, perhaps without yet fully understanding its importance as an aesthetic form, utilised walking – the most natural and everyday act of man – as a means by which to investigate and unveil the *unconscious of the city*, those parts that elude planned control and constitute the unexpressed, untranslatable component in traditional representations.' Careri, pp. 87–8

[13] Careri, p. 83

[14] André Breton, *Manifestoes of Surrealism*, trans. by Richard Seaver & Helen Lane, Ann Arbor, MI: University of Michigan, 1972, p. 14

[15] Aragon, p. 28

[16] Michael Sheringham, *Everyday Life: Theories and Practices from Surrealism to the Present*, Oxford: Oxford University Press, 2006, p. 75

[17] Aragon, p. 50

[18] The historian of Surrealism, Maurice Nadeau, writes: 'Something of a problem presents itself in the form of books like *Nadja* and *Paysan de Paris*. Both are direct personal accounts of a short period spent in pursuit of "surreality", plus lengthy reflections on the very meagre events reported. Their frankness and the occasional power of the prose make up for the desultory form and the unblinking egoism of every page. But they fall about halfway between purely experimental writing and exposition.' Maurice Nadeau, *The History of Surrealism*, trans. by Richard Howard, London: Jonathan Cape, 1968, p. 27

[19] Michael Sheringham describes the narrator of *Paris Peasant* as adopting 'the guise of an ethnographer seeking to piece together the mythology of a society on the basis of close scrutiny of its material culture, and participatory observation in its rituals (notably in the sphere of consumption: eating, drinking, sex, and shopping).' Sheringham, p. 75

[20] Susan Buck–Morss, *The Dialectics of Seeing: Walter Benjamin and the Arcades Project,* Cambridge, MA: MIT Press, 1991, p. 33

[21] Simon Watson-Taylor, ed., Aragon, *Paris Peasant*, Introduction, p. 9

[22] Nadeau, p. 151

[23] Mark Polizzotti, ed., André Breton, *Nadja*, trans. by Richard Howard, London: Penguin, 1999, Introduction, p. ix

[24] Breton, *Nadja*, p. 32

[25] Breton, *Nadja*, pp. 63–4

[26] Breton, *Nadja*, p. 116

[27] Breton, *Nadja*, p. 113

[28] Philippe Soupault, *The Last Nights of Paris*, trans. by William Carlos Williams, New York: Full Court Press, 1982, pp. 73–4

[29] Soupault, p. 41

[30] The Lettrist International (1952–7), itself the product of the earlier Lettrist Group (1948), and a forerunner to The Situationist International (1957–72), was to identify the act of walking as a means of challenging the *status quo*: 'The practice of walking in a group, lending attention to unexpected stimuli, passing entire nights bar-hopping, discussing, dreaming of a revolution that seemed imminent, became a form of rejection of the system for the Lettrists: a means of escaping from bourgeois life and rejecting the rules of the art system.' See Careri, p. 92. Those seeking a detailed understanding of the short-lived, and often invisible, series of movements and counter movements that characterise the pre-Situationist decade before 1957 should consult Stewart Home's *The Assault on Culture: Utopian Currents from Lettrisme to Class War*, Edinburgh: AK Press, 1991

[31] Guy Debord, 'Introduction to a Critique of Urban Geography' (1955), in Ken Knabb, ed., *Situationist International Anthology*, Berkeley, CA: Bureau of Public Secrets, 1981, p. 5

[32] Debord, 'Introduction to a Critique of Urban Geography', in Knabb, p. 7

[33] Debord, 'Theory of the Dérive', in Knabb, p. 50

[34] Sadie Plant writes: 'Unlike surrealist automatism, the *dérive* was not a matter of surrendering to the dictates of an unconscious mind or irrational force [...] Nor was everything subordinated to

the sovereignty of choice: to *dérive* was to notice the way in which certain areas, streets, or buildings resonate with states of mind, inclinations, and desires, and to seek out reasons for movement other than those for which the environment was designed. Sadie Plant, *The Most Radical Gesture: The Situationist International in a Postmodern Age*, London: Routledge, 1992, p. 59

[35] Simon Sadler, *The Situationist City*, Cambridge, MA: MIT Press, 1982, p. 81

[36] Ralph Rumney, *The Consul*, trans. by Malcolm Imrie, London: Verso, 2002, pp. 65–66. Rumney was the founder member (the only member) of The London Psychogeographical Committee and was present at the formation of the Situationist International in July 1957 at Cosio d'Arroscia in Italy. While Rumney was clearly gripped by the idea of the *dérive*, he was also openly dismissive of the notion that such a concept was one which originated with the Situationists: 'Of course, it wasn't a new discovery', he writes, 'it had always existed [...] The Letterists gave it a name and a methodology [...] At the level of ideas, I don't think we came up with anything which didn't already exist.' Rumney, p. 37

[37] Debord, 'Theory of the Dérive', in Knabb, p. 53

[38] Antony & Henry, eds., *Lonely Planet Guide to Experimental Travel*, London: Lonely Planet, 2005, p. 22

[39] Greil Marcus, *Lipstick Traces: The Secret History of the Twentieth Century*, London: Secker & Warburg, 1990, p. 385

[40] Sadler, p. 80

[41] Guy Debord, *Society of the Spectacle*, trans. by Ken Knabb, London: Rebel Press, 1992, p. 97

[42] Merrifield, pp. 81–2

[43] Merrifield, pp. 119–20

The Return of the Walker

Nobody wants to be thought of as a 'shallow topologist.' Geoff Nicholson[1]

I've taken to long-distance walking as a means of dissolving the mechanised matrix which compresses the space-time continuum, and decouples human from physical geography. So this isn't walking for leisure – that would be merely frivolous, or even for exercise – which would be tedious. Will Self[2]

In Geoff Nicholson's *Bleeding London* (1997) his protagonist, Stuart London, has a peculiar secret; Stuart is married to Anita Walker and by day they run a company offering guided walks of the city, called, naturally enough, The London Walker. These excursions along London's established heritage trails are offset, however, by Stuart's true passion for the lost and overlooked quarters of the city. To this end he is attempting to walk every street in London, meticulously erasing each corresponding entry from his *A to Z* as he does so. In this way he hopes to perform an act of erasure which will, when complete, culminate in his own suicide. *Bleeding London* has since garnered little critical attention, and yet as a knowing parody of the growing fashion for psychogeographical excursions through London's edgelands, Nicholson's book highlights the degree of cultural significance with which, by the mid-1990s, in London at least, the act of walking had become imbued. For over the last thirty years we have witnessed a marked revival in the literary representation of walking, a revival which has been mirrored in film, performance, and visual art. Looking back over this period and commenting upon the accretion of arcane and frequently bizarre motivations with which walking has since become associated, Nicholson is in little doubt as to whom he holds responsible:

> To devise your own system of walking in London isn't easy, it requires resolve and maybe even perversity. The true London walkers avoid the obvious even if that means pursuing some grand, illogical, Quixotic, agenda. They walk in search of lines of force, unrecognised symbols, secret bunkers, evidence of conspiracy, seeking the Land of Cockayne or a new Jerusalem. Personally I blame the author Iain Sinclair for a lot of this.[3]

Born in Wales but resident in London for the last forty years, much of Iain Sinclair's work over this period falls within the boundaries of what he has described as his 'London Project', a series of poems and novels, as well as documentary studies and films, which celebrate London's lost spaces and reclaim for the city its dominant position within the pedestrian canon.[4] Sinclair's work has little overt connection with the ideological agenda of the Situationists but is heavily indebted both to the surrealist drift of Breton and Aragon and to the visionary tradition of London writers from William Blake to Arthur Machen. It was Sinclair's early work *Lud Heat* (1975) which first established his reputation, albeit retrospectively; for Sinclair's prose poem remained in some obscurity until the publication of Peter Ackroyd's acclaimed novel *Hawksmoor* (1985) a decade later, which was to acknowledge the influence of his ideas. Proposing an occult alignment between the architect, Nicholas Hawksmoor's, surviving London churches, *Lud Heat* argues that 'lines of force' can be mapped between these churches to reveal the true but hidden relationship between the city's financial, political and religious institutions:

> A triangle is formed between Christ Church, St George-in the-East and St Anne, Limehouse. These are centres of power

for those territories; sentinel, sphinx-form, slack dynamos abandoned as the culture they supported goes into retreat. The power remains latent, the frustration mounts on a current of animal magnetism, and victims are still claimed. St George, Bloomsbury, and St Alfege, Greenwich, make up the major pentacle-star. The five card is reversed, beggars in snow pass under the lit church window; the judgement is 'disorder, chaos, ruin, discord, profligacy.' These churches guard or mark, rest upon, two major sources of occult power: The British Museum and Greenwich Observatory.[5]

Some twenty years later, Sinclair was to describe a walk across London to the burial place of the Elizabethan Magus, Dr Dee, in Mortlake, summarising this excursion as 'a marriage of convenience between chiropody and alchemy'[6]; and it is precisely this union between the search for occult aspects of London's history and his attempts to uncover them on foot that has since become the hallmark of his work. Indeed, his entire project is underpinned by an unwavering belief in the significance of the act of walking, not merely as a means of accessing the city's neglected spaces but as an intrinsic part of the creative process itself. For Sinclair sees the walker–writer as a hybrid figure, whose work can clearly be distinguished from that of his more stationary counterparts:

I buy into a union between writing and walking. I think there is as much of that going on – or more – than what could be described as psychogeography. I have this notion that there are two kinds of writers: there's one called 'pods', and there's another called 'peds'. Peds are the kind of writers who very definitely have, within their writing, this rhythm of journeys and walks and pilgrimages and quests. And pods are these other writers who sit in a room and just draw the world to them in whatever ways they want to. And there is a very distinct gap between the two.[7]

While walking has always been bound up with Sinclair's work, from his earliest and most obscure publications from the late 1960s onwards, it was not until the release of *Lights Out for the Territory* (1997) that the true extent of this relationship between walking and his work was first revealed. Subtitled an account of 'nine excursions in the secret history of London', *Lights Out for the Territory* is as much a performative exercise as it is a literary one, as Sinclair and his companions use a series of walks across the city to trace out the occulted, or hidden message that lies beneath:

> The notion was to cut a crude V into the sprawl of the city, to vandalise dormant energies by an act of ambulant signmaking [...] (I had developed this curious conceit while working on my novel *Radon Daughters*: that the physical movements of the characters across their territory might spell out the letters of a secret alphabet. Dynamic shapes, with ambitions to achieve a life of their own, quite independent of their supposed author. Railway to pub to hospital: trace the line on the map. These botched runes, burnt into the script in the heat of creation, offer an alternative reading – a subterranean, preconscious text capable of divination and prophecy. A sorcerer's grimoire that would function as a curse or a blessing.)[8]

Lights Out for the Territory was the book which first brought Sinclair's work to the attention of a mainstream audience, and it is a work which reiterates his belief in the power of walking to shape our perception of the landscape. Yet just as Sinclair is alert to the avant-garde heritage of Aragon and Debord, he is no *flâneur*, for he is equally aware of the transformation this figure has been forced to undergo in order to face up to the rigours of the modern city:

> Walking is the best way to explore and exploit the city; the changes, shifts, breaks in the cloud helmet, movement of light

on water. Drifting purposefully is the recommended mode, tramping asphalted earth in alert reverie, allowing the fiction of an underlying pattern to reveal itself. To the no–bullshit materialist this sounds suspiciously like *fin-de-siècle* decadence, a poetic of entropy – but the born–again *flâneur* is a stubborn creature, less interested in texture and fabric, eavesdropping on philosophical conversation pieces, than in noticing *everything*.[9]

The *flâneur* has evolved: the bystander is now the participant; the aimless drift has given way to a more purposeful mode of travel; the stroller has become the stalker:

> The concept of 'strolling', aimless urban wandering, the *flâneur*, had been superseded. We had moved into the age of the stalker; journeys made with intent – sharp-eyed and unsponsored. The stalker was our role-model: purposed hiking, not dawdling, nor browsing. No time for the savouring of reflections in shop windows, admiration for the Art Nouveau ironwork, attractive matchboxes rescued from the gutter. This was walking with a thesis. With a prey [...] The stalker is a stroller who sweats, a stroller who knows where he is going, but not why or how.[10]

Sinclair's peculiar form of historical and geographical research is overlaid by a mixture of autobiography and literary eclecticism. But beneath this allusive surface lies a political engagement and a clear anger directed against the legacy of both Thatcherite and Blairite redevelopment. This political dimension owes little to the revolutionary fervour of the Situationists but shares a great deal with the mood of frustration and dismay to be found in the pages of Aragon's *Paris Peasant*. For *Lights Out for the Territory*, with its exploration of the hidden city and memorial to a lost London, replicates Aragon's anger at the destruction of the Parisian Arcades, highlighting the similarly destructive effects of London's recent redevelopment.

In an interview with *Fortean Times* Sinclair acknowledges his debt to the Surrealist stroll: 'I liked the notion of it', he claims, 'but it wasn't exactly what I was doing. I liked their notion of finding strange parks at the edge of the city, of creating a walk that would allow you to enter into a fiction.'[11] And yet as Sinclair exposes in *Lights Out*, London is increasingly a city in which the walker is under threat, repeatedly denied access, his progress resisted or curtailed, his movements closely monitored and recorded. In such an environment, in which the centre remains hostile to the pedestrian unwilling to align his movements to the heritage trail, the stroller, the stalker, must turn his back and strike out for the perimeter.

'One may sail easily around England, or circumnavigate the globe', wrote Ford Madox Ford in 1907, 'but not the most enthusiastic geographer [...] ever memorized a map of London. Certainly no one ever walks round it.'[12] A little less than a century later, however, and that was exactly the task which Iain Sinclair was to undertake in *London Orbital* (2002), an account of his epic journey on foot around London's orbital motorway, the M25. 'Everything I did was always based on walking', says Sinclair, 'so having decided that the M25 more or less described this perimeter fence of London, then the only way to deal with it from my point of view was to walk it.'[13] Sinclair's method of 'dealing' with the M25 involved a series of monthly walks taken over the course of a year, accompanied by many of the usual suspects from previous expeditions. Travelling in a counter-clockwise direction, the M25 walk began in January 1998 in Enfield, and over the next twelve months Sinclair and his companions recorded a journey through the unloved and often unregarded landscapes of London's outer limits. Those looking for a reason for such an excursion, however, a meaning to be derived from such an unlikely trajectory, will be disappointed. As always with Sinclair, the walk requires no justification, no excuses; it is a wholly self-fulfilling activity which accepts the implicit challenge presented by an environment so overtly hostile to the pedestrian. A more occult interpretation, however, is the suggestion that such a walk, taken in an anti-clockwise fashion, might, by reversing the passage of time, erase the past, the walk becoming a ritualistic attempt to 'exorcise the unthinking malignancy of the [Millennium] Dome, to celebrate the sprawl of London.'[14]

Travelling through a landscape so often characterised by invisible institutions, the motif of Sinclair's walk is the asylum and their forgotten inhabitants, a population which Sinclair regards as somehow emblematic of this suburban interzone. And so, as he approaches Shenley (formerly home to Shenley Hospital for psychiatric illness) Sinclair begins to interpret the walk as itself symptomatic of madness, an act of wilful forgetting, a dreamlike progression into a state of fugue:

> I try to explain my notion of our walk as a fugue [...] I found the term *fugueur* more attractive than the now overworked *flâneur*. Fugueur had the smack of the swear word, a bloody-minded Tommy muttering over his tobacco tin in the Flanders trenches. *Fugueur* was the right job description for our walk, our once-a-month episodes of transient mental illness. Madness as voyage [...] The fugue is both drift *and* fracture. The story of the trip can only be recovered by some form of hypnosis, the memory prompt of the journal or photo-album. Documentary evidence of things that may never have happened [...] In twentieth-century representations of the fugue, the walker disappears from the walk [...] The walker becomes a control freak, compulsively logging distances, directions, treading abstractions into the Ordnance Survey map. Scripting minimalist asides, copywriting haikus.[15]

London Orbital marks a further stage in the evolution of the walker in Sinclair's work, as we move from the *flâneur* to the stalker and now, finally, the *fugueur*. From detached observer to madman, Sinclair's metaphor demonstrates the ways in which the act of walking not only allows us a new understanding of our environment, but also how it can distance the walker from his surroundings, the metronomic rhythm of one's footsteps disengaging the memory and allowing it to float free from its moorings. For just as Virginia Woolf was to describe the loss of identity she experienced in the crowd, so too has Sinclair indicated the way in which the walker can lose himself in unfamiliar terrain: 'Walking where there is nothing familiar, nothing to stimulate personal memory, we are not ourselves; we must begin afresh, and that is the excitement'; 'I'm not really there when I'm walking', confesses Sinclair, and what he describes elsewhere as 'ambulatory amnesia' remains both an occupational hazard and an opportunity for renewal.[16]

Of course, the term with which Iain Sinclair is popularly associated today has more to do with the *dérive* than the fugue, for he is considered (regardless of the merits of the appellation) to be, above all else, a *psychogeographer*. Quite what this amounts to is difficult to assess, for as Geoff Nicholson has observed, in its current format, psychogeography appears to be little more than 'a way for clever young men to mooch around cities doing nothing much, claiming that they're [...] doing something really, you know, significant, and often taking Iain Sinclair as their role model.'[17] This is by no means a new development, however, for as early as 1991 the historian Patrick Wright was identifying the effects of Sinclair's growing reputation, noting that: 'In recent years, Sinclair's renegade charting of the city has provoked a whole industry.'[18] Indeed, regardless of Sinclair's oft-stated bemusement at the ubiquity of this term, it seems that psychogeography in its current incarnation is here to stay. For so successful, so recognisable and so widespread has Sinclair's method become that he appears to have inaugurated an entirely new genre of topographical writing centred upon London which has gone some way towards displacing Debord and situationism as the official psychogeographical brand. Alert, as ever, to this development, Sinclair writes:

For me, it's a way of psychoanalysing the psychosis of the place in which I happen to live. I'm just exploiting it because I think it's a canny way to write about London. Now it's become the name of a column by Will Self, in which he seems to walk about the South Downs with a pipe, which has got absolutely nothing to do with psychogeography. There's this awful sense that you've created a monster. In a way I've allowed myself to become this London brand. I've become a hack on my own mythology, which fascinates me. From there on in you can either go with it or subvert it.[19]

Despite Sinclair's comments, and those of other commentators who have questioned the authenticity of his psychogeographic credentials, Will Self has certainly written a great deal and walked a huge distance in support of this particular discipline.[20] He has described himself as engaged on a mission 'to untangle human and physical geography', an undertaking which began in the late, 1980s: 'My epiphany came in 1988, when one day I found myself standing in Central London with a day to kill.' Realising that despite having spent his entire life in London, he had never seen the mouth of the Thames, Self immediately got into his car and drove there. 'Needless to say it was nothing like I imagined', he says, and yet it was the realisation of 'how strongly this human-defined geography still holds sway', exerting unseen control over our every movement, that set him on the path he has followed subsequently.[21] And while he may be a relative latecomer to the burgeoning ranks of the psychogeographical community, his walking career has much deeper roots, as he explains in his foreword to Duncan Minshull's collection of walking scenes, *The Burning Leg* (2010):

I was raised to be a walker by my father. And when I say he was a walker, I mean 24-hour traverses of Dartmoor with only a few squares of chocolate and an apple for sustenance [...] I have come to prize his legacy, which was this: all those thoughts divulged at walking pace; the steady 4/4 beat of his metre as he read the landscape then interpreted it for me [...] Since his death the impulse I've always had to walk – but which was hobbled by the fetters of grosser housebound pleasures – has grown irresistible. It began conventionally enough with picturesque ascents in the Scottish hills and rambles along the Suffolk coast, yet soon enough I felt frogmarched towards a different kind of walking: an anti-Romantic pursuit of the sublime, not in nature, but in those portions of civilisation that are awesomely unregarded.

So it is that for the past six years, each summer, I have walked out from my home in South London along one of the cardinal compass lines: north then north-west, south then south-east – and so on. I have become fixated on the hinterland of the city – only closely observable on foot – that other travellers simply leap over by train and car. I have delighted in the curious oxbows of farmland left marooned by the course of fluvial motorways, and felt like an insurgent, tiptoeing along bramble-lined paths through a landscape devoid of people – until, that is, I reached a road.[22]

Self's reincarnation as a born-again pedestrian coincided with the termination of his previous incarnation as a much heralded drug user, a habit that came to an end shortly after his ejection from the then Prime Minister, John Major's, plane in 1997, having allegedly snorted heroin in the bathroom. Self's new habit rapidly took hold, however, and he was soon propelled on ever-longer journeys, as walks of 10 or even 20 miles gave way to treks of up to 100 miles at a stretch.[23] For as he explains, these gargantuan strolls simply replaced one form of elective torpor with another, granting access to exactly that state of fugue that Sinclair describes, in which the roles of writer and walker coalesce:

Of course, all my little walking tours were methods of legitimizing. Towards the end of my drug addiction it had occurred to me that the manias of cocaine, the torpors of heroin and the psychoses of the hallucinogens – all these were pre-existing states of mental anguish that only appeared to be self-induced, and so, perhaps, controllable, because of the drugs. So it was with the walking, which was a busman's holiday; for, while I trudged along, through fields, over hills, beside bypasses, I remained sunk deep in my own solipsism – then I returned to the chronic, elective loneliness of the writing life. The only real difference I could see between walking and writing was that engaged in the former my digestion achieved a certain [...] regularity, while when I wrote I became terribly constipated: a stylite typing atop a column of his own shit.[24]

Between 2003 and 2008, Self wrote a weekly column for *The Independent*, entitled 'Psychogeography', a selection of which were subsequently published as *Psychogeography* (2007) and its sequel *Psycho Too* (2009). In awarding psychogeography such mainstream recognition, however, Self's column merely reaffirmed the distance this term had travelled since its initial appearance in the *samizdat* publications of 1950s Paris, provoking a degree of scepticism in the minds of those who retained an affection for the radicalism of Debord's ideas. Of course, Self's column, as Sinclair rightly suggests, has little in common with the practice of psychogeography as originally conceived. Self does, however, display a truly original take on the idea of the long-distance walk, massively extending the scope of this activity through the simple, but revolutionary, expedient of inserting a train journey, or more frequently a flight, into the otherwise pedestrian itinerary. Applying such a technique, Self is able to transform a weekend break into a pedestrian epic, without, of course, having to experience the prolonged discomfort of the unabbreviated version:

In Toulouse, I would walk to my hotel, walk to the theatre [...] walk to dinner, limp to bed, and in the morning I'd do the whole thing in reverse: a nice weekend's stroll, covering some

1,300 miles. My wife, ever sceptical of these peregrinations, always says the same thing: 'Will you walk up and down the train?' She refuses to accept the musicality of my giant steps, their alternation of rhythmic striding and the fermata of the rail compartment.[25]

The scepticism displayed by Self's wife certainly seems legitimate, and yet to be fair to Self, his most far-flung excursions appear to deliver him to some of the world's most inhospitable pedestrian cities. Indeed, it is journeys to two such cities – Dubai and Los Angeles, along with an earlier account of a walk to New York, which are the subjects of his most extended commentaries. The first of these walks took place in November, 2006, as Self, describing himself as an 'ambulatory time traveller', sets sail for New York on a pedestrian voyage of discovery:

I resolved to walk to New York; in the interests of writing about the experience, certainly, yet also with objectives at once more pedestrian and more ambitious [...] I resolved to walk to New York because I wanted to explore. Here was a true Empty Quarter, and, as with other long walks I have taken out of my native city, I had the strong hunch that this would be the first time in the post-industrial era that anyone had ventured across it. True, I had walked from central London to Heathrow before, and I had heard of one adventurer who had walked from JFK to Manhattan, but I was certain I would be the first person to go the whole way, with only the mute, incurious interlude of a club class seat to interfere with the steady, two-mile-an-hour, metronomic rhythm of my legs, parting and marrying, parting and marrying.[26]

While Self's marathon excursion is undertaken, at least in part, as a foray into the unknown, an attempt to walk where no one has walked before, his motives are multiple, and the spirit of adventure is allied to deeper requirements, less easily remedied:

I resolved to walk to New York because I had business there, to explore; and, also, because in so doing, I hoped to suture up one of the wounds in my own, divided psyche: to sew together my American and my English flesh, my mother's and my father's body bags, sundered by marriage, rived by death. And maybe even, at a more grandiose level [...] to expiate the sense of weird culpability that had dogged me, ever since 11 September 2001 [...] Could my own, slow advance, needle-limbs piercing and repiercing the fabric of reality, sew up this singularity, this tear in the space-time continuum through which medievalism had prolapsed?[27]

There have been many motivations at work behind the feats of pedestrian endurance outlined in this book, but none surely can quite eclipse the dizzying ambition on display here, as Self attributes to the act of walking hitherto unsuspected reserves of temporal and psychic power. In the pages that follow, however, as we witness his progress across the city, these hopes are momentarily obscured, if not wholly deflated, by the more mundane realities of New York's eastern suburbs. For the landscape that Self encounters on his walk is an unremittingly dispiriting array of blighted apartment blocks and rubbish-strewn sidewalks; a marginal and disputed territory, in which the act of walking becomes an incongruous and highly visible means of transportation. In the end, however, with the walk safely completed, and with his psyche no doubt healed, Self is able to declare his mission a success:

It had worked, though, walking to New York. It had done exactly what I wanted it to do: the Atlantic had been siphoned off, the continental shelf jacked up, and Hayes, Middlesex, had been rammed unceremoniously into South Ozone Park.

That I had walked, continuously, from Stockwell in south London to Rivington Street in the Lower East Side of Manhattan, could not be denied – for my body told me that this was so; that it had covered some thirty-five miles over the past two days. And the body's awareness is so much more plangent than that of any mere mind. Bodies like mine have been walking distances like these for hundreds – Yea! thousands – of millennia; what can a few score years of powered rolling and whistling flight mean set beside this immemorial trudge?[28]

Self has described himself as a modern-day *flâneur*, and yet the journey which he records in *Walking to Hollywood* (2010) highlights the very real difficulties such a figure faces in a city which is so clearly designed with the driver, rather than the pedestrian, in mind. For just as Los Angeles, like so many American cities, is widely presumed, by Europeans at least, to pose almost insurmountable problems for the would-be walker, Self's experiences reveal not so much a hostile environment, as one in which the walker is simply presented with too many options:

Counter-intuitively, a grid-plan city forces more decisions on the walker than the winding folkways of an older more haphazard urbanity. Since diagonal progress can be made equally effectively by any given series of horizontal and perpendicular traverses, at each intersection the choice of two directions remains, maddeningly.[29]

If Self's observation is true, then cities such as New York and Los Angeles are, by their very nature, resistant to walking, possessing an inbuilt architectural aversion to the pedestrian, or at least to the *purposeless* pedestrian. For while their straightforward pattern may well aid the swift transit of those walking for a clearly defined reason, it is this very simplicity which somehow repels the digressive and meandering drift of the *dérive*, forcing the would-be *flâneur* to make choices, decisions, to plot a route rather than to let the city guide him. In short, it is precisely through helping the walker to find their way that these street plans deny one the possibility of getting lost; and it is perhaps for this reason that the older and more labyrinthine layout of cities such as Paris and London has proved historically more conducive to the aimless stroll.

Walking to Hollywood is not written as a documentary account of Self's journey, but rather forms the basis of a kind of fictional autobiography, a hallucinatory journey in which Self's walk elides into a truly bizarre exploration of identity and celebrity, in which all the characters of the book – Self included – are 'played' by Hollywood actors. In this way, Self's journey becomes less the subject of a book than of a film, albeit an uncut version shot in a single take:

Walking is so much slower than film – especially contemporary Hollywood movies, with their stuttering film grammar of split-second shots – and it isn't framed, when you walk you're floating in a fishbowl view of the world. There can't possibly be any editing: no dissolves, no cuts, no split-screens – and, best of all, no special effects, no computer-cheated facsimiles of the world.[30]

In contrast to *Walking to Hollywood*, with its mood of surreal intensity, Self's walk to Dubai is undertaken in a rather more reflective spirit. The walk begins at the house of JG Ballard in Shepperton, and was written up shortly before Ballard's death in 2009. For this reason, perhaps, the walk is overshadowed by the presence of Ballard himself, a figure whose own work both anticipates and celebrates the outlandish and hyper-real playground that Self's walk explores. For the ultimate destination of Self's essay 'Walking to the World' is 'The World' itself, an archipelago of 300 artificial islets, forming an 'exclusive' peninsula off the coast of Dubai.

Whereas Los Angeles presented Self with too many choices, Dubai appears to offer the pedestrian too few, if any at all. As Self soon discovers, walking in the city is seen principally as a 'leisure activity inseparable from retail opportunities' and as such is conducted within the air-conditioned splendour of the shopping mall.[31] For those foolhardy enough to walk elsewhere, however, a different fate awaits, that of invisibility; for despite his acutely incongruous transit across motorways and through endless construction sites, Self's unauthorised excursion is greeted with complete disregard: 'I saw plenty of pedestrians on my walk to The World', he writes, 'but without exception they all had black or brown skins.'[32] As the possessor of a white skin, Self is granted a status which seemingly permits him to walk unmolested and unquestioned, truly an invisible spectator in a landscape populated by an all too visible underclass.

Self completes what is, at times, an arduous journey and returns home. But throughout the walk, he seems preoccupied by the ultimate purpose of such an excursion. Can such a walk truly be said to offer an insight into the landscape denied to other modes of travel? Beyond the simple fact of having reached one's destination how can such a walk be judged to have been a success? Anticipating such questions, Self appears to challenge the very principles upon which walks such as his would seem to depend. For unless the 'method' he employs can deliver some kind of meaning, then why, he asks himself, is he there at all?:

I cursed myself for a fool, labouring along the pavement, past air-conditioned bus shelters. This time the airport walk hadn't worked; on previous journeys – from my house to New York, Los Angeles and even Zurich – the mediation of distance by legs alone, with only the dull pause of an airline seat interpolated, had pulled these landmasses into crushing proximity: it felt as if I had walked all the way [...] It struck me that it must have been because I had walked from Jim Ballard's house in Shepperton rather than my own, that the desired spatial consummation had not been achieved [...] as it was I felt tired, alienated and began to doubt the validity of my quest: what was the point of these rambles anyway? They told me nothing that I didn't know already, or, rather, my method imposed on the raw data of experience a prefabricated narrative: everywhere was the same; everyone was forced to follow the same road/rail/flight path, only I had escaped the man/machine matrix to saunter, barefoot, along the median strip.

But wasn't the truth that I was just as determined? Moreover, in eschewing my ground transport, my view of these alien lands was grossly circumscribed, while my ambitious mileages meant that I had no time to stop and stare [...] Instead, driven full speed ahead by my ambulatory engine, I sat inside the hot, rubbery compartment of my skull, maddened with frustration, staring out through the windscreen of my own eyes.[33]

Self's account of his walks, whether through New York, Los Angeles, or Dubai, all conform to a similar pattern, not simply in their structure, but in their mood: the enthusiasm of departure gradually giving way to a more questioning tone as tiredness sets in and the purpose of the walk becomes less clear. This, no doubt, is simply a natural response to the physical demands of covering such long distances, but in Self's case the Dubai walk, in which he experiences the outlandish automotive epiphany outlined above, seems to have been a walk too far, and marks the end of the series of long-haul excursions he had been conducting over the previous few years.

'But', concludes Self, 'might the need to feel our peregrinations have a purpose be part of our problem? In other words: should we perhaps not simply accept that all we are doing is going for a walk?'[34] It is this question of what, if any, meaning we should ascribe to the act of walking, which has been answered, if not lived, by a friend, and sometime walking companion of Self's, whose own journey through London's outer limits provides a domestic, but no less remarkable, equivalent to Self's feats of international pedestrianism.

First published in 1925, a year after Machen's *The London*

Adventure, James Bone's *The London Perambulator* is a similarly unclassifiable account, written in a dreamlike style that shares something of Machen's delight at the otherworldly nature of the city. Bone was the London Correspondent for the Manchester Guardian and 'The London Perambulator' was the pseudonym he employed for his column. Today, however, Bone's title has been resurrected, this time as the name of a documentary film exploring the work of another memorialist of London's hinterland, the self-proclaimed 'deep topographer', Nick Papadimitriou.

'I always walked a lot', recalls Papadimitriou. 'As a child growing up in Finchley, in the borough of Middlesex, walking was the way in which I got to know my world.'[35] Born in 1958, over the last twenty years Papadimitriou has been conducting, in a state of almost unwavering obscurity, an exhaustive and minutely detailed topographical examination of North London and Middlesex that has, somewhat belatedly, seen him assume the mantle of psychogeographer *par excellence*. Abandoning this term, however, in favour of what is, for the time being at least, the less hackneyed label of 'deep topographer', Papadimitriou has now become a figure of some reverence. Indeed, Iain Sinclair, in his recent introduction to Richard Mabey's *The Unofficial Countryside*, describes Papadimitriou as 'the most submerged inheritor' of a genealogy that stretches back to include such luminaries as Cobbett and Defoe; 'a solid invisible, tramping and haunting Mabey's familiar turf, the Colne Valley: the canals, reservoirs and sewage farms of the Watford–to–Heathrow corridor.'[36] Papadimitriou has also been a regular companion to Will Self on his psychogeographic journeys, including the outward leg of his 'walk' to New York, in which Self describes his friend as 'a walking compendium of fact, opinion and supposition: a great Blue Nile of verbiage, that, when it's diverted to mingle with my own thoughtful tributary, completely alters its hue.'[37] While earlier in the same account, Self describes Papadimitriou's position within what he calls, with some disdain, the 'psychogeographic fraternity':

Others, such as my friend Nick Papadimitriou, pursue what he prefers to term 'deep topography': minutely detailed, multi-level examinations of select locales that impact upon the writer's own microscopic inner-eye. He manufactures slides, in which are pinned ecology, history, poetry, sociology. Nick points out that most of the psychogeographic fraternity [...] are really only local historians with an attitude problem. Indeed, real, professional local historians view us as insufferably bogus and travelling – if anywhere at all – right up ourselves.[38]

Of course, establishing exactly what deep topography amounts to, let alone attempting to differentiate it from other forms of topographical activity, has proved difficult, not least because Papadimitriou has published so little on the subject (although his memoir *Scarp*, which takes its name from the truly unsung North Middlesex Tertiary Escarpment, is due to be published in 2012).[39] In conversation with the director of *The London Perambulator*, John Rogers, however, Papadimitriou has attempted to clarify his position:

What is deep topography? It's not a programme. It's an acknowledgement of the magnitude of response to landscape. Something that I don't see in most accounts that I read of landscape. I find there's two ways that descriptions of landscape go. One of them puts the person who is experiencing at the centre; and it always seems a little narcissistic to me: 'I respond to this', 'I spotted that'. It's more about them than about the landscape. And the other way it goes, it tends to be greened or touristed, one of the two. So there's either an attempt to place the landscape within a framework of mainstream green philosophy, or else it goes the other way, which is it just becomes touristic: 'The fields are really nice in April'. That sort of thing.[40]

Papadimitriou's 'Bedfont Court Estate', his contribution to Iain Sinclair's anthology, *London: City of Disappearances* (2009), provides a brief demonstration of deep topography in action. For while it begins in the manner of the local historian, albeit a historian whose chosen edge-land locale almost guarantees him pre-eminence in his field, Papadimitriou's meticulous account of an intensely unpromising landscape of abandoned sewage works and heavily policed perimeter fencing, manages, against all the odds, to convey a magical sense of place:

> All through the summer, drawn by the raw, unswerving energy of the jets, I returned obsessively to Heathrow Airport and environs. I was fascinated by the squat utility buildings of the 1940s and 1950s, but it was the unmapped zone, out beyond the airport's Western Perimeter Road, that attracted me most [...] I would take my camera and my plant recognition manuals and set out with an open eye for roadside skips and empty houses. I have spent years building up an archive of material – old photos, documents, household objects – recording traces of lives lived in the old county of Middlesex. Retrieving discarded letters, diaries and borough guides from these unofficial time capsules was one of the pleasures of my walks.[41]

Like Will Self, Papadimitriou's walking career has coincided with a protracted battle with addiction, the two often taking place in tandem and going some way to explain, if not account for, the intensity of his vision. Radiating outwards from his home in Child's Hill, North London, Papadimitriou's Middlesex odyssey has resulted in the creation of a vast archive of found objects: books, papers and assorted souvenirs of his journeys which reveal, in miniature, the compressed history of his local landscape. Papadimitriou dates the origin of his pedestrian obsession to July 1989 when he took what he calls his first 'conscious' walk, a journey between Amersham and Rickmansworth.[42] Ever since he has been tracing and retracing this invisible landscape, attempting to recover the lost history of a place which seems to hold immunity from the cultural and temporal imperatives which govern the centre. Here, amidst this liminal zone, Papadimitriou's topographical excavations have revealed a twofold depth, the vertical descent through time past provoking an equally deep emotional response to place:

> Behind the houses, across land dense with thistles and docks, a flimsy wire fence marked the lower slopes of the gravel mounds. It was hard to shake off the feeling that something disastrous had happened here. It was as if a major contamination of the site had occurred, an unreported Chernobyl emptying the area of its inhabitants. Folk memories had been replaced by the blur seen in a moment's glance from cars speeding through the new terminal.
>
> Yet the particular resonance didn't arise from relics left behind by previous users: the broken fences lost in weeds, a burned-out caravan parked in a yard, the dying damson bushes. There was a knotty multifariousness, a strata of cultural associations, evident in the broader brushstrokes of the place.[43]

'My ambition', claims Papadimitriou, 'is to hold my region in my mind. So that I am the region. So that when I die I literally become Middlesex in some kind of way. For me that is my highest spiritual aspiration.'[44] It is an aspiration which makes Papadimitriou the natural figure with which to conclude this account, for his particular obsession with lost landscapes, his articulacy in recording them, and, of course, his determination to carry out the necessary legwork, all confirm his position within the unbroken tradition of visionary walker-writers that have populated the preceding chapters. For in recording this 'knotty multifariousness' of place and the magnitude of his response to it, Papadimitriou has elevated the act of walking to something far beyond the commonplace. Here, once again, walking has proved itself capable of inspiring not merely an act of remembrance, but of initiating, in those who know how to look, a means of reading the landscape anew, exposing a vision of our local environment entirely at odds with that of the accepted or promoted version.

Notes
[1] Nicholson, *The Lost Art of Walking*, p. 117
[2] Will Self, 'South Downs Way' in *Psychogeography*, London: Bloomsbury, 2007, p. 69
[3] Nicholson, *The Lost Art of Walking*, p. 46
[4] 'That was the beginning of a London Project', writes Sinclair, 'I realised that what I was going to do for some time was cope with the mythology and the matter of London, incorporating diary material from my everyday life and essay-type explanatory and exploratory journeys and so on.' Iain Sinclair, *Entropy* (2; Summer 1997), qtd. in *Waterstone's Guide to London Writing*, ed. by Nick Rennison, Brentford: Waterstone's Booksellers, 1999, p. 190
[5] Iain Sinclair, *Lud Heat & Suicide Bridge*, London: Granta, 1997, p. 15
[6] Iain Sinclair & Marc Atkins, 'Watching the Watchman', in *Liquid City*, London: Reaktion, 2007, 83–85, p. 84
[7] Interview with Iain Sinclair, *Varsity*, 27 February 2009. Sinclair has restated repeatedly his belief in a transformative bond between walking and writing. In *Liquid City* (1997), for example, he writes of: 'Walks for their own sake, furiously enacted but lacking agenda. Strategic walks [...] as a method of interrogating fellow pilgrims. Walks as portraits. Walks as prophecy. Walks as rage. Walks as seduction. Walks for the purpose of working out the plot [...] Walks that release delirious chemicals in the brain as they link random sights [...] Savagely mute walks that provoke language.' Sinclair, *Liquid City*, p. 15
[8] Iain Sinclair, *Lights Out for the Territory*, London: Granta, 1997, p. 1. Sinclair's 'curious conceit' recalls that of Paul Auster's novel *City of Glass* (1985) in which the solitary detective, Quinn, wanders through a labyrinthine New York City, his daily walks spelling out, letter by letter, 'THE TOWER OF BABEL.' Sinclair's attempts to translate the equally unreadable nature of

his own city provide an equivalent to Quinn's pedestrian signature: 'I wait outside, toying with the notion that each essay so far written for this book can be assigned one letter of the alphabet. Obviously, the first two pieces go together, the journey from Abney Park to Chingford Mount: **V**. The circling of the City: an oval **O**. The history of *Vale Royal*, its poet and publisher: an **X** on the map. **VOX**. The unheard voice that is always present in the darkness.' Sinclair, *Lights Out*, p. 162

[9] Sinclair, *Lights Out*, p. 4

[10] Sinclair, *Lights Out*, p. 75

[11] 'City Brain' (2002), an interview with Iain Sinclair at www. forteantimes.com/features/interviews/37/iain_sinclair.html

[12] Ford Madox Ford, *The Soul of London* (1907), London: Phoenix Press, 1995, p. 31

[13] Iain Sinclair, *The Verbals: Iain Sinclair in Conversation with Kevin Jackson,* Tonbridge, Worple Press, 2003, p. 135.

[14] Iain Sinclair, *London Orbital*, London: Granta, 2002, p. 342

[15] Sinclair, *London Orbital*, pp. 119–121. In explaining his notion of the *fugueur*, Sinclair draws upon Ian Hacking's *Mad Travelers: Reflections on the Reality of Transient Mental Illness* (1998). Hacking describes the fleeting epidemic which was to originate in Bordeaux in the late nineteenth century, compelling its victims to embark upon random and seemingly compulsive pedestrian journeys across Europe. The first and most celebrated case to be recorded was that of Albert Dadas, an occasional employee of the local gas company, who was to become notorious for his involuntary travels, which were to take him as far as Algeria, Moscow and Constantinople. It all began 'one morning last July', wrote the then medical student, Philippe Tissié, in 1886, 'when we noticed a young man of twenty-six crying in his bed in Dr. Pitres's ward. He had just come from a long journey on foot and was exhausted, but that was not the cause of his tears. He wept because he could not prevent himself from departing on a trip when the need took him; he deserted family, work, and daily life to walk as fast as he could, straight ahead, sometimes doing 70

kilometers a day on foot, until in the end he would be arrested for vagrancy and thrown in prison.' Ian Hacking, *Mad Travelers: Reflections on the Reality of Transient Mental Illness*, Charlottesville, VA: University Press of Virginia, 1998, p. 7

[16] Iain Sinclair, *Ghost Milk: Calling Time on the Grand Project*, London: Hamish Hamilton, 2011, pp. 171 & 34

[17] Nicholson, *The Lost Art of Walking*, pp. 49–50

[18] Patrick Wright, *A Journey Through Ruins: The Last Days of London*, London: Radius, 1991, p. 164. In confirmation of Wright's observation, Sinclair's trek around the M25 has itself provoked a similar, and equally unlikely, expedition along the M62. For an account of this walk, undertaken by the Liverpool vicar, John Davies, in 2007, see 'Walking the M62' at http://johndavies. typepad.com/walking_the_m62/. Sinclair's own response to this walk can be found in *Ghost Milk*, pp. 311–313

[19] Iain Sinclair in interview with Stuart Jeffries, *The Guardian*, Saturday April 24, 2004. Also available at www.classiccafes.co.uk/ isinclair.htm

[20] Geoff Nicholson writes: 'You could argue that Will Self came a little late to the psychogeography party. Some have said that he isn't really a psychogeographer at all, which strikes me as just plain silly. If you want to call your newspaper column and your book *Psychogeography*, then hell, a psychogeographer is what you are.' Nicholson, *The Lost Art of Walking*, p. 117

[21] Will Self, 'On Psychogeography and the Places that Choose You', Interview with Frank Bures, *Worldhum*, 17 December 2007, at http://www.worldhum.com/features/travel-interviews/will_ self_on_psychogeography_and_the_places_that_choose_you_20 071217/

[22] Will Self, *The Burning Leg: Walking Scenes from Classic Fiction*, ed. by Duncan Minshull, London: Hesperus, 2010, foreword, pp. vii–ix. In revealing his obsession with London's overlooked hinterland, Self is describing an area that is by no means as unregarded as he suggests. Indeed, over the last forty years these interstitial 'non-places' have increasingly formed the backdrop to

an emerging literature which seeks to bring them to public scrutiny. The principal figure here is JG Ballard, a writer whose home in Shepperton has become something of a shrine for literary walkers since his death in 2009, and which features in walks conducted by Iain Sinclair, Will Self and Geoff Nicholson. Novels such as *Crash* (1973) and *Concrete Island* (1974) have been enormously influential in demarcating this perimeter, and alongside Richard Mabey's *The Unofficial Countryside* (1973), they can be regarded as the key texts in establishing the tradition which Self describes. Iain Sinclair has obviously taken up the mantle as chief celebrant for such spaces in his documentary accounts of the city, while, as we shall see, Self has continued, and dramatically extended, the scope of such excursions. The most recent addition to this particular canon is Paul Farley and Michael Symmons Roberts's *Edgelands* (2011).

[23] Will Self, 'On Psychogeography and the Places that Choose You', *Worldhum*, 17 December 2007

[24] Will Self, 'Spurn Head', in *Walking to Hollywood*, London: Bloomsbury, 2010, 327–428, pp. 336–7

[25] Will Self, 'So Long Toulouse', in *Psycho Too*, London: Bloomsbury, 2009, 166–168, p. 166

[26] Will Self, 'Walking to New York', in *Psychogeography*, London: Bloomsbury, 2007, 11–66, pp. 11–13

[27] Self, 'Walking to New York', in *Psychogeography*, pp. 13–14

[28] Self, 'Walking to New York', in *Psychogeography*, p. 61

[29] Self, *Walking to Hollywood*, p. 177. Elsewhere, however, Self provides an alternative, or rather an additional, explanation: 'People always say that you can't walk in American cities – implying that the very sidewalks curl up in front of your feet, or that the traffic mows you down. But that isn't it: no one walks through East New York, I'm forced to conclude, because it's so fucking dull.' Self, 'Walking to New York', in *Psychogeography*, p. 54

[30] Self, *Walking to Hollywood*, pp. 124–5

[31] Will Self, 'Walking to The World', in *Psycho Too*, 11–73, p. 27

[32] Self, 'Walking to The World', in *Psycho Too*, pp. 34–5

[33] Self, 'Walking to the World', in *Psycho Too*, pp. 37–8

[34] Self in discussion with Geoff Nicholson at http://joysofpedestriansim.blogspot.com/

[35] Nick Papadimitriou in *The London Perambulator*, dir. John Rogers, London, Vanity Projects, 2009

[36] Iain Sinclair in Richard Mabey, *The Unofficial Countryside* (1973), Dorset: Little Toller Books, 2010, Introduction, 7–13, p. 11. Sinclair has expressed great enthusiasm for the term 'deep topography', arguing that it has grown out of a characteristically practical tradition of English naturalism, in contrast with what he regards as the more conceptual and predominantly European tradition that gave rise to psychogeography. See Rogers, *The London Perambulator* (2009)

[37] Self, 'Walking to New York', in *Psychogeography*, p. 35

[38] Self, 'Walking to New York', in *Psychogeography*, pp. 11–12

[39] Many of Papadimitriou's collaborations with filmmaker John Rogers can be accessed online. Of particular interest is a series of talks recorded for Resonance FM in 2009, entitled *Ventures and Adventures in Topography*, in which their discussions of walks taken in and around London are interspersed with excerpts from early twentieth-century topographical accounts of the region. See http://venturesintopography.wordpress.com/podcasts/

[40] Nick Papadimitriou in conversation with John Rogers. In *The London Perambulator* (2009), Papadimitriou responds to the question, 'What is deep topography?' with the answer: 'It's about getting a very, very, dangerous balance between finding the overlooked, and showing it to the other people who have an eye for the overlooked and not making the overlooked into something that is gazed at [...] like people looking through the bars of a monkey house while some baboon plays with his penis or picks his arse. Which is probably a pretty good description of what me and Sinclair do anyway.'

[41] Nick Papadimitriou, 'Bedfont Court Estate', in *London: City of Disappearances*, ed. by Iain Sinclair, London: Hamish Hamilton, 2006, 612–619, p. 612

[42] According to Papadimitriou, his career as a writer also originates in the act of walking. Not as one might expect, however, as the result of having harnessed the act of walking for its creative potential, but rather more straightforwardly as a consequence of having come across a notebook lying in the road during a three-day walk north of St Albans. If, then, his career can be said to originate, literally, in the street, so too is Papadimitriou equally willing for his work to return there in due course: 'I'd like my work to be found in a skip in Southgate, or somewhere, in forty years time.' See Rogers, *The London Perambulator* (2009)

[43] Papadimitriou, 'Bedfont Court Estate', p. 615

[44] Rogers, *The London Perambulator* (2009)

Bibliography

On the long stroll through the literature and history of walking there are several milestones along the way: from the late nineteenth century onwards one comes across titles such as Alfred Barron's *Foot Notes, or, Walking as a Fine Art* (1875) and Arnold Haultain's *Of Walks and Walking Tours: An Attempt to Find a Philosophy and a Creed* (1914). The first major overview of the subject, however, and an undisputed classic in its own right, is Morris Marples' *Shanks's Pony* (1959). Following closely in Marples' footsteps, Miles Jebb's *Walkers* (1986) covers similar territory, while in recent years there have been a number of major contributions to the subject. Of these, Rebecca Solnit's *Wanderlust: A History of Walking* (1999); Joseph A. Amato's *On Foot: A History of Walking* (2004); and Geoff Nicholson's *The Lost Art of Walking: The History, Science, Philosophy and Literature, Theory and Practice of Pedestrianism* (2010) all proved particularly valuable in researching this account. The final word, however, should go to Francesco Careri's *Walkscapes: Walking as an Aesthetic Practice* (2002), a brilliant analysis of the aesthetic function of walking from its earliest biblical sources through to the avant-garde movements of the twentieth century.

In addition to the histories outlined above there are also a number of anthologies which gather together the finest examples of the many essays, poems and novels the act of walking has inspired. Amongst these, the best selection is to be found in *The Pleasures of Walking* edited by Edwin Valentine Mitchell (1934). More recently, Duncan Minshull has edited two further collections, *The Vintage Book of Walking* (2000) and *The Burning*

Leg: Walking Scenes from Classic Fiction (2010). Mention here should also be made of Bruce Chatwin's *The Songlines* (1987) which contains a broad selection of quotation and observation on the subject of walking and nomadism, culled from his notebooks.

Ackroyd, Peter, *Dickens*, London: Sinclair-Stevenson, 1990
 — *Blake*, London: Sinclair-Stevenson, 1995
 — *Poe: A Life Cut Short*, London: Chatto & Windus, 2008
Amato, Joseph A., *On Foot: A History of Walking*, New York: New York University Press, 2004
Andreotti, Libero & Costa, Xavier, eds., *Theory of the Dérive and Other Situationist Writings on the City*, Barcelona: Museu d'Art Contemporani, 1996
Antony, Rachael & Henry, Joel, eds., *The Lonely Planet Guide to Experimental Travel*, London: Lonely Planet Publications, 2005
Aragon, Louis, *Paris Peasant*, trans. by Simon Watson-Taylor, Cambridge, MA: Exact Change, 1995
Auster, Paul, *City of Glass*, Los Angeles, CA: Sun & Moon Press, 1985
Avery, George C., *Inquiry and Testament: A Study of the Novels and Short Prose of Robert Walser*, Philadelphia: University of Pennsylvania Press, 1968
Baker, Phil, 'Secret City: Psychogeography and the End of London', in *London from Punk to Blair*, ed. by Joe Kerr and Andrew Gibson, London: Reaktion, 2003
Barrell, John, *The Idea of Landscape and the Sense of Place 1730–1840: An Approach to the Poetry of John Clare*, Cambridge: Cambridge University Press, 1972
Barron, Alfred, *Foot Notes, or, Walking as a Fine Art*, Wallingford, CT: Wallingford Printing Company, 1875
Barta, Peter I, *Bely, Joyce, and Döblin: Peripatetics in the City Novel*, Gainesville, FL: University Press of Florida, 1996
Bate, Jonathan, *John Clare: A Biography*, London: Picador, 2003
Baudelaire, Charles, *Intimate Journals*, trans. by Christopher

Isherwood, London: Picador, 1990

– *The Painter of Modern Life & Other Essays*, ed. and trans. by Jonathan Mayne, London: Phaidon, 1995

Bauman, Zygmunt, 'Desert Spectacular' in *The Flâneur*, ed. by Keith Tester, London: Routledge, 1994

Belloc, Hilaire, *The Path to Rome*, London: George Allen, 1902

– 'The Idea of Pilgrimage' in *Hills and the Sea*, London: Methuen, 1906

Benjamin, Walter, *Charles Baudelaire: A Lyric Poet in the Era of High Capitalism*, trans. by Harry Zohn, London: New Left Books, 1973

– *One-Way Street and Other Writings*, trans. by K. Shorter & E. Jephcott, London: Verso, 1979

– *Reflections: Essays, Aphorisms, Autobiographical Writings*, ed. by Peter Demetz, New York: Schocken, 1986

Blake, William, *The Complete Poems*, ed. by Alicia Ostriker, London: Penguin, 2004

Blanchard, Marc Eli, *In Search of the City: Engels, Baudelaire, Rimbaud*, Saratoga, CA: Stanford University, Dept. of French & Italian, 1985

Bone, James, *The London Perambulator*, London: Jonathan Cape, 1925

Boseley, Mark, *Walking in the Creative Life of John Cowper Powys: The Triumph of the Peripatetic Mode*, Västeras, Sweden: Mälardalens Högskola, 2001

Bradbury, Ray, 'The Pedestrian', in *The Golden Apples of the Sun*, London: Hart–Davis, 1953

Brant, Clare & Whyman, Susan E., eds., *Walking the Streets of Eighteenth-Century London: John Gay's Trivia (1716)*, Oxford: Oxford University Press, 2007

Breton, André, *Manifestoes of Surrealism*, trans. by Richard Seaver & Helen Lane, Ann Arbor, MI: University of Michigan, 1972

– *Nadja*, ed. by Mark Polizzotti, trans. by Richard Howard, London: Penguin, 1999

Briggs, Julia, *Virginia Woolf: An Inner Life*, London: Penguin, 2005

Buck–Morss, Susan, *The Dialectics of Seeing: Walter Benjamin and the Arcades Project,* Cambridge, MA: MIT Press, 1991

Bunyan, John, *The Pilgrim's Progress*, ed. by Roger Sharrock, Harmondsworth: Penguin, 1965

Cappelorn, Niels Jorgen; Garff, Joakim; Kondrup, Johnny, eds., *Written Images: Soren Kierkegaard's Journals, Notebooks, Booklets, Sheets, Scraps, and Slips of Paper*, trans. by Bruce H Kirmmse, Princeton, NJ: Princeton University Press, 2003

Careri, Francesco, *Walkscapes: Walking as an Aesthetic Practice*, Barcelona: Editorial Gustavo Gili, 2002

Chatwin, Bruce, *The Songlines*, London: Viking, 1987
– 'Werner Herzog in Ghana', in *What Am I Doing Here?*, London: Jonathan Cape, 1989

Chesterton, GK, *Charles Dickens*, London: Wordsworth Editions, 2007

Clare, John, *The Journal, Essays, The Journey from Essex*, ed., by Anne Tibble, Manchester: Carcanet New Press, 1980
– *John Clare: Everyman's Poetry*, ed. by RKR Thornton, London: Phoenix, 1997
– *Major Works*, ed. by Eric Robinson, David Powell and Tom Paulin, Oxford: Oxford University Press, 2004

Coverley, Merlin, *Psychogeography*, Harpenden: Pocket Essentials, 2006

Dante, Alighieri, *The Portable Dante*, ed. by Paolo Milano, Harmondsworth: Penguin, 1977
– *The Divine Comedy: Purgatory*, trans. by Dorothy L Sayers, London: Penguin, 2004
– *The Divine Comedy*, ed. by David H Higgins and trans. by CH Sisson, Oxford: Oxford World's Classics, 2008

Davidson, Robyn, ed., *Journeys: An Anthology*, London: Picador, 2001

Davies, W.H., *The Autobiography of a Super-Tramp*, Oxford: Oxford University Press, 1980

Debord, Guy, *Society of the Spectacle*, trans. by Ken Knabb, London: Rebel Press, 1992 de Botton, Alain, *The Art of Travel*, London: Hamish Hamilton, 2002

de Certeau, Michel, *The Practice of Everyday Life*, trans. by Steven Rendall, Berkeley, CA: University of California Press, 2002

de Maistre, Xavier, *A Journey Around my Room*, ed. and trans. by Andrew Brown, with a foreword by Alain de Botton, London: Hesperus, 2004

de Quincey, Thomas, *Recollections of the Lake Poets*, ed. by David Wright, Harmondsworth: Penguin, 1970
– *Confessions of an English Opium Eater and Other Writings*, ed. by Barry Milligan, London: Penguin, 2003
– 'Walking Stewart' (1823) at http://www.readbookonline.net/readOnLine/47766/

Dexter, Gary, ed., *Poisoned Pens: Literary Invective from Amis to Zola*, London: Frances Lincoln, 2009

Dickens, Charles, *The Old Curiosity Shop: A Tale*, ed. by Norman Page, London: Penguin, 2000
– *Martin Chuzzlewit*, ed. by Patricia Ingham, London: Penguin, 2004
– *The Uncommercial Traveller*, Stroud: Nonsuch Publishing, 2007

Dun, Aidan Andrew, *Rimbaud: Psychogeographer*, London: Bookchase, 2006

Espedal, Tomas, *Tramp: Or the Art of Living a Poetic Life*, trans. by James Anderson, London: Seagull Books, 2010

Farley, Paul, & Roberts, Michael Symmons, *Edgelands: Journeys into England's True Wilderness*, London: Jonathan Cape, 2011

Ferris, Joshua, *The Unnamed*, London: Viking, 2010

Ford, Ford Madox, *The Soul of London*, London: Phoenix Press, 1995

Gilbert, Roger, *Walks in the World: Representation & Experience in Modern American Poetry*, Princeton NJ: Princeton University Press, 1991

Gleber, Anke, *The Art of Taking a Walk: Flanerie, Literature, and Film in Weimar Culture*, Princeton, NJ: Princeton University Press, 1999

Graham, Stephen, ed., *The Tramp's Anthology*, London: Peter Davies, 1928

Gray, Timothy, *Urban Pastoral: Natural Currents in the New York School*, Iowa City, IA: University of Iowa Press, 2010

Grayeff, Felix, *Aristotle and his School*, London: Duckworth, 1974

Grohmann, Alexis, & Wells, Caragh, *Digressions in European Literature: From Cervantes to Sebald*, Basingstoke: Palgrave Macmillan, 2011

Hacking, Ian, *Mad Travelers: Reflections on the Reality of Transient Mental Illness*, Charlottesville, VA: University of Virginia Press, 1998

Hampson, Robert & Montgomery, Will, eds., *Frank O'Hara Now: New Essays on the New York Poet*, Liverpool: Liverpool University Press, 2010

Harman, Claire, *Robert Louis Stevenson: A Biography*, London: HarperCollins, 2005

Harman, Mark, ed., *Robert Walser Rediscovered: Stories, Fairy-Tale Plays, and Critical Responses*, Hanover, NE: University Press of New England, 1985

Haultain, Arnold, *Of Walks and Walking Tours: An Attempt to Find a Philosophy and a Creed*, London: T Werner Laurie Ltd, 1914

Hayes, Kevin J, *Edgar Allan Poe*, London: Reaktion, 2009

Hazlitt, William, 'On Going a Journey', in *Selected Essays*, ed. by George Sampson, Cambridge: Cambridge University Press, 1917

Herzog, Werner, 'Minnesota Declaration' (1999) at http://www.wernerherzog.com/52.html

    – *Herzog on Herzog*, ed. by Paul Cronin, London: Faber, 2002

    – *Of Walking in Ice: Munich-Paris 23 November – 14 December 1974*, trans. by Marje Herzog & Alan Greenberg, New York: Free Association, 2007

Holloway, Julia Bolton, *The Pilgrim and the Book: A Study of Dante, Langland and Chaucer*, New York: Peter Lang, 1992

Holmes, Richard, *Footsteps: Adventures of a Romantic Biographer*, London: Vintage, 1985

– *The Age of Wonder: How the Romantic Generation Discovered the Beauty and Terror of Science*, London: HarperPress, 2008

Home, Stewart, *The Assault on Culture: Utopian Currents from Lettrisme to Class War*, Edinburgh: AK Press, 1991

Hooper, Barbara, *Time to Stand and Stare: A Life of W.H. Davies, Poet & Super-Tramp*, London: Peter Owen, 2004

Hou Je Bek, Wilfried, 'Pedestrian Culture Through the Ages'(2002), at http://www.scenewash.org/lobbies/chainthinker/situationist/debord/reviews/walking.html

Huizinga, Johan, *Homo Ludens: A Study of the Play Element in Culture*, trans. by RFC Hull, Boston, MA: Beacon Press, 1955

Huysmans, Joris-Karl, *Against Nature*, ed. by Nicholas White, trans. by Margaret Mauldon, Oxford: Oxford University Press, 1998

Ingold, Tim, *Lines: A Brief History*, London: Routledge, 2007
– *Being Alive: Essays on Movement, Knowledge and Description*, London: Routledge, 2011

Ingold, Tim & Vergunst, Jo Lee, eds., *Ways of Walking: Ethnography and Practice on Foot*, Surrey: Ashgate Publishing, 2008

Jarvis, Robin, *Romantic Writing and Pedestrian Travel*, Basingstoke: Macmillan, 1997

Jebb, Miles, *Walkers*, London: Constable, 1986

Johnson, Barbara A., *Reading Piers Plowman and The Pilgrim's Progress: Reception and the Protestant Reader*, Carbondale, IL: Southern Illinois University Press, 1992

Kerouac, Jack, *Rimbaud*, San Francisco, CA: City Lights Books, 1960

Kierkegaard, Søren, *The Journals of Kierkegaard: 1834–1854*, ed. and trans. by Alexander Dru, London: Fontana, 1958

Knabb, Ken, ed., *Situationist International Anthology*, Berkeley, CA: Bureau of Public Secrets, 1981

Lachman, Gary, *The Dedalus Book of the Occult: A Dark Muse*, Sawtry: Dedalus, 2003

Landry, Donna, *The Invention of the Countryside: Hunting, Walking and Ecology in English Literature 1671–1831*, Basingstoke: Palgrave, 2001

– 'Radical Walking' (2001) at www.opendemocracy.net/ecology–climate_change_debate/article_465.jsp

Langan, Celeste, *Romantic Vagrancy: Wordsworth and the Simulation of Freedom*, Cambridge: Cambridge University Press, 1995

Langland, William, *Piers Plowman*, ed. and trans. by AVC Schmidt, Oxford: Oxford University Press, 1992

Lee, Hermione, *Virginia Woolf*, London: Chatto & Windus, 1996

Lindop, Grevel, *The Opium-Eater: A Life of Thomas De Quincey*, London: JM Dent, 1981

Lopate, Phillip, 'On the Aesthetics of Urban Walking and Writing', (2004) at http://mrbellersneighborhood.com/2004/03/on-the-aesthetics-of-urban-walking-and-writing

Mabey, Richard, *The Unofficial Countryside*, with an introduction by Iain Sinclair, Dorset: Little Toller Books, 2010

Macauley, David, 'A Few Foot Notes on Walking', *The Trumpeter: Journal of Ecosophy* (10: 1; Winter, 1993) at http://trumpeter.athabascau.ca/index.php/trumpet/article/view/403/651

Macfarlane, Robert, *The Wild Places*, London: Granta, 2007

Machen, Arthur, *Things Near and Far*, London: Martin Secker, 1923

– *The London Adventure, or, the Art of Wandering*, London: Martin Secker, 1924

– *Tales of Horror and the Supernatural*, ed. by Philip Van Doren Stern, London: Richards Press, 1949

– *The Collected Arthur Machen*, ed. by Christopher Palmer, London: Duckworth, 1988

– *The Secret of the Sangraal & Other Writings*, Leyburn: Tartarus Press, 2007

– *N*, Leyburn: Tartarus Press, 2010

Mandelstam, Osip, 'Conversation about Dante', in *The Selected Poems of Osip Mandelstam*, trans. by Clarence Brown & WS Merwin, New York: New York Review of Books, 2004

Marcus, Greil, *Lipstick Traces: The Secret History of the Twentieth Century*, London: Secker & Warburg, 1990

Marples, Morris, *Shanks's Pony: A Study of Walking*, London: Dent, 1959

McDonough, Tom, ed., *Guy Debord and the Situationist International: Texts and Documents*, Cambridge, MA: MIT Press, 2002

Merrifield, Andy, *Guy Debord*, London: Reaktion, 2005

Miller, Sally M. & Morrison, Daryl, *John Muir: Family, Friends and Adventure*, University of New Mexico Press, 2005

Milton, John, *Paradise Lost*, ed. by John Leonard, London: Penguin, 2003

Minshull, Duncan, ed., *The Vintage Book of Walking*, London: Vintage, 2000
– ed., *The Burning Leg: Walking Scenes from Classic Fiction*, London: Hesperus, 2010

Mitchell, Edwin Valentine, ed., *The Pleasures of Walking*, Bourne End, Bucks: Spurbooks, 1975

Mock, Roberta, ed., *Walking, Writing & Performance*, Bristol: Intellect Books, 2009

Muir, John, *The Unpublished Journals of John Muir*, ed., by LM Wolfe, Madison, WI: University of Wisconsin Press, 1979
– *A Thousand-Mile Walk to the Gulf*, New York: Mariner Books, 1998

Nadeau, Maurice, *The History of Surrealism*, trans. by Richard Howard, London: Jonathan Cape, 1968

Nicholl, Charles, *Somebody Else: Arthur Rimbaud in Africa (1880–91)*, London: Jonathan Cape, 1995

Nicholson, Geoff, *Bleeding London*, London: Gollancz, 1997
– *The Lost Art of Walking: The History, Science, Philosophy, Literature, Theory and Practice of Pedestrianism*, Chelmsford: Harbour Books, 2010

Nietzsche, Friedrich, *The Twilight of the Idols*, ed. and trans. by Duncan Large, Oxford: Oxford University Press, 2008
– *Thus Spoke Zarathustra*, ed. and trans. by Graham Parkes, Oxford: Oxford University Press, 2008

O'Hara, Frank, *Lunch Poems*, San Francisco, CA: City Lights Books, 1964

– *The Collected Poems of Frank O'Hara*, ed. by Donald Allen, New York: Alfred A. Knopf, 1972

– *The Selected Poems of Frank O'Hara*, ed. by Donald Allen, New York: Vintage, 1974

– *Standing Still and Walking in New York*, ed. by Donald Allen, Bolinas, CA: Grey Fox Press, 1975

Papadimitriou, Nick, 'Bedfont Court Estate' in Iain Sinclair, ed., *London: City of Disappearances*, London: Hamish Hamilton, 2006

– *Ventures and Adventures in Topography* (podcasts; 2009), at http://venturesintopography.wordpress.com/podcasts/

– *Scarp*, London: Sceptre, 2012 (forthcoming)

Photinos, Christine, 'The Tramp in American Literature, 1873–1939', (2008) at http://ejournals.library.vanderbilt.edu/ameriquests/viewarticle.php?id=71&layout=html

Plant, Sadie, *The Most Radical Gesture: The Situationist International in a Postmodern Age*, London: Routledge, 1992

Plato, *Phaedrus*, ed. and trans. by Robin Waterfield, Oxford: Oxford University Press, 2002

Poe, Edgar Allan, 'The Man of the Crowd', in *The Fall of the House of Usher and Other Tales*, ed. by David Galloway, London: Penguin, 2003

Polizzotti, Mark, *Revolution of the Mind: The Life of André Breton*, London: Bloomsbury, 1995

Réda, Jacques, *The Ruins of Paris*, trans. by Mark Treharne, London: Reaktion Books, 1996

Rickett, Arthur, *The Vagabond in Literature*, London: Dent, 1906

Rimbaud, Arthur, *Rimbaud Complete*, ed. and trans. by Wyatt Mason, London: Scribner, 2003

Robb, Graham, *Rimbaud*, London: Picador, 2000

Robinson, Jeffrey, *The Walk: Notes on a Romantic Image*, Norman, OK: University of Oklahoma Press, 1989

Rogers, John, dir., *The London Perambulator* (film), London: Vanity Projects, 2009 at http://londonperambulator.wordpress.com/

Rousseau, Jean-Jacques, *Confessions*, trans by JM Cohen, Harmondsworth: Penguin, 1954

– *Émile, or On Education*, trans. by Allen Bloom, New York: Basic Books, 1979

– *Reveries of a Solitary Walker*, trans. by Peter France, London: Penguin, 2004

Rumney, Ralph, *The Consul*, trans. by Malcolm Imrie, London: Verso, 2002

Sadler, Simon, *The Situationist City*, Cambridge, MA: MIT Press, 1982

Salter, Elizabeth, *Piers Plowman: An Introduction*, Oxford: Blackwell, 1969

Sebald, WG, *The Rings of Saturn*, trans. by Michael Hulse, London: Harvill, 1998

Self, Will, *Psychogeography*, London: Bloomsbury, 2007

– *Psycho Too*, London: Bloomsbury, 2009

– *Walking to Hollywood*, London: Bloomsbury, 2010

Shakespeare, Nicholas, *Bruce Chatwin*, London: Vintage, 2000

Sheppard, Robert, *Iain Sinclair*, Tavistock: Northcote House, 2007

Sheringham, Michael, *Everyday Life: Theories and Practices from Surrealism to the Present*, Oxford: OUP, 2006

Sinclair, Iain, *Lights Out for the Territory: 9 Excursions in the Secret History of London*, London: Granta, 1997

– *Lud Heat & Suicide Bridge*, London: Granta, 1997

– *Liquid City*, (with Marc Atkins), London: Reaktion, 1999

– *London Orbital: A Walk Around the M25,* London: Granta, 2002

– *The Verbals: Iain Sinclair in Conversation with Kevin Jackson,* Tonbridge, Worple Press, 2003

– *Edge of the Orison: In the Traces of John Clare's Journey Out of Essex*, London: Hamish Hamilton, 2005

– *London: City of Disappearances*, ed., by Iain Sinclair, London: Hamish Hamilton, London, 2006

– *Blake's London: The Topographic Sublime*, London: The Swedenborg Society, 2011

– *Ghost Milk: Calling Time on the Grand Project*, London: Hamish Hamilton, 2011

Slater, Michael, *Charles Dickens*, London: Yale University Press, 2009

Smith, Hazel, *Hyperscapes in the Poetry of Frank O'Hara: Difference/Homosexuality/Topography*, Liverpool: Liverpool University Press, 2000

Smith, Phil, 'A Short History of the Future of Walking', *Rhizomes* (2003) at http://www.rhizomes.net/issue7/smith.htm

Solnit, Rebecca, *Wanderlust: A History of Walking*, London: Viking, 1999

Soupault, Philippe, *The Last Nights of Paris*, trans. by William Carlos Williams, New York: Full Court Press, 1982

Speer, Albert, *Spandau: The Secret Diaries*, trans. by Richard & Clara Winston, London: Collins, 1976

Stephen, Leslie, 'In Praise of Walking', in *The Pleasures of Walking*, ed. by Edwin Valentine Mitchell, Bourne End, Bucks: Spurbooks, 1975

Stevenson, Robert Louis, 'Walking Tours' in *The Magic of Walking*, ed. by Aaron Sussman & Ruth Goode, New York: Simon and Schuster, 1980

— *Travels with a Donkey in the Cévennes and the Amateur Emigrant*, ed. by Christopher MacLachlan, London: Penguin, 2004

Sumption, Jonathan, *Pilgrimage: An Image of Medieval Religion*, London: Faber, 1975

Sussman, Aaron & Goode, Ruth, *The Magic of Walking*, New York: Simon & Schuster, 1967

Sutherland, John, 'Clarissa's Invisible Taxi', in *Can Jane Eyre be Happy? More Puzzles in Classic Fiction*, Oxford: OUP, 1997

Svevo, Italo, *Zeno's Conscience*, ed. and trans. by William Weaver, London: Penguin, 2002

Taplin, Kim, *The English Path*, Sudbury, Suffolk: The Perry Green Press, 2000

Tester, Keith, ed., *The Flâneur*, London: Routledge, 1994

Thelwall, John, *The Peripatetic*, ed. by Judith Thompson, Detroit, MI: Wayne State University Press, 2001

Thomas, Edward, *Collected Poems*, London: Faber, 1979

Thoreau, Henry David, 'Walking', in *The Pleasures of Walking*, ed. by Edwin Valentine Mitchell, Bourne End, Bucks: Spurbooks, 1975

Urry, John, *Mobilities*, Cambridge: Polity Press, 2007

Valentine, Mark, *Arthur Machen*, Bridgend: Seren, 1995

Wallace, Anne D., *Walking, Literature, and English Culture: The Origins and Uses of the Peripatetic in the Nineteenth Century*, Oxford: Clarendon, 1993

Walser, Robert, *The Walk*, ed. by Susan Sontag & trans. by Christopher Middleton, London: Serpent's Tail, 1992
– *Masquerade & Other Stories*, ed. by William H. Gass & trans. by Susan Bernofsky, London: Quartet, 1993
– *The Microscripts*, ed. and trans. by Susan Bernofsky, New York: New Directions, 2010

Wells, HG, 'The Door in the Wall', in *The Country of the Blind and Other Selected Stories*, ed., by Patrick Parrinder, London: Penguin, 2007

Werner, James V., *American Flaneur: The Cosmic Physiognomy of Edgar Allan Poe*, London: Routledge, 2004

White, Edmund, *The Flâneur: A Stroll through the Paradoxes of Paris*, London: Bloomsbury, 2001

Whitman, Walt, *Leaves of Grass*, ed. by Jerome Loving, Oxford: Oxford University Press, 2008

Wolff, Janet, 'The Invisible Flâneuse: Women and the Literature of Modernity' (1985) at http://www.fll.vt.edu/Johnson/431405paristexts/wolff.pdf

Woolf, Virginia, *The London Scene: Five Essays by Virginia Woolf*, London: Hogarth Press, 1982
– *Mrs Dalloway*, ed. by Elaine Showalter, London: Penguin, 1992
– 'Street Haunting', in *Selected Essays*, ed. by David Bradshaw, Oxford: OUP, 2008

Wordsworth, Dorothy, *The Grasmere and Alfoxden Journals*, ed. by Pamela Woof, Oxford: Oxford University Press, 2008

Wordsworth, William, *The Collected Poems of William Wordsworth*,

Ware, Hertfordshire: Wordsworth Editions, 1994

– *The Major Works: Including The Prelude*, ed. by Stephen Charles Gill, Oxford: Oxford University Press, 2008

Wright, Patrick, *A Journey Through Ruins: The Last Days of London*, London: Radius, 1991

Paul Zweig, *Walt Whitman: The Making of the Poet*, Harmondsworth: Penguin, 1986

Online Sources

http://walkart.wordpress.com/
Walking and Art: A blog about the uses of walking in art
http://www.mis-guide.com/ws/about.html
Wrights & Sites
http://www.walkinginplace.org/converge/iprh/index.htm
Walking as Knowing as Making: A Peripatetic Investigation of
    Place
http://www.timwright.typepad.com/L_O_S/
Tim Wright: BlakeWalking
http://www.theflaneur.co.uk/
Official Website of La Société des Flâneurs Sans Frontières
    (Liverpool chapter)
http://goldenrulejones.com/walser/
Wandering with Robert Walser: A Project dedicated to Swiss
    author Robert Walser (1878–1956)
http://londonperambulator.wordpress.com
The London Perambulator
www.walkwalkwalk.org.uk/index.html
walkwalkwalk: An archaeology of the familiar and the forgotten
http://www.mythogeography.com/
Phil Smith – Mythogeography
http://johndavies.typepad.com/walking_the_m62/
John Davies: Walking the M62
http://www.talkingwalking.net/public/Talking_Walking/Talking_
    Walking.html
Talking Walking: activism, art, gossip, interviews, and news from
    the world of walking

www.middlesexcountycouncil.org.uk
Nick Papadimitriou website
http://www.thelondonadventure.co.uk/
The London Adventure: Explorations into Hidden Literary
    London
http://joysofpedestrianism.blogspot.com/
Geoff Nicholson & Will Self discuss the joys of walking

Index

I would like to acknowledge here the support that I have received from the Society of Authors. It was thanks to their generosity in granting me an Author's Foundation Award that I was able to complete this book.

OCCULT LONDON

London, more than any other city, has a secret history concealed from view. Behind the official façade promoted by the heritage industry, lies a city of esoteric traditions and obscure institutions, of lost knowledge and hidden locations. *Occult London* rediscovers this hidden history, unearthing the secret city and its forgotten inhabitants. Encompassing a historical panorama from the Elizabethan age to the present day, we are introduced to the magic of Dr Dee and Simon Forman, the rise of the Kabbalah and the occult designs of Wren and Hawksmoor. Elsewhere we meet figures such as Spring-Heeled Jack and the Highgate Vampyre, and occult organizations from the Invisible College to the Golden Dawn. Coverley explores this revival of interest in the occult tradition, one that accords well with emerging New Age philosophies, the interest in London's Ley Lines, in alternative histories and psychogeography.

978-1-904048-88-6	**(print)**	**£9.99**
978-1-84243-949-4	**(epub)**	**£5.99**

UTOPIA

For more than 2,000 years utopian visionaries have sought to create a blueprint of the ideal society: from Plato to HG Wells, from Cloudcuckooland to Shangri-La, *Utopia* takes the reader on a journey through these imaginary worlds, charting the progress of utopian ideas from their origins within the classical world, to the rebirth of utopian ideals in the Middle Ages. Later we see the emergence of socialist and feminist ideas; while the twentieth century was to be dominated by expressions of totalitarian oppression.

Today, it is claimed that we are witnessing the death of utopia, as increasingly the ideals that give rise to them are undermined or dismissed. These arguments are explored and evaluated here, and contemporary examples of utopian thought used to demonstrate the enduring relevance of the utopian tradition.

978-1-84243-316-4	**(print)**	**£7.99**
978-1-84243-873-2	**(epub)**	**£5.99**

PSYCHOGEOGRAPHY

From the urban wanderer to the armchair traveller, from the *dérive* to *détournement*, psychogeography provides us with new ways of apprehending our surroundings, transforming the familiar streets of our everyday experience into something new and unexpected.

This original bestseller, now in its fifth printing conducts the reader through this process, offering both an explanation and definition of the terms involved, and an analysis of the key figures and their work. A very useful introduction.

'A short, but valuable book' – *Daily Telegraph*

'A short guide to psychogeography for beginners'
– *New Statesman*

978-1-84243-347-8	**(Print)**	£7.99
978-1-84243-870-1	**(epub)**	£5.99

LONDON WRITING

In this book, Merlin Coverley examines the major themes in the development of the London novel from its origins in the Victorian metropolis and onward to the present day and the revival of London writing. On the way he explores the Occult Tradition and London Noir, the Disaster Novel and the rise of Psychogeography, and alongside the recognised classics of the genre he recovers some of those lost London writers whose works have been unjustly neglected.

London has continued to generate a series of fantastic visions. The humorous and the tragic, the grotesque and the bizarre, everything is possible here as Merlin Coverley explains.

978-1-904048-48-0	**(print)**	£4.99
978-1-84243-947-0	**(epub)**	£5.99